Charlie Hore is a retired bookseller living in London. He joined the International Socialists in 1974, and was a member of the Socialist Workers Party until 2013. In 2014 he became a founder member of Revolutionary Socialism in the 21st Century (rs21). He has written on China and other subjects for many publications and websites including *International Socialism*, *International Socialist Review*, *Jacobin*, *rs21*, *Socialist Review*, *Socialist Worker (Britain)* and *Socialist Worker (US)*.

The road to Tiananmen Square
by Charlie Hore

First published by Bookmarks in 1991

This edition published by Red Flag Books
Melbourne, 2025

ISBN: 978-1-922927-16-3

Red Flag Books is an imprint of Socialist Alternative
redflag.org.au // sa.org.au
books@redflag.org.au

Edited by Matthias Radja
Cover photo: Student protest, 19 May 1989, Tiananmen
Square, Bejing, China. Photographer: Edgar Bauer/dpa.
Cover design by Susan Miller
Interior layout by Susan Miller

Printed by IngramSpark

THE ROAD TO TIANANMEN SQUARE

CHARLIE HORE

R

**RED FLAG
BOOKS**

CONTENTS

Introduction to second edition   1

I   Why 1989 still matters   3
II   China's expansion since 1989   11
III   Social and political change   25
IV   Resistance from below   31
V   Xi Jinping, repression and Covid   55
VI   Conclusion   68

Introduction to first edition   75

The road to Tiananmen Square

1   The first Chinese revolution   81
2   The road to power   101
3   1949: A socialist revolution?   117
4   'It is right to rebel' – the Cultural Revolution   131
5   'The socialist market' – China's economy after Mao   149
6   Waiting for reforms – opposition 1978-88   169
7   'We are still ruled by wolves' – the revolt of 1989   203
8   Revolt and repression   221
9   What next?   247

Further reading   255
Acknowledgements   262
A note on transliterating Chinese names   263

Introduction to second edition

This book was written in another century, and in a very different world.

In 1991, when the first edition was published, the Chinese economy was only just recovering from the turmoil that culminated in the 1989 mass movement known as 'Tiananmen Square' (though it extended across almost all of China). GDP growth fell to just 4.2 percent in 1989, and declined even further in 1990, with zero or negative industrial growth from mid-1989 to mid-1990.[1] Despite some recovery in 1991, economic strategy was at an impasse – the market-led strategy of the 1980s was discredited, but when conservatives inside the CCP tried to reimpose central state planning controls, this quickly made things worse.

By contrast, the USA was at its strongest since the 1960s. The eastern European revolutions of 1989, the collapse of the Soviet Union, and the crushing defeat of Iraq in the first Gulf War, all seemed to confirm America's position as the world's only superpower. The Cold War had been won, and Francis Fukuyama's assertion that this represented the 'end of history' seemed all too plausible. In that context, the downbeat prognosis for China's

---

1   Barry Naughton, *Growing out of the plan*, (Cambridge University Press, Cambridge, 1995), page 287.

economic reforms in the final chapter was consonant with most forecasts – and just as wrong.

Fast-forward thirty-three years, and how differently things look now. China is the world's largest manufacturing economy and goods exporter, the top trading partner of over 120 countries, and the second largest economy overall. The Belt and Road Initiative (BRI), first announced in 2013, is by some distance the largest overseas investment framework in the history of capitalism, far outstripping the amounts involved in the post-1945 Marshall Plan.[2]

Meanwhile, America's political and military might has been greatly weakened by failed adventures in Afghanistan and Iraq, whilst the crash of 2008 led to the longest recession since World War II, and low growth rates across the world economy ever since. China has become the main engine of growth in the world economy, and a political, military and economic challenger to American hegemony across much of Asia and Africa. Even if economic growth has slowed recently, the prediction that this will be China's century in the same way as the last century was America's still seems a real possibility,

For socialists, understanding China's rise and role in world capitalism today is more important than ever before. This book was originally written to explain China's history in the 20th century and, in particular, to document the economic and social pressures that produced the explosion of May and June 1989. That history remains crucial to understanding 21st century China. In this introduction, I aim to do three things: firstly, to explain why the events of 1989 remain so important today; secondly, to outline what has been learned about 1989 since this

---

2 Estimates vary, but one 2020 study said that the sums involved were seven times the amount spent on the Marshall Plan, after adjusting for inflation. Jonathan E Hillman, *The emperor's new road – China and the project of the century*, (Yale University Press, New Haven, CT, 2020), page 4.

book was first published; and thirdly, to sketch a history of major economic and social developments since 1991, including China's rise to becoming a world power, and how the very successes of growth produced new waves of struggle.

I Why 1989 still matters

The events of 1989, which spread to every province and major city in China, were a watershed in modern Chinese history, comparable only to the revolutions of 1925-27 and 1949. For the Chinese Communist Party (CCP), 1989 represented the most profound and widespread challenge to its control since 1949. The events were not a revolutionary movement – the demonstrators' demands, insofar as they were clearly articulated, did not go beyond the removal of a few officials and official recognition that the revolt was justified. But the movement's dynamic carried the promise of going much further, while the founding of the student and workers' Autonomous Federations opened up the possibility of civil society organisations outside the CCP's control, which would challenge its monopoly of power.

The organisation of industrial workers in the movement was on a scale not seen since the Cultural Revolution. This raised, in particular, the spectre of a repeat of the Solidarity experience in Poland, which had quickly developed from being a grass-roots trade union to becoming a 'beacon for all the other oppressed and exploited layers of class-divided society.'[3]

The Cultural Revolution had seen much greater turmoil, including armed clashes between rival gangs of Red Guards, and

---

3   Colin Barker, 'Poland 1980-81 – the self-limiting revolution' in Colin
      Barker (ed), *Revolutionary rehearsals*, (Bookmarks, London, 1987),
      page 170.

massacres by the armed forces.[4] However, almost all the fighting took place between groups loyal to different factions inside the CCP. In 1989, though there were CCP insiders advising the student leaders in Tiananmen Square behind the scenes, the movement wasn't backing one leader against another, but rather challenging the bureaucracy's monopoly of power.

The potential for any mass gathering to turn to 'disorder' was – and remains – a crucial concern for the CCP. When Deng Xiaoping died in 1997, spontaneous public mourning was banned or heavily policed lest it turn into anti-government protests.[5] And one astute, if rather disgruntled, factory owner summed up a widespread view in 2007:

> China is different from other countries. In the West, it is the rich people who influence politics and the government fears the rich. Now, in China, it is the rich who fear the government and the government fears the poor. The poor have a high potential to threaten social stability and social order.[6]

'Long-term social stability' is seen by the CCP as equally important as economic development, but one of the lessons it drew from 1989 is that heavy-handed repression has to be the last resort, not least because, while the repression silenced China's campuses, it did not scare people off the streets. A *New York Times* article in 1991 quoted a CCP internal report complaining that:

---

4   See for instance Roderick MacFarquhar and Michael Schoenhals, *Mao's last revolution*, (Harvard University Press, Cambridge, MA, 2006), pages 177-80 and 216-17, and pages 135-141 below.

5   James Miles, *The legacy of Tiananmen*, (University of Michigan Press, Ann Arbor, MI, 1997), page xi.

6   Quoted in Chris King-Chi Chan, *The challenge of labour in China*, (Routledge, Abingdon, 2010), page 161.

Protesters frequently seal off bridges and block roads, storm party and government offices, coercing party committees and government, and there are even criminal acts such as attacking, trashing, looting and arson.[7]

Many of these were rural environmental protests, but 1992 and 1993 saw the return of widespread strikes and worker unrest across China's cities in response to high inflation and layoffs.[8] The decades since have seen levels of struggle rise and fall, but never die away completely.

The Chinese state – in particular the local state – lacks the means to repress all outbreaks of struggle, and has learned that partial repression often draws more people in. They have thus developed an array of techniques for managing dissent within certain limits. One key technique is making swift concessions to demands, and the larger the protest, the more likely this is to happen; one researcher noted that 'My collection of 261 cases shows that actions involving more than 4,000 participants rarely failed.'[9]

The other side of this unwritten 'social contract' is a general acceptance of the limits set by the CCP. Strikes are allowed – organising independent trade unions is not. Local mobilisations making easily conceded demands on local authorities may meet initial repression but, provided they stay essentially peaceful, will not bring in police or the army from outside. Part of the reason such struggles proliferate is that substantial economic power has been devolved to local authorities and factory managements, so that immediate economic demands can be realised without challenging the central state.

---

7   Quoted in Elizabeth C Economy, *The river runs black*, (Cornell University Press, Ithaca, NY, 2010), page 91.

8   Orville Schell, *Mandate of heaven*, (Little, Brown, London, 1995), pages 419-21.

9   Yongshun Cai, *Collective resistance in China*, (Stanford University Press, Stanford, CA, 2010), page 126.

This 'repressive tolerance' even has certain advantages for the central state: it keeps struggles localised, partial and immediate, and ensures that they do not generalise into wider political challenges; and it allows for a 'safety valve' which also functions as a 'stress test' for local officials. But it also encourages further struggles, and it is important to understand that the limits of this tolerance are set both by the streets and the central state. One of the key limits is that, even when repression is used, there is a conscious effort to avoid death or serious injury.[10]

Under Xi Jinping, however, the pendulum has swung back towards repression, with high-profile arrests of students organising in support of striking workers, closure of NGOs supporting workers' rights, and a widespread crackdown on the beginnings of an independent feminist movement in China.[11] This has been part of a wider attempt at reasserting the power of the central state through crackdowns on corrupt local officials, increased policing of the media and online spaces, and the attack on Hong Kong's autonomy in 2019/20. While this has reduced both street protests and strikes over the last few years, it comes at a cost, as one recent study noted:

> All of this signifies the end of the 'pragmatic authoritarianism' that characterized the efforts of previous CCP regimes to contain discontent and safeguard stability. The regime's flexibility in containing unrest – i.e., its ability to adapt its strategy by applying different forms of leadership and appropriately

---

10   Tibet and Xinjiang are important exceptions to this: the highest points of struggle have repeatedly been directed against Chinese rule, and thus against the central state; and the police and army have far less compunction about killing or seriously injuring protesters. I return to this below.

11   For the last, see Leta Hong Fincher, *Betraying Big Brother – the feminist awakening in China* (Verso, London, 2018).

combining repression, concession and co-optation – is, to say the least, hampered.[12]

In late 2022, protest returned to China's cities on a scale not seen since state-sanctioned anti-Japanese protests in 2005, with demonstrations in many towns and cities (including central Beijing), on at least fifty university campuses, and even in Hong Kong, which quickly turned into wider protests against draconian Covid restrictions.

The protests died down as quickly as they had flared up, but represented both the biggest popular mobilisations of the Xi Jinping era, and the first direct challenges to central government policies of this century. And the government flinched, removing the lockdown restrictions they had reimposed just a couple of weeks previously.[13] The repression of 1989 still casts a long shadow, but it constrains the government as well as the street, and has not prevented multiple eruptions of anger.

Keeping the memory alive

'Tiananmen Square' is in many ways a misnomer for both the movement and the massacre of 1989. The movement spread to every provincial capital city, as well as many other cities and towns and some rural areas, particularly in the days after the massacre. And while students were killed in the square itself, the worst of the killing occurred in the west of Beijing as the army broke through the barricades in working-class districts of the city.

For almost two months central Beijing was on front pages and television screens across the world, while the movement

---

12 Ralf Ruckus, *The communist road to capitalism*, (PM Press, Oakland, CA, 2021), page 126.

13 For a longer analysis, with links to other reports, see my 'Back on the streets in China', *rs21*, 30 November, 2022: https://www.rs21.org.uk/2022/11/30/back-on-the-streets-in-china/ and pages 64-66 below.

elsewhere in Beijing and in the rest of China gained much less coverage. In part this was simply because of state censorship, which could not be enforced in the areas barricaded after the declaration of martial law. But it was also in part because the student protests offered articulate English-speaking leaders making simple arguments for democracy and against oppression, which chimed with Western journalists and the assumptions that they brought to their reporting.

That gap in reporting is reproduced in the literature that has appeared since 1989. In this section, I am going to highlight some of the most useful books that have appeared since the first edition of this book, but this is no way a comprehensive survey. Although censorship still puts obstacles in the way of researchers, there is a substantial literature on 1989 which is crucial to keeping the history alive.

Two of the students who were at the heart of the movement have written important memoirs – *Almost a revolution* by Shen Tong,[14] and *A heart for freedom* by Chai Ling,[15] who was the 'commander' of the student headquarters and one of the few female student leaders. Both are centred on the student organisation in the Square – and defending the quite different perspectives that each brought to the movement – but they are particularly valuable for insights into student organising before 1989.

The most comprehensive accounts of the movement in Beijing are *Black hands of Beijing*, by George Black and Robin Munro[16] and Craig Calhoun's *Neither gods nor emperors*.[17] *Black hands of Beijing* is a journalistic account, which relates events

14 Shen Tong, *Almost a revolution*, (Harper Perennial, New York, NY, 1991).

15 Chai Ling, *A heart for freedom*, (Tyndale, Carol Stream, IL, 2011).

16 George Black and Robin Munro, *Black hands of Beijing*, (Wiley, New York, NY, 1993).

17 Craig Calhoun, *Neither gods nor emperors*, (University of California Press, Berkeley, CA, 1994).

from the perspectives of two intellectuals advising the students behind the scene, and Han Dongfang, founder of the Beijing Autonomous Workers' Federation (BWAF). The very different perspectives give a much wider account of the movement's development than most histories, and bring out in particular some of the class tensions that emerged as the movement evolved. There is also a fuller account of the BWAF's history in a 1993 academic paper available online.[18] *Neither gods nor emperors* is an academic work that focuses more narrowly on the students at the heart of the movement and their motivations, informed by surveys of protesters. For the end of the movement Timothy Brook's *Quelling the people*[19] is the definitive account to date of the massacre itself and the scale of the resistance.

Louisa Lim's *The people's republic of amnesia: Tiananmen revisited* is likewise mostly about Beijing,[20] but there is a substantial chapter recording both the movement and the bloody repression after June 4 in Chengdu, Sichuan province, when a vicious police baton attack left hundreds dead and injured. This was the only recorded instance of mass killings outside Beijing, and from talking to eyewitnesses, she draws a full and graphic picture of both the repression and the resistance:

> Chengdu became a focal point for marchers, who flocked in from the surrounding regions from as far west as the Tibetan prefecture of Aba to take part in the protests…By nightfall on June 4th, angry mobs were setting fire to anything belonging to

---

18   Andrew G. Walder and Gong Xiaoxia, 'Workers in the Tiananmen Protests: The Politics of the Beijing Workers' Autonomous Federation', *The Australian Journal of Chinese Affairs* (1993), 29: 18: http://www.tsquare.tv/links/Walder.html

19   Timothy Brook, *Quelling the people*, (Oxford University Press, New York, NY, 1992).

20   Louisa Lim, *The people's republic of amnesia: Tiananmen revisited*, (Oxford University Press, New York, NY, 2014)

the state. The crowd threw stones, tiles and gasoline bottles at a police station near the square where detained protesters had been beaten, and eventually set it on fire.[21]

Lim uses individual reminiscences to structure a wider narrative which highlights the continuing importance of 1989 to both China's rulers and many of those who were involved, though she is clear-sighted about the successes of the government's campaign of erasure.

A more recent book provides the fullest account of the movement outside Beijing for several decades – Jeremy Brown's *June Fourth*.[22] Brown writes as a social historian who wants to correct class, racial and gender biases in previous histories, highlighting:

> … [a] diverse mix of people whose actions and choices were far more significant than those of students from a few elite universities: ordinary residents of Beijing, worker activists pushing to establish independent unions, people outside China's capital, including Muslims and Tibetans…[23]

His account of the spread of the movement outside Beijing tells us more about the breadth of mobilisation than about the details in any one city, though he does give a valuable account of the pan-Muslim campaign against an Islamophobic book,[24] which erupted at the same time as the 1989 protests (discussed on pages 187-188 below), which features only very briefly in more recent histories of Xinjiang. But as valuable as his wider perspective is, the book highlights how much is still unknown about the extent

---

21 As above, pages 185 and 189.
22 Jeremy Brown, *June Fourth – the Tiananmen protests and Beijing massacre of 1989*, (Cambridge University Press, Cambridge, 2021)
23 As above, pages xi-xii.
24 As above, pages 164-167.

of the movement outside Beijing.[25] While the CCP has been unable to completely erase memories of what happened in Beijing, it has had more success in suppressing the wider history.

II   China's expansion since 1989

That success would not have been possible, however, without the economic boom of the past thirty years, an expansion unprecedented in the history of capitalism – the nearest parallel is the USA's industrialisation in the late 19th century. Deng Xiaoping's 'southern tour' of early 1992, which hailed the success of Special Economic Zones such as Shenzhen in attracting foreign investment, marked a fundamental turning point in China's economic development.

However, as one study noted:

> The immense economic growth that followed in the 1990s and 2000s was not the result of a grand plan of CCP leaders or the China Model; the reforms relied on the attraction of foreign investment to the PRC, and they coincided with the search of companies from capitalist core states for investment opportunities.[26]

'Export-processing zones' blossomed across Africa and Asia in the 1990s, as documented by Naomi Klein's *No logo*,[27] but

---

25   One other source which gives very brief accounts and numbers of protesters for many cities is Zhang Liang (compiler), *The Tiananmen papers*, (Little, Brown, London, 2001), but there is controversy over its accuracy: see for example *June Fourth*, page xvi, and 'Poring over the Tiananmen paper trail', *The Globe and Mail*, 26 July, 2004: https://www.theglobeandmail.com/news/world/poring-over-the-tiananmen-paper-trail/article1138348/

26   Ruckus, *The communist road to capitalism,* page 111.

27   Naomi Klein, *No Logo*, (Flamingo, London, 2000).

China had two particular advantages over other countries. The first was the ready availability of Chinese diaspora capital from Hong Kong and Taiwan. Hong Kong capitalists were eager to take advantage of the much cheaper land and labour across the border; by 2000 some five million workers in southern China were employed by Hong Kong companies, and another three million by Taiwanese firms.[28] Hong Kong's formal reintegration into China in 1997 was preceded by an effective economic integration from the early 1990s onwards.

Capital is no use without labour, however; China's second advantage was the 'surplus' rural population created by the agricultural reforms of the 1980s, who flocked to both the 'township and village enterprises' (TVEs – small factories in the countryside) and rapidly expanding new cities such as Shenzhen. The growth of the TVEs defied superlatives – by the end of 1998, they employed one in five of the total workforce, producing a third of GDP and half of all exports.[29]

But their very success gave rise to a number of new headaches for the ruling class. Firstly, their growth was highly uneven, concentrated in an arc of the southern coast between Shanghai and Guangzhou. Inequality both within and between provinces became one of the defining features of China's growth. Secondly, a part of their success came at the expense of older state-owned enterprises (SOEs), which were losing money even faster than previously. This prompted a massive restructuring programme from the mid-1990s onwards, and in particular a jobs massacre – the 1990s saw a net loss in manufacturing employment, despite China becoming the 'workshop of the world'.[30]

---

28   Nicholas R Lardy, *Integrating China into the global economy*, (Brookings Institution Press, Washington, DC), page 57.

29   Bruce Gilley, *Model rebels*, (University of California Press, Berkeley, CA, 2001), page 149.

30   Ho-fung Hung, *The China boom*, (Columbia University Press, New York, NY, 2015), page 68.

Lastly, the export-processing model relied on continuous growth in export markets – which essentially meant the USA: imports of raw materials, components and fuels resulted in China running a trade deficit with the rest of the world apart from the USA for much of this period. Given the limited recovery in the American economy, double-digit growth in imports was simply unsustainable.

The export boom stuttered briefly as a result of the Asian currency crisis of 1997, which hit smaller TVEs hard, but the central state's control over currency rates meant that China was far less affected than its neighbours. China's accession to the World Trade Organisation in 2001 further expanded export markets, while also accelerating the tendency towards over-production.

The world financial crisis of 2008 brought this phase of growth to a close, with an immediate and precipitous drop in exports which saw some 25 to 30 million workers lose their jobs as tens of thousands of factories closed. Ironically, China's growth was a contributory factor to the crash, with China's foreign exchange reserves, which had risen from US$212 billion in 2001 to US$1.9 trillion in 2008, being mostly invested in American financial markets, which fuelled the unsustainable real estate bubble.

China's rulers reacted swiftly with a US$500 billion economic stimulus package, which involved central and local state spending on power and transport infrastructure, as well as consumer credit. The economy quickly rebounded, with growth rates by 2011 well above those of other leading economies. However, it was a reactive move, rather than a fully-rounded economic strategy, and swapped one set of problems for another.

Firstly, the sheer pace of infrastructure construction was neither economically nor environmentally sustainable. There are physical limits to the number of airports, new cities or roads that can be built, and housing construction in particular has been outstripping demand over the past ten years.

Secondly, there has been the runaway expansion of credit as

the primary driver of economic growth, with debt as a percentage of GDP more than doubling between 2008 and 2016 – on one estimate, China accounted for half of all new credit created world-wide between 2005 and 2016.[31] That credit has been mobilised above all to keep a boom in housing construction going that is both essential to continued economic growth, and a major factor in increasing economic instability – in computing language, both a feature and bug.

The property and debt booms are routinely described as unsustainable in Western analysis, but much of this commentary misunderstands the nature of debt in China. Three factors are particularly important. Firstly, almost all debt is held internally, with just five percent of the total held outside China.[32] Secondly, almost all debt is corporate or government (at all levels), with household debt underpinned by high levels of personal savings, concentrated among the most well-off – one survey found that the richest ten percent of households save 60 percent of their income, making up almost three-quarters of total personal savings.[33]

Lastly, the state-owned banks hold the great bulk of debt, which makes it easier for the central government to simply roll over the debts of state-owned or state-controlled enterprises. 'Unsustainable' levels of debt (in monetarist terms) turn out to be quite sustainable if the political will is there. As one writer rather crudely put it: 'When considering domestic 'debt' in China, what we're really discussing is the amount of money the Communist Party owes to the Communist Party.'[34]

---

31 George Magnus, *Red flags – why Xi's China is in jeopardy*, (Yale University Press, New Haven, CT, 2018), page 77.

32 2021 figures, from a Bank of Finland report: https://www.bofit.fi/en/monitoring/weekly/2021/vw202104_3/

33 Thomas Orlik, *China – the bubble that never pops*, (Oxford University Press, New York, NY, 2020), page 76.

34 Wade Shepard, *Ghost cities of China*, (Zed Books, London, 2015), page 190.

The downsides of this are firstly that propping up unviable companies or SOEs uses up capital or credit that could be more profitably deployed elsewhere. The second is that it does nothing to resolve the underlying weaknesses of the economy, with unprofitable banks and enterprises that are 'too big to fail' still dragging down overall profit rates.

The CCP can do this because one key aspect of China's rise has been a very high level of capital accumulation, which peaked at 48 percent of GDP in 2011, and remains over 40 percent. The other side of this is that the level of consumption is correspondingly low, and fell throughout the years of highest growth (though higher growth rates meant that living standards were rising, as workers were getting a smaller share of a much larger economy). The CCP had long understood that the economy was unbalanced, and even before the 2008 crash took steps to increase household spending, with some success – from 2005 to 2017 household spending grew by just under 10 percent a year, with urban living standards rising considerably.[35] The Covid pandemic reversed this trend, however, and as of late 2024 recovery remained sluggish, despite yet another stimulus package.

China and the world since 1989

The great crash of 2008 was very obviously a watershed in China's economic growth. It marked both the end of the export-led boom, and of the generally favourable conditions in the world economy that had facilitated China's growth. Massive investments in infrastructure helped to pull China out of recession and, through demand for imports, restore a degree of growth across the world economy, but these were only a stop-gap – a new long-term economic strategy would become necessary.

However, 2008 was also an opportunity. The crash

---

35 Figures from Magnus, *Red flags*, pages 56-57.

highlighted the continuing relative economic decline of the USA, and consequently enabled China to extend its political and economic influence. Although the economic reforms evolved in response to specific conditions of the Chinese economy, rather than mirroring the neo-liberal turn in world politics, the economy's runaway growth depended greatly on the neo-liberal world economy. Once that framework was broken, however, shaping the world economy into something that better fitted China's needs was both an opportunity and a necessity. Put another way, for almost two decades the CCP had been lucky, but from now on they would have to make their own luck.

One key component of the post-2008 economic strategy has been overseas investment, much of it channelled through the Belt and Road Initiative (BRI). As of September 2023, the BRI, best understood as a development framework rather than a fixed programme, involved projects in 154 countries[36] (though a significant proportion of China's investment goes to the most developed countries that lie outside the BRI). China has now become the world's second-largest exporter of capital, recycling the huge trade surpluses it has accumulated from exports to the USA and Europe. It has also become the largest exporter and second-largest importer of goods and services, moving towards becoming one of the world's major imperialist powers.[37] And though the BRI involves private companies as well as state and private partnerships, it is a centrally planned and directed

---

36 Shannon Tietzi, 'How China's Belt and Road Took Over the World', *The Diplomat*, 12 September, 2023: https://thediplomat.com/2023/09/how-chinas-belt-and-road-took-over-the-world/

37 Two useful accounts of China's emergence as an imperialist power are Au Loong-yu (interview), 'China's rise as a world power', *International Socialist Review* 112, Spring 2019: https://isreview.org/issue/112/chinas-rise-world-power/ and Pierre Rousset, 'China: a new imperialism emerges', *International Viewpoint*, 18 November, 2021: https://internationalviewpoint.org/spip.php?article7401

campaign of capital export which ties investment directly to political advantage.

For the USA, China's rise represents a threat to the political, military and economic hegemony it has taken for granted since the collapse of the USSR, a problem made all the more intractable by the fact that the American economy is both dependent on and threatened by China's economic rise. Since 2008, and in particular since Xi Jinping's accession to power in 2012, China has been using its economic and political power to develop a number of Asian- or China-centric institutions which directly or indirectly challenge American hegemony: the Asian Infrastructure Investment Bank (AIIB); the Regional Comprehensive Economic Partnership, covering much of south-east Asia; and the Shanghai Co-Operation Organisation (SCO), a military and political alliance dating back to 1996 which now includes most central and south Asian countries.

This is in addition to the BRICS partnership (Brazil, Russia, India, China, South Africa), a wider alliance of 'emerging' economies, whose recent expansion to BRICS+ has been compared to the 'Bandung Movement' of non-aligned countries set up in 1955 to challenge the Cold War framework of American and Russian power. The comparison is mistaken, however, as Tithi Bhattacharya and Gareth Dale noted:

> BRICS+, a grouping of countries led by the aspirant hegemon, challenges the established world order, but ultimately their animating spirit is the same: capital accumulation. Their struggle is with who rules the roost, and not with the pecking order itself. It is no surprise that debt forgiveness is nowhere on its agenda, given that China is the world's biggest creditor nation.[38]

---

38 Tithi Bhattacharya and Gareth Dale, 'Is BRICS+ an anti-colonial formation worth cheering from the left? Far from it.' *rs21*, 14 September, 2023: https://www.rs21.org.uk/2023/09/14/

Ho-fung Hung underlines that this is about China's integration into the existing world order:

> The China boom has been dependent on the global neoliberal order, which is based on expanding, unfettered transnational flow of goods and capital, and it is in China's vested interest to maintain the status quo, though China might seek to change the balance of power within this arrangement. More, China's own imbalanced development path is a key source of rather than the solution to the global economic imbalance that led to the global financial crisis.[39]

The AIIB, like the New Development Bank set up by the BRICS countries in 2015, is complementary to the traditional institutions of world capital such as the IMF and World Bank, both of which China has become increasingly enmeshed with.

China replicates the approach of other imperial powers in seeing much of Africa and Latin America (and to a lesser extent Australia[40]) as sources of raw materials or energy, with development skewed towards the needs of the Chinese economy rather than benefiting the host country. One study of recent African history argues that:

> China is no kinder, gentler imperial power: just like nineteenth-century colonialists, when the Chinese build roads and schools, the goal is to facilitate resource extraction and build allegiances... Chinese investment and infrastructure building

---

is-brics-an-anti-colonial-formation-worth-cheering-from-the-left-far-from-it/ .

39 Ho-fung Hung, *The China boom*, page 5.

40 Tom Bramble, 'Trading places? Australia, China and US imperialism', *Red Flag*, 19 November, 2014: https://redflag.org.au/article/trading-places-australia-china-and-us-imperialism

has reproduced the social and economic inequality and unevenness that likewise accompany imperialism in its Western form.[41]

A similar pattern has been at work in Latin America:

The vast majority of Latin American exports to China are in a handful of primary commodities in a small set of countries in South America. Such a pattern of trade with China is quite distinct relative to Latin America's trade patterns with the rest of the world, and China's imports from the rest of the world... For commodities, anyway, Latin America is a uniquely important source of supply for China.[42]

The sluggish nature of the world economy since the crash has made China a more important trading partner for many countries. The sheer size of the Chinese economy also means that China's increased or reduced demand for particular commodities greatly affects world prices, which has been a further cause of instability since the onset of the Covid pandemic.

China has overtaken the USA as the primary trading partner for almost all of Asia and Africa, and much of South America and Europe. It is primarily this economic competition, and the consequent increase in China's political influence and 'soft power', that has led successive US administrations to see China as the major challenger to American hegemony. For many commentators, this amounts to a 'new Cold War', and certainly much of the language used by Western politicians reflects that era.

But in reality, the differences are much more important than the similarities. The world today has changed out of all

---

41   Lee Wengraf, *Extracting profit*, (Haymarket Books, Chicago, IL, 2018), page 109.

42   Kevin P Gallagher, *The China triangle*, (Oxford University Press, New York, NY, 2016), page 45.

recognition since the classic Cold War era, where the world was essentially divided into two opposing blocs whose competition was primarily expressed in military terms. The rise of China, and of other major economies in the 'Global South', means that both the USA and Russia are politically weaker and less influential than they were at the height of their powers, but also that economic, political and military competition between great powers are once again intertwined, in ways that resemble the 'classic' Marxist accounts of imperialism as presented by Lenin, Bukharin and Luxemburg.[43]

One fundamental difference, however, is that the world is no longer simply divided into oppressor and oppressed nations. As a consequence, smaller states have much greater room for manoeuvre between the great powers. The USA's closest military allies in east Asia (Japan, Taiwan and Vietnam) are also some of China's most important trading partners. India straddles all camps: Russia's longest-standing Asian ally, a member of the Chinese-influenced AIIB and SCO, but also one of the four nations in the US-sponsored Quad anti-China alliance (and so rather undermining the 'anti-imperialist' stance of the BRICS+).

One recent analysis of imperialism's evolution highlights:

...the increasing assertiveness of lower-ranked powers in the global hierarchy of states. This phenomenon is based on the rise of independent centres of capital accumulation outside the historic core of the capitalist system... A similar process has also repeated itself among the second, third and fourth-ranked powers. The fusion of economic and military competition, which characterises capitalist imperialism, is not confined to rivalries

---

43 For an account of some of the similarities, see Ho-fung Hung, 'Rereading Lenin's Imperialism at the time of US–China rivalry, *Spectre*, 10 December, 2021: https://spectrejournal.com/rereading-lenins-imperialism-at-the-time-of-us-china-rivalry/

among the largest powers, but is also structured into how smaller states and capitals interact. The changing balance between the global powers and the retreat of old empires, far from creating opportunities for a more peaceful international order, has instead acted as a spur to even more frenzied competition as the middle-sized predators muscle in and fill the gap.[44]

Although China's rise to a global power has primarily been through the expansion of economic and political power, the last thirty years have also seen greatly increased military spending, from US$10 billion in 1997 to over US$140 billion in 2015,[45] and a higher military profile, especially in asserting Chinese claims to Taiwan and in the South China Sea.[46] This has led China into military and coastguard confrontations with the Philippines, South Korea, Taiwan and Vietnam, especially over the disputed Paracel and Spratly islands. Military tensions in the region have been further increased by a growing American military presence in the region and American arms sales to China's neighbours, and more recently the AUKUS nuclear-powered submarine partnership between the USA, Australia and Britain.[47]

While China's multiple economic links with Taiwan might seem to militate against any military takeover, the risk of either a provocation (from either side) or a misunderstanding

---

44 Anne Alexander, 'Revisiting the dynamics of imperialism in the Middle East', *International Socialism* 2:182, spring 2024: https://isj.org.uk/ revisiting-imperialism-middle-east/

45 Richard Javed Heydarian, *Asia's new battlefield*, (Zed Books, London, 2015), page 15.

46 For a map showing China's claimed 'territorial waters', see: https://www. nationsonline.org/oneworld/map/South-China-Sea-political-map.htm

47 Tom Bramble, 'AUKUS and the US alliance: Australian imperialism in the Indo-Pacific', *Marxist Left Review*, 15 February, 2022: https://marxistleftreview.org/articles/ aukus-and-the-us-alliance-australian-imperialism-in-the-indo-pacific/

escalating into full-blown fighting remains very real.[48] The idea that wars between economically linked countries are necessarily 'irrational' and therefore avoidable has been repeatedly disproved over the past 150 years. At a certain point, the logic of military competition comes to take on a life of its own.

Barack Obama's twin-track approach of a military 'pivot to Asia' and the economic Trans-Pacific Partnership (TPP) free-trade project marked perhaps the high point of the USA's attempts to build a durable coalition against China. However, both strategies proved difficult to put into practice, and were scrapped by Donald Trump in favour of a more directly aggressive approach, which backfired badly. Trump's imposition of tariffs on Chinese exports led to a retaliation, which ended up having a greater effect on the American economy than on China, while the USA's relative decline was underlined by the 2018 decision of the other countries involved in the TPP to revive it without the USA.

Under Joe Biden, the USA moved to an 'imperialist Keynesianism' approach which combined parts of Trump's break from neo-liberalism with elements of Obama's strategy.[49] One key aspect of Trump's approach that Biden kept was 'decoupling' – an attempt to partially unravel the interconnections between the American and Chinese economies, in particular around information technology and especially the microchip industry. While it was relatively easy for the USA to block Chinese companies such as Huawei, and use tariffs as a

---

48 There is no space here to further develop an analysis of the China-Taiwan relationship. For more background, see my 'Pelosi, Taiwan and China, *rs21*, 16 August, 2022: https://www.rs21.org.uk/2022/08/16/pelosi-taiwan-and-china/ and Mick Armstrong, 'Taiwan's independence and the new Cold War', *Red Flag*, 25 June, 2021: https://redflag.org.au/article/taiwans-independence-and-new-cold-war

49 Ashley Smith, 'Imperialist Keynesianism', *Tempest*, 18 May, 2021: https://www.tempestmag.org/2021/05/imperialist-keynesianism/

blunt instrument to reduce imports, this both imposed increased costs on American companies and threatened shortages if no replacement for Chinese products could be found.[50] China's attempts to reduce their reliance on Taiwan's near-monopoly in high-performance chips, through the 'Made in China 2025' policy, have similarly run up against the limits of technological backwardness and a globalised supply chain. As a result, many companies and governments are now pursuing the more limited policy of 'de-risking',[51] which accepts that international interconnections can't simply be undone.

Both China and the USA also face the reality that they are far from the only strategic actors in east and southeast Asia. As one historian sees it:

> …the US allies – from the Philippines to Vietnam and Japan – have been playing their own strategic games simultaneously using America's commitment to regional (or bilateral) security, and China's ability to exercise self-restraint… Outside this theatre of strategic jostling, states such as Indonesia – the informal leader of ASEAN – are most interested in preventing a brewing Sino-American rivalry from turning into a direct confrontation, desperately trying to manage a region splintering along conflicting allegiances and competing national interests.[52]

China's rise is neither the cause of America's relative decline, nor simply a direct product of it. The two have separate but

---

50   For a more detailed account of some of the obstacles, see 'Four years into the trade war, are the US and China decoupling?', *Peterson Institute for International Economics*, 20 October, 2022: https://www.piie.com/blogs/realtime-economics/four-years-trade-war-are-us-and-china-decoupling

51   'China decoupling versus de-risking: What's the difference?', *Hinrich Foundation*, 12 December, 2023: https://www.hinrichfoundation.com/research/article/trade-and-geopolitics/china-decoupling-vs-de-risking/

52   Heydarian, *Asia's new battlefield*, page 209.

interlocking dynamics. But the more China exerts power over the world market, the more it is vulnerable to that market's weaknesses and pressures. As Ho-fung Hung put it:

> Although China's presence has not severed developing countries' ties to the developed world, it does increase the plurality of their investors and trade partners, thus enhancing their bargaining power in the world market. It is in this sense that the capitalist boom in China is altering the power relations between the developing world and the developed... China is therefore both a facilitator of developing countries' autonomy from the developed ones and a status quo power that joins hands with traditional core powers to help reproduce a global neoliberal order.[53]

That increased autonomy has also been turned against China, in particular since the onset of Covid. BRI projects have been cancelled by governments in Bangladesh, Egypt, Malaysia, Pakistan, Sri Lanka and Tanzania. They have also run into environmental or workers' protests, as well as corruption scandals in many more countries – one study found that 35 percent of BRI projects had 'encountered major implementation problems' from these.[54] The vast majority of BRI financing comes as loans, and for many countries this has led to huge levels of debt, with 12 countries owing China the equivalent of 20 percent of their GDP. In part this is simply because those countries that most need Chinese investment have the least resources to repay debt, but it is also because BRI investment is primarily driven by China's needs, rather than

---

53 Ho-fung Hung, *The China boom*, page 175.
54 'Banking on the Belt and Road', *AidData*, (William and Mary College, Williamsburg, VA), 29 September, 2021: https://www.aiddata.org/publications/banking-on-the-belt-and-road

those of its recipients.[55] Though the BRI is only part of China's expansion across the world economy, it highlights a growing problem for the CCP: the more China's influence extends across the world, the more they risk imperial overstretch.

III   Social and political change

In the last thirty years China has changed from a primarily rural country to a primarily urban one, one of the fastest such transformations in world history, with profound social, political and environmental consequences. Here I want to focus on just two aspects of this transformation: environmental damage; and the contradictory changes in the status of women. In the next section I will attempt an overview of some of the many strands of resistance from below that have also characterised this period of monumental change.

The environment
China under Mao was an environmental disaster area, with some of the worst damage done during the Great Leap Forward.[56] However, unregulated industrial development and runaway urban construction since 1991 have made the situation far worse. The reliance on coal and oil as primary energy sources led to China overtaking the USA in 2005 as the world's largest greenhouse gas emitter – between 1990 and 2017 carbon dioxide emissions more than quadrupled.[57] Huge amounts of agricultural land have been lost to development, with one

---

55   For a good overview, see Economy, *The world according to China*, page 88-127, as well as Magnus, *Red flags*, pages 173-192.

56   Judith Shapiro, *Mao's war against nature*, (Cambridge University Press, Cambridge, 2001) is the best overall history.

57   Richard Smith, *China's engine of environmental collapse*, (Pluto Press, London, 2020), pages xiii-xiv.

(undated) survey finding that 16 percent of rural families had lost land or their homes to development, and another reporting that one million villages had simply disappeared in a decade.[58] Air and water pollution is some of the worst in the world, with China having the world's third and fourth most-polluted rivers in the world, and the Yangzi river depositing more plastic into the ocean than any other river.[59]

That pollution is not confined to urban areas, with groundwater levels dropping dangerously across the north China plain, threatening both drinking and agricultural water supplies. In one best-selling book about the changing countryside, the author noted that in her home village, the river had become so polluted that 'where the river eddies, you can use a lighter to ignite the foam, and with a "whoomp" the fire will race along the riverbank.' Large-scale sandmining had also made it a deathtrap for swimmers, with a dozen or so people drowning every year (this from a village of some 1,400 people).[60]

The combination of local power and the central drive for growth has also stymied the CCP's project of moving away from reliance on coal and (imported) oil towards renewable energies. While China has become the world leader in solar and wind power, with more solar capacity than every other country combined, coal and oil still account for almost three-quarters of China's energy usage[61]. New coal-fired power stations are also still being built, despite a pledge to reach 'net zero' carbon emissions by 2060. That reliance on fossil fuels has also characterised Beijing's investments abroad, with almost 40 percent of overseas energy investments being in coal projects.[62]

---

58   Shepherd, *Ghost cities*, pages 24-27

59   Smith, *China's engine*, page 56.

60   Liang Hong, *China in one village*, (Verso, London, 2021), page 50.

61   'China – energy country profile', *Our world in data*: https://ourworldindata.org/energy/country/china

62   Economy, *The world according to China*, pages 102-103

Extreme weather events resulting from climate change have also worsened the environmental malaise. In 2022 China underwent the worst heatwave and consequent drought in 60 years, and in 2023 the heatwave began even earlier in the year, while Beijing suffered the heaviest rainfall ever recorded. Worse was to come in 2024, with six typhoons, record rainfall in the north and heatwaves across much of the south.[63] And on the Tibetan plateau, global warming threatens both the permafrost on which much recent development has been built (including the railway to Lhasa, built in 2006) and the region's glaciers, with predictions that parts of the plateau could lose more than half of their glacier mass by the end of the century.[64] Yet China is stepping up mining and other industrial activity in Tibet, which can only add to the damage already done. Here as in the rest of China, the CCP, like other ruling classes across the globe, is caught between the realities of global warming and the demands of 'growth'.

The 'demographic deficit' and the changing status of women

The explosive growth from 1991 onwards was dependent above all on a seemingly inexhaustible reservoir of cheap labour from the countryside, young men and women willing to work very long hours in atrocious conditions because life as a migrant worker offered more than remaining in their villages.

But as early as 2006, export-processing industries in Guangdong province were reporting labour shortages, as migrant workers moved to better-paying jobs further north. By 2012, China's labour force had begun to shrink, as more people died or retired than joined the workforce. And in 2022, the population fell for the first time

---

63   'China's most devastating summer yet, by the numbers', *Sixth Tone*, 25 September, 2024: https://www.sixthtone.com/news/1015942

64   'The Qinghai-Xizang plateau is turning into a vast grassland, study finds', *Sixth Tone*, 23 August, 2024: https://www.sixthtone.com/news/1015741 (Xizang is the Chinese name for Tibet).

since the early 1960s, with live births falling by 10 percent from 2021 figures. Covid has accelerated this fall, but it has been primarily driven by the 'one-child policy' (see pages 154-155), which saw China's fertility rate fall from 2.8 births per woman in 1979 to 1.6 in 2015. The bias towards male children inherent in the one-child policy further exacerbates the long-term consequences of this fall, with a skewed sex-ratio of 113 boys born for every hundred girls in the same year.[65]

The one-child policy was abolished completely in 2016, with the government announcing a three-child policy aim in 2021. However, the birth rate continued to drop even before Covid, and there are few reasons to believe that changes in government policy will reverse this. Rapid economic growth and urbanisation have greatly expanded the economic choices open to women; marriage and childbirth, once inevitable for the vast majority of women in China, are now options that can be taken or refused:

> A May 2017 survey by Zhaopin, one of China's largest job-recruitment websites, found that just over 40 percent of working women in China without children do not want to have babies at all. Almost two-thirds of working mothers with one child do not want to have a second child. The women surveyed said their top reasons for not wanting children were "not enough time and energy", "concerns over career development", and "too expensive to raise children".[66]

That last comment highlights one of the major social changes over the reform period, which has seen the costs of social reproduction almost entirely privatised. As one study noted:

---

65 Fincher, *Betraying Big Brother*, pages 171-172. The 'normal' sex ratio is 102-106 to 100 (official figures on fertility and sex ratios assume a simple female/male binary, taking no account of trans or intersex people).

66 As above, page 178.

Health and education reforms in the past twenty years have dismantled what were once state-provided systems that served as models for the third world and replaced them by market models, in which health and education are provided as commodities… between 1994 and 2005, the consumer price index increased by less than 40 percent, but the price of health care services increased by 226 percent and the price of tuition by 370 percent… Individual expenditure on education was five times greater in 2004 than in 1996, and on health it was 3.6 times.[67]

One aspect of the CCP's responses to the growing 'demographic deficit' has been a sustained attack on women who don't marry (childbirth outside marriage, while not illegal, is still heavily stigmatised almost everywhere in China). Official media have described single women over 27 as 'leftover women' since 2007,[68] and part of the reassertion of the CCP's control over society under Xi Jinping has been a hardening of gender norms and expectations. This has included growing restrictions on LGBTQ spaces, both online and in the real world, as well as media campaigns against 'sissy men' and 'abnormal gender aesthetics'.[69] Despite these attacks, however, China now has one of the largest LGBTQ communities in the world, estimated by one marketing agency at 70 to 80 million people.[70]

China is far from being the only state responding to a declining birth-rate with natalist 'culture wars', which assert the

---

67 Michael Webber, *Making capitalism in rural China*, (Edward Elgar, Cheltenham, 2012), page 180.

68 Leta Hong Fincher, *Leftover women*, (Zed Books, London, 2014), page 3.

69 'China's government is targeting 'sissy' men, with devastating consequences', *Gal-Dem*, 26 January, 2022: https://gal-dem.com/china-sissy-men-lgbtq/

70 'China now has the biggest LGBT economy in the world, but still no same-sex marriage', *Pink News*, 21 February, 2020: https://www.thepinknews.com/2020/02/21/lgbt-economy-world-china-same-sex-marriage-rights-conversion-therapy-alibaba-pink-yuan/

importance of 'family values' and strict gender roles. Far-right politicians across Europe and the Americas have in recent years linked campaigns to protect marriage and the family with racist attacks on migration and 'woke' challenges to conservative values. The equivalent in China is the CCP's promotion of the 'harmonious society', in which the patriarchal family is the guarantor of social stability.

However, in China as elsewhere, the natalists face a fundamental contradiction: the women that they want to force back into the home as wives and mothers are also essential to the modern urban economy. They are also increasingly unwilling to step back into traditional restrictive gender roles. According to official statistics quoted in a *China Labour Bulletin* (*CLB*) report of September 2023, women make up over a third of the migrant working class, and almost 44 percent of the total working class.[71] However, gender inequality remains high, and has markedly increased for older and rural women in particular, though one report claimed that the gender pay gap had narrowed in 2023 to 12.6 percent, down from 23.5 percent in 2019.[72]

In the countryside, the introduction of the 'household responsibility system' in the early 1980s saw the return of the patriarchal household as an economic unit (see page 154), as well as the return of arranged marriages, child marriages and bride prices, with girls and young women disproportionately taken out of school to work in the fields or rural industry.[73] The economic boom of the 1990s saw several hundred million people leave the villages to become migrant workers, though leaving behind

---

71 'Migrant workers and their children', *China Labour Bulletin*, 6 September, 2023: https://clb.org.hk/en/content/migrant-workers-and-their-children

72 'Gender wage gap narrows, but work discrimination remains', *China Daily*, 3 August, 2023: https://www.chinadaily.com.cn/a/202303/08/WS6407e66ca31057c47ebb3044.html

73 Elizabeth Croll, *From heaven to earth*, (Routledge, London, 1994), pages 164-170.

tens of millions of children with relatives for lack of schools and other facilities.[74]

In the cities, the massive wave of redundancies and workplace closures that began in the mid-1990s discriminated hugely against women. One 1997 survey found that over 62 percent of those laid off or unemployed were women, though they made up less than 39 percent of the urban workforce. Between 1995 and 2000 over 14 million women lost their jobs, the vast majority in manufacturing.[75] In part, this was because the closures were worst in those sectors which employed most women (particularly textiles), but it was also because married women were singled out for redundancy.

For young women coming from the countryside, however, the cities opened up many more opportunities in the new export-processing industries and services. One journalist who studied them found that:

> Their tolerance for risk was extraordinary. If they didn't like a factory or a boss or a coworker, they jumped somewhere else and never looked back... Their parents back home were only dimly aware of what their daughters were up to. Existence, to the factory girls, was a perpetual present which seemed immensely liberating but also troubling.[76]

IV   Resistance from below

The making of the modern migrant working class – arguably the largest population movement in human history – has

---

74   On the costs of such separations, see Orna Naftali, *Children in China*, (Polity Press, Cambridge, 2016) pages 144-153

75   Wang Zheng, 'Gender, employment and women's resistance', in Elizabeth Perry and Mark Selden (eds), *Chinese Society: Change, Conflict and Resistance (2nd edition)*, (RoutledgeCurzon, London, 2003), page 161.

76   Leslie T Chang, *Factory girls*, (Picador, London, 2009), page 25.

transformed Chinese society. One key aspect of that transformation is frequent waves of resistance from below, as different groups of workers and peasants have both reacted to, and attempted to shape, the 'liberating but also troubling' changes happening to them. I use the term 'waves' rather than 'movements' because one author's description of peasant resistance is more generally true:

> The events in each township and county were isolated, with little evidence that people in other jurisdictions came to the support of each other. Despite common circumstances and collectively held meanings of place and cultural attachments, these separate acts of protest never coalesced into a movement; they were just groups of people reacting in similar ways.[77]

These waves have been widely separated both in time and geographically, and have taken many diverse forms, both violent and non-violent, driven both by the combined force of individual aspirations and collective struggle. Collective struggles have overwhelmingly targeted local officials and managements as the people with the power to grant their demands, but they have often aimed at ensuring that higher officials knew of the issues involved. This tactic draws on the traditional folk belief that 'the emperor is wise, but his officials are corrupt', which has obvious advantages for both central government and for protesters – it both limits and legitimises protests.[78]

In the process, workers and peasants repeatedly have tested and extended the limits to dissent that the state would allow. I focus below on economic and livelihood-driven protests, but

---

77 Webber, *Making capitalism in rural China*, page 83.
78 For a longer discussion of this (and the extent to which peasants actually believe it, as opposed to using it as a mobilising tool), see Kevin J O'Brien and Lianjian Li, *Rightful resistance in rural China*, (Cambridge University Press, Cambridge, 2006), pages 42-49.

the 2000s also saw large numbers of environmental protests against pollution and the proposed construction of toxic chemical plants. One protest in the southern coastal city of Xiamen saw the first large-scale use of mobile phones as an organising tool, with organisers claiming to have sent a million texts.[79] The decade also saw a number of large-scale riots in small towns against local officials' abuses of power, many involving migrant workers, which required armed police to bring them to an end.[80]

However, in the 1990s and early 2000s, two of the biggest waves of organised resistance came from two quite different groups left behind by the boom: peasants in central China, and laid-off workers in state-owned industries, especially in the northeast.

Peasant struggles

By 1989 the peasants' gains from the agricultural reforms of the early 1980s had largely dried up, while they faced ever-increasing tax demands from local officials. One best-selling study of Anhui province in central China reported that:

> …peasants' average yearly income from 1994 to 1997 was only 1.91 percent more than it had been in 1993 – but the tax burden for 1997 was nine times the average of the previous four years.[81]

The study listed taxes on every aspect of village life over five pages, from management fees and officials' wages to building and farming regulation, including an 'attitude tax' levied on

---

79 Economy, *The river runs black*, page 271.

80 See for instance 'Residents in central China protest over death' *Reuters*, 20 June, 2009: https://www.reuters.com/article/latestCrisis/ idUSPEK69469/

81 Chen Guidi and Wang Juntao, *Will the boat sink the water?* (4th Estate, Sydney, 2006), page 139.

anyone who challenged or resisted the tax collector![82] The earliest known mass protest was in Renshou county, Sichuan province, in 1993, which drew some 15,000 peasants and lasted for some six months. An official report complained that protesters had:

> ...stormed the township and district governments and schools, beat up cadres and teachers, smashed public and private property, and illegally detained grassroots cadres [local officials] and public security personnel.[83]

When the police tear-gassed the protesters, they took police hostages and set fire to their cars. Renshou was far from an isolated case – an internal CCP report found over 6,000 instances of 'violent collective action' in the same year, with over 8,000 injuries or deaths. The police, and on occasion the army, were deployed in 340 cases, with over 2,000 casualties including almost 400 deaths. A Hong Kong journal reported that the 1990s had seen over 50,000 incidents with some five million participants, though this included peaceful demonstrations and boycotts as well as riots.[84]

The tax protests did eventually force national reform, with agricultural taxes being abolished in 2006, but as one researcher noted:

> ...local governments had already found another way to generate funds: the sale of village land to public and private investors and developers for the construction of infrastructure, housing or

---

82   As above, pages 151-155.

83   Quoted in Marc Blecher, 'Collectivism, contractualism and crisis in the Chinese countryside', in Robert Benewick and Paul Wingrove (eds), *China in the 1990s*, (Macmillan, Basingstoke, 1995), page 117.

84   Thomas P Bernstein and Xiaobo Li, *Taxation without representation in contemporary rural China*, (Cambridge University Press, Cambridge, 2003), pages 124-125.

industrial buildings. Peasants were often driven off the land by local cadres, who then sold collective land not just to raise money for local governments, but also to line their own pockets... By the mid-2000s, tens of millions of peasants had lost the land allocated to them.[85]

The land grabs provoked a new wave of protests, many of which were larger than the 1990s tax protests. The largest was in 2004 in Hanyuan county, Sichuan province: up to 100,000 people tried to block the construction of a dam, and fought the police sent to evict them. People were killed on both sides, and the county government had to send 10,000 militia to repress the demonstration. The protesters won increased compensation and the sacking of the local party secretary, but at the cost of almost 30 convictions.[86]

The high point of this wave was the 2011 revolt in Wukan village, Guangdong province, where protesters threw out local officials and police following the police murder of a protest leader, and barricaded the village, gaining international media coverage.[87] Armed police surrounded the village, cutting food, water and electricity supplies, but the blockade was lifted following promises of remedies from the provincial government. However, the promises weren't kept, and in 2016 the new village head called new protests, which were met with a vicious police crackdown involving tear gas and rubber bullets.[88]

---

85 Ruckus, *The communist road to capitalism*, page 125.

86 Yongshun Cai, *Collective resistance in China*, pages 115-116, 119.

87 See 'Gleaning the welfare fields', *Chuang*, issue 1 (2016): https://chuangcn.org/journal/one/gleaning-the-welfare-fields/ and 'Wukan: China's Democracy Experiment' *Al-Jazeera*, 3 April, 2017: https://www.aljazeera.com/program/featured-documentaries/2017/4/3/wukan-chinas-democracy-experiment

88 See 'Revisiting the Wukan uprising of 2011', *Chuang*, issue 1 (2016): https://chuangcn.org/journal/one/revisiting-the-wukan-uprising-of-2011/ and 'Wukan: The end of a democratic uprising in China', *Al-Jazeera*,

The number of rural protests peaked in 2014, and diminished steadily until the Covid lockdown of 2019. This was largely because of the general increase in state control and repression under Xi Jinping, though increased media controls also meant less reporting of protests. The fall also reflected reduced peasant numbers because of migration, as well as the general slowdown in economic growth which meant that less land was being taken for development.[89]

State-sector workers

Among state-sector workers, militancy revived very quickly after 1989, with one source reporting over 1,600 protests across China involving some 37,000 workers in 1990, and the growth of illegal organisations, with the largest having possibly 300 members.[90] Most of the disputes were defensive, triggered by redundancies and pensions shortfalls.

From 1997 onwards there was a major change in the state sector, as mass sackings sparked a more violent – and on occasion near-insurrectionary – series of disputes over unemployment pay, welfare benefits and pensions. The first of these exploded in the city of Mianyang, Sichuan province, in July 1997, where some 10,000 workers from three state-owned factories:

> ...took to the streets to denounce graft and demand unemployment relief after their factories were declared bankrupt. Armed police were sent in to impose a citywide curfew, after more than

10 June, 2017: https://www.aljazeera.com/features/2017/6/10/wukan-the-end-of-a-democratic-uprising-in-china

89   Chih-Jou Jay Chen, 'Peasant protests over land seizures in rural China', *Journal of Peasant Studies*, (2020), 47/6, pages 1327/1347L https://doi.org/10.1080/03066150.2020.1824182

90   Willy Wo-Lap Lam, *China after Deng Xiaoping*, (John Wiley, Singapore, 1995), page 273.

one hundred workers were injured in violent clashes with the police and eighty workers were reportedly arrested.[91]

The Mianyang protest was important both because of the scale of the demonstration, and because it united workers from a number of different enterprises. That same year the nearby city of Nanchong saw a 20,000-strong demonstration that kidnapped a factory manager to demand back pay, drew in thousands of workers from other enterprises – and won![92]

The mass lay-offs were spread unevenly, with the worst-affected region being northeastern China, with one researcher told of a 70 percent lay-off/unemployment rate in Benxi city, Liaoning province.[93] The same province saw almost 1,000 'mass incidents' between 2000 and 2002 involving some 830,000 people.[94] The largest of these, in Liaoyang city in 2002, saw the biggest workers' mobilisation since 1989. Workers from closed factories had for months been petitioning for the payment of back wages and social security. After the head of the provincial government said on television that there was no unemployment in the city, up to 100,000 workers from 20 different factories marched to demand his sacking.

The same year saw a movement among oil-field workers that spanned at least four provinces, after up to 50,000 workers from the Daqing oilfield took to the streets to protest a cut in heating subsidies. According to the *CLB* website:

---

91 Ching Kwan Lee, *Against the law*, (University of California Press, Berkeley, CA, 2007), page 101.

92 Ching Kwan Lee, 'Pathways of labour insurgency', in Perry and Selden (eds), *Chinese society*, page 81.

93 William Hurst, *The Chinese worker after socialism*, (Cambridge University Press, Cambridge, 2009), page 32.

94 Ching Kwan Lee, *Against the law*, page 5.

Workers from the Xinjiang, Shengli (close to Shandong Province) and Liaohe (Liaoning Province) oilfields staged solidarity demonstrations when they heard about the Daqing workers' struggle. Most significantly, the workers have set up their own union, the Daqing PAB Retrenched Workers' Provisional Union Committee, and elected representatives. The local authorities responded by sending paramilitary police, and deploying a PLA tank regiment. 'The workers have stood up to fight, and they will not be threatened [by the military presence],' the local official exclaimed.[95]

Few if any of the protests were against the enterprise closures as such, aiming instead at obtaining the lay-off pay and other benefits that workers had been promised. They won significant national concessions, including the government taking over payment of lay-off benefits. This, combined with the decline in the number and scale of closures, led to a drop in large-scale protests after 2005. However, as late as 2009 steelworkers in Jilin province hit the headlines after killing a company executive involved in a takeover which threatened thousands of jobs.[96]

The state's willingness to pay off grievances was part of a larger pattern. As Ho-fung Hung noted:

…the Chinese state, aided by increasing financial and fiscal means arising from the economic boom has been able to keep this unrest under control by making concessions to protesters' demands.[97]

---

95   'CLB Press Release on Daqing Oilfield Workers' Protests', China Labour Bulletin: https://clb.org.hk/en/content/clb-press-release-daqing-oilfield-workers-protests

96   'Chinese state steel workers beat private firm boss to death', Guardian, 26 July, 2009: https://www.theguardian.com/world/2009/jul/26/china-steel-workers-riot

97   Ho-fung Hung, The China boom, page 177

But while the combination of economic concessions and repression kept struggles fragmented and directed at the lowest levels of the state or individual managements, it also kept them coming. One of the lessons workers drew was that strikes, demonstrations and riots could win concessions. This was to be especially true as militancy grew among migrant workers in central and southern China.

Migrant workers

The migrant working class grew from around 60 million in the mid-1990s to over 270 million in 2014.[98] Migrant workers were both 'pushed' by diminishing opportunities in the villages and 'pulled' by the lure of higher wages and greater life chances in the cities. Many early accounts of China's industrialisation saw migrant workers as a pliable, inexhaustible and disposable source of cheap labour, willing to put up with long hours and atrocious working conditions for low wages that were nevertheless better than what they could earn in the villages. Tellingly, as late as 2011, one researcher felt it necessary to write that 'the stereotype of Chinese workers as passive victims of capitalist globalization and authoritarian government does not fit the reality of industrial relations in China.'[99]

There is no question that the hours and conditions which most migrant workers had to endure were atrocious, nor that they were often paid far below a living wage because:

...the wage that a migrant receives from working in the factory is not for supporting their livelihood in the city, but it is presumed that the costs of the social reproduction of the workers is absorbed in the rural communities. This means that

98   Pun Ngai, *Migrant labour in China*, (Polity Press, Cambridge, 2016), page 30.
99   Tim Pringle, *Trade unions in China*, (Routledge, London, 2011), page 8.

their family, marriage, procreation, childrearing, and retirement are taken care of in the original rural location from which they migrated... In short, the salary they receive is not for them to live in the industrial cities but to prepare them for return to their rural homelands.[100]

The *hukou* system of household registration which still denies migrants access to welfare benefits, education and housing also meant that it was easy for the government to remove them from the cities; following the 2008 stock market crash, one in seven migrant workers returned to their villages after being laid off.[101] Until 2003, migrants were regularly detained and forcibly expelled from the cities by police checking temporary permits, a system that had much in common with apartheid South Africa's pass laws.[102] The practice was only abolished following a nation-wide outcry after police beat a detainee to death.[103]

However, the toxic combination of long hours, unsafe working conditions, management violence and sexual abuse, and low wages (often paid late or not at all) sparked many forms of resistance, from simply walking off the job (either singly or as a group) to filing an official grievance. In Shenzhen, which had one of the biggest concentrations of migrant workers, arbitrated labour cases went from just 359 in 1990 to over 13,000 in 1999. In the same year there were 110 large-scale strikes and 540 'spontaneous incidents'.[104]

---

100 Pun Ngai, *Migrant labour in China*, pages 33-34.
101 Hsiao-Hung Pai, *Scattered sand*, (Verso, London, 2012), page 11.
102 For a detailed comparison between South Africa and China see Peter Alexander and Anita Chan, 'Does China have an apartheid pass system', *Journal of Ethnic and Migration Studies*, Vol 30, No 4, July 2004; https://doi.org/10.1080/13691830410001699487
103 'Why it is important to remember Sun Zhigang', *China Labour Bulletin*, 17 April, 2013: https://clb.org.hk/en/content/why-it-important-remember-sun-zhigang
104 Ching Kwan Lee, *Against the law*, pages 162-164.

From 2003 onwards, there was a relative labour shortage in Shenzhen and the surrounding Pearl River Delta, as workers either moved north for better-paying jobs or returned to their villages, and this further stimulated militancy. There are no reliable figures for the numbers of strikes, but one researcher quoted an NGO worker saying 'at least half of the workers she met had experience of striking'.[105] Another researcher found a young woman who, at the age of 22, had worked for more than 20 companies since she was 16, and had led strikes in three of them![106]

She was almost certainly an outlier, but she exemplified the leading role of women in strikes across the Pearl River Delta. The same researcher reported on a 2002 strikers' demonstration:

> The male strike leaders were consciously pushed to the core or the back of the crowd, while female workers stood in the periphery or the front. Many female workers who used to be docile and obedient on the job became very brave and militant; they stood in the front to protect the male strikers... Workers were aware that male workers were more likely to be arrested if they confronted the police, while female workers were relatively safe given that police would not dare touch them.[107]

The global crisis of 2008 destroyed tens of millions of jobs and broke for a while workers' ability to strike. But while there were fewer strikes, organisation became more sophisticated, as was particularly shown in the 2010 wave of auto industry strikes. These began in one Honda plant, and quickly spread across the industry and beyond. The wave crested with widespread strikes

---

105 Chris King-Chi Chan, *The challenge of labour in China*, page 37.
106 Zhongjin Li, Eli Friedman and Hao Ren, *China on strike* (Haymarket, Chicago, IL, 2016), pages 115-127.
107 As above, page 70.

across the northern city of Dalian involving over 70,000 workers, with several companies giving pre-emptive wage increases to head off strikes.[108]

These were offensive strikes for above-inflation wages, involving high levels of organisation including 'dark web' websites that allowed workers from different plants to contact each other. Several of the strikes called for wage parity with other plants, and there were repeated calls for independent trade unions. Almost all of the strikes won significant wage increases, and workers in some plants won unofficial bargaining rights; at the first Honda plant to strike, workers won another even higher increase in 2011 without striking.[109]

Employers could afford such rises as wages were so low, but they were also facing labour shortages, and pressures from central and local governments to raise wages. Strike numbers continued to rise, peaking in 2015 and 2016 before falling off. Post-lockdown figures have suggested a new rise, with the *CLB* Strike Map recording more strikes in 2023 than any year since 2016.[110]

The vast majority of strikes are still defensive (mostly over unpaid wages) and independent union organisation remains strictly banned. In that sense, there is still no Chinese workers' movement. But while strikes are not officially legal, they cannot be repressed out of existence, and the dilemma that a leading CCP official identified in 2011 remains true today:

---

108 Eli Friedman, *Insurgency trap*, (Cornell University Press, Ithaca, NY, 2014), pages 140-150.

109 Hsiao-Hung Pai, *Scattered sand*, page 185.

110 'An introduction to *China Labour Bulletin*'s Strike Map', *China Labour Bulletin*, 10 January 2024: https://clb.org.hk/en/content/introduction-china-labour-bulletin%E2%80%99s-strike-map The Strike Map doesn't claim to record every single strike, but it seems reasonable to assume that the proportion of strikes they do record remains roughly constant over time.

In other countries, the strike is only a last resort and frequently is used as a threat; domestically, employees strike first and then negotiate. That is to say, they use strikes and other extreme measures to win the right to negotiate. First, the production line stops, and then they consider how to resolve the problem.[111]

The state-run All-China Federation of Trade Unions remains part of the problem, unable to represent workers' interests because it is run by the CCP, and so strengthens the impetus to 'strike first, talk later'. While the CCP is able to set effective limits to worker militancy, it is unable to prevent the news of fully or even partially successful strikes spreading. Even after the increased repression under Xi Jinping and the Covid lockdown, the dynamic identified by a *CLB* writer in 2014 still applies today:

Just about every factory worker... has a cheap smartphone and can post news about their strike and the response of management and the local government to it on social media and have that information circulate within a matter of minutes... And the fact that there are so many strikes means that workers have less to fear by staging protests, there is safety in numbers and in many cases, they have nothing to lose by going out on strike. Younger workers, especially, have higher expectations and are no longer willing to tolerate the abuse and exploitation their parents had to endure.[112]

Tibet and Xinjiang
Across most of China the CCP deals with strikes, protests and demonstrations through a mixture of concessions and sporadic

---

111 Quoted in Friedman, *Insurgency trap*, page 151
112 'Q&A: Strikes on the rise in China with new generation of interconnected workers', *South China Morning Post*, 13 August, 2014: https://www.scmp.com/news/china-insider/article/1572050/qa-strikes-peak-china-new-generation-interconnected-blue-collar

repression aimed at reinforcing the 'red lines' beyond which dissent will not be tolerated. Almost all acts of protest stay within those restraints, targeting local officials or individual managers rather than the CCP as a ruling class. In Tibet and Xinjiang, however, things are very different. Although the dynamics are quite different in the two places, the past thirty years has seen huge challenges to CCP rule, and state repression follows quite different rules of engagement to those used elsewhere.

In Tibet, repression continued after 1989 (see page 191), with further restrictions on monasteries and religious activities, while at the same time economic development led to huge environmental damage and high inflation. But most Tibetans were excluded from the economic growth they could see around them.

Tensions exploded in 2008, following police attacks on monks in Lhasa demonstrating in support of the Dalai Lama. As larger numbers protested against mass arrests, Chinese security forces first used tear-gas and cattle-prods, and then live ammunition. By the end of the week thousands of people were fighting back with stones against a massive police and army presence, and rioters briefly controlled large parts of Lhasa. The government claimed that 19 people had died, while Tibetan exile sources put the figure at over 80.

The protests quickly spread beyond Lhasa and Tibet province to the whole of 'historic Tibet', which includes Qinghai province and parts of Gansu, Sichuan and Yunnan provinces. The government admitted opening fire and killing demonstrators in the towns of Luhuo and Aba in Sichuan,[113] while in Gansu the *Guardian* website showed video footage of several thousands of people demonstrating in the town of Xiahe where protesters

---

113 'State admits police shot protesters "in self-defence"', *Guardian*, 21 March, 2008: http://www.theguardian.com/world/2008/mar/21/tibet. china

were tear-gassed.[114] The repression was particularly fierce as the CCP was concerned to put down the protests before the start of the 2008 Olympic Games, a major showcase announcing China's arrival as a world power.

This was the largest and most widespread protest wave across Tibetan areas since the 1950s, with the majority of the protests outside Tibet province, which illustrated the extent to which this had become a pan-Tibetan movement.[115]

The same areas were again at the centre of student protests in 2010 and 2011 against the marginalisation of the Tibetan language in education reforms,[116] a movement which was to overlap with one of the most arresting and disturbing protest movements of this century – suicide by fire, or self-immolation.

The Tibetan author Tsering Woeser documented every incident to July 2015 in her book *Tibet on fire*, and summarised what is known about the 145 who killed themselves (or tried to):

> Most of these individuals are men, though some are women. Many were parents who left behind young children. The oldest was sixty-four and the youngest sixteen... many were ordinary people: seventy-four were nomads or peasants. In general, the

114 'Tibet protests spread to neighbouring provinces', *Guardian*, 16 March, 2008: http://www.theguardian.com/world/video/2008/mar/16/xiahe. gansu

115 For the extent of the revolt and the subsequent repression, see Warren W Smith Jr, *Tibet's last stand?*, (Pentagon Press, New Delhi, India, 2010), pages 11-75. A map on the Uprising Archive website shows the extent of the protests (the blank areas are mostly uninhabited): https://uprisingarchive.org/Resources/Tibet%20Protest%20Map%20 2008%20.jpg

116 See Clémence Henry, 'The Chinese education system as a source of conflict in Tibetan areas', in Ben Hillman and Gray Tuttle (eds), *Ethnic conflict and protest in Tibet and Xinjiang*, (Columbia University Press, New York, NY, 2016), pages 111-114.

profiles of the self-immolators are diverse, including high-school students, workers, vendors, a carpenter…[117]

The government passed new laws making it illegal to self-immolate, to help anyone else to do so, to spread the news of a self-immolation, or even to organise prayers for someone who had died. Collective punishments were imposed on families, monasteries, nunneries, and sometimes whole villages. Since 2012, Lhasa has been essentially closed to Tibetans from outside the city. However, that same year:

> At the Eighteenth Chinese Communist party Congress held in Beijing in November 2012, officials insisted that 'Lhasa is the happiest city in China,' while guards stood outside on Tiananmen Square armed with fire extinguishers, in case anyone should try to light themselves on fire.[118]

The combination of repression and the commitment required has reduced the numbers in more recent years, with only 16 self-immolations taking place since those recorded in *Tibet on fire*, the last in March 2022.[119] China's campaign of forcible assimilation has been intensified, with hundreds of thousands of nomads and inhabitants of remote villages relocated to newly-built settlements (for which those removed have to pay), and further restrictions on religious freedoms. Dam and mining projects, forced resettlement, the increasing numbers of Chinese tourists and settlers, and more recently, the further restrictions of Covid lockdowns, all combined

---

117 Tsering Woeser, *Tibet on fire*, (Verso, London, 2016), pages 5/6.

118 Emily Yeh, *Taming Tibet: landscape transformation and the gift of Chinese development* (Cornell University Press, Ithaca, NY, 2013), page 270.

119 'Factsheet on self-immolation', *Central Tibetan Administration* (the Dalai Lama's government in exile), last updated 14 March 2022: https://tibet.net/important-issues/factsheet-immolation-2011-2012/

to put the continued existence of the Tibetan language and culture under increasing threat.

Xinjiang's history since 1989 has been even more turbulent. The province has become increasingly important to China's economic development in this period. It is a major source of oil and natural gas, and increasingly a site for solar power development, as well as China's biggest cotton producer. It is also a key link in the 'belt' of the BRI, with major trading routes to west and south Asia and beyond.

The well-documented attacks on Xinjiang's Muslims have occasioned much hypocrisy from Western governments, despite China making explicit connections between its campaigns of repression and the 'global war on terror' since 2001.[120] The first major confrontation was in the town of Baren in April 1990, when a protest outside government offices was attacked by police, which triggered further resistance and was finally suppressed by the army, with up to 50 people killed. In February 1997, thousands of people protested and rioted in the town of Ghulja against the banning of a Muslim youth organisation, with armed police again opening fire. The same month saw three bombs explode on buses in Urumqi, killing nine people. The government would later claim that 'terrorist acts' in the 1990s killed 162 people and injured over 400, and carried out thousands of arrests and at least 190 executions of 'terrorists'.[121]

Protests were sparked by a combination of increased repression of expressions of Muslim identity, reversing the religious and political liberalisation of the 1980s, and a growing sense of exclusion from economic development in Xinjiang. The province's economy grew very fast in the 1990s (though from a

---

120 See for instance Nick Holdstock, *China's forgotten people*, (IB Tauris, London, 2015), pages 158-165.

121 James A Millward, *Eurasian crossroads*, (Christopher Hurst, London, 2021), pages 317-327.

low base), driven by trade with the newly-independent states in central Asia, cotton-growing, oil and construction. Agricultural and industrial development largely excluded Uyghurs and other Muslims, and were dominated by Han Chinese migrants from other provinces. The result was that by the early 2000s per capita income in Uyghur-majority southern Xinjiang was half the provincial average.[122]

This toxic mix of poverty and religious discrimination exploded in the Urumqi riots of 2009, some of the worst violence seen anywhere in China since 1989. It began with a peaceful Uyghur protest in the city centre against the murder of several migrant Uyghur workers in Guangdong, which was savagely attacked by the police, who reportedly fired into the crowds.[123] In response, Uyghurs attacked symbols of Chinese power, but also some individual Han Chinese migrants, with almost 200 people reported killed. Repression was swift and savage, with the whole province placed under martial law and a mobile phone and internet blackout, as well as thousands of arrests. Han Chinese vigilantes who armed themselves to retaliate were treated far more leniently by the security forces, with at least one documented incident of open collaboration.[124]

Violent incidents multiplied over the next few years. There were increasing confrontations between Uyghurs and security forces, as well as with Han migrants. From 2014 onwards acts of individual terror multiplied, including car and bus attacks (one in Beijing), bombings, and a group knife attack in the south-western city of Kunming that killed 31 people and injured over 180. As the CCP increasingly came to treat almost all Uyghurs as actual or potential terrorists, this became a self-fulfilling prophecy, with increasing numbers of Uyghurs being drawn

---

122 As above, page 298.
123 See above, pages 370-371.
124 Nick Holdstock, *China's forgotten people*, page 192.

to Islamist groups, especially among the growing number of refugees fleeing the province.

Attacks on Uyghur and Muslim culture accelerated following Xi's declaration in 2014 of a 'People's War on Terror'. This entailed constant identity checks, electronic surveillance, mass arrests, the demolition of religious buildings, as well attempts to outlaw expressions of religious belief such as beards, hijabs, and fasting during Ramadan. This campaign explicitly drew on Western Islamophobia, including recruiting former Blackwater mercenaries from service in Iraq. One researcher quoted the current head of China's National Ethnic Affairs Commission, as saying that China 'should learn from the United States', Russia's, and Israel's colonial methods to introduce Han settlers to its western frontier.'[125]

And there are also the infamous camps, which have imprisoned between one and two million Muslims across Xinjiang. This represents something like one in ten of the adult population, the largest internment of civilians since World War II.[126] A Google Earth search in 2018 documented the building of 94 such camps across Xinjiang:[127]

> Uyghur, Kazakh, Kyrgyz and Uzbek internees were not tried before internment, but simply rounded up on suspicion of being likely to commit future crimes. A list used by police to help them meet detainment quotas included as 'extremist' such mundane Islamic practices as avoiding alcohol, fasting, veiling, wearing a beard or owning a Qur'an, as well as stranger criteria such as quitting smoking or owning a tent... Former detainees

---

125 Promise Li, 'China and Israel Have a Long History of Cooperating in Repression', *Jacobin*, 21 October, 2023: https://jacobin.com/2023/10/china-israel-repression-military-trade-palestine-technology

126 Darren Byler, *In the camps*, (Atlantic Books, London, 2022), is the best source for first-hand accounts of life inside the camps.

127 Sean R Roberts, *The war on the Uyghurs*, (Manchester University Press, Manchester, 2020), page 214.

who managed to leave China reported crowded cells, unsanitary condition, poor food, beating, psychological and physical torture, systematic rape, as well as forced IUD-insertion and sterilization, and administration of anti-fertility drugs within the camps.[128]

The camps have also become notorious for both forced labour, in which many well-known Western companies and brands are implicated, and for forced labour transfers to other parts of China. As in Tibet, the imposition of Covid lockdown restrictions intensified the repression of both Uyghur and Muslim culture, which then spread across all parts of China with a Muslim population. A *Financial Times* report of 2023 identified over 1,700 mosques which have been 'altered, stripped or destroyed'.[129]

In recent years Western politicians have increasingly taken up the plight of both Tibetans and Uyghurs as part of a growing campaign against the rise of China as a world power. This is sheer hypocrisy – China's repression in Tibet and Xinjiang mirrors past assaults on Indigenous peoples and cultures in the USA, Canada, Australia and elsewhere, and the continuing assaults on the Palestinian people.

Nevertheless, as one researcher argued:

Acknowledging the shortcomings of this style of advocacy should in no way diminish international solidarity with the Uyghur people. Some self-identified "anti-imperialists" have cited US support for Uyghur activism to cast doubt on claims of mass repression in Xinjiang and the existence of the internment camps. But progressives who criticise racism and Islamophobia

---

128 Millward, *Eurasian crossroads*, page 399.
129 'How China is tearing down Islam', *Financial Times*, November 27, 2023: https://ig.ft.com/china-mosques/

in the West while turning a blind eye to it in China only end up discrediting the left, and entrenching the emerging Cold War dynamics on this issue. It is perfectly possible to condemn China's actions in Xinjiang, while at the same time remaining clear-eyed about Washington's efforts to utilise the issue for its own ends.[130]

Hong Kong

Although Hong Kong reverted to China in 1997, it did so under the 'one country, two systems' arrangement whereby Hong Kong kept its existing political and social structures. This included an element of popular election for parts of the government, and basic democratic rights such as the freedoms to publish, to strike and to demonstrate. Crucially, this meant that Hong Kong was the only place in China where it was legal to commemorate the June 4 massacre. In the years from the 20th anniversary in 2009 to 2019, over 100,000 people turned out each year to the annual commemorations, including significant numbers of people from mainland China.

There were large-scale protests in Hong Kong in 2014 for universal suffrage in government elections. The 'Umbrella Movement' – so called because demonstrators used umbrellas as protection against tear gas – brought hundreds of thousands onto the streets at its height, but was repressed after almost 80 days of street occupations.[131]

The 2019 movement started in response to a proposed extradition bill which would allow China to extradite anyone from

---

130 David Brophy, 'Confronting China's war on terror, *rs21*, 14 December, 2018: https://www.rs21.org.uk/2018/12/14/confronting-chinas-war-on-terror/

131 See Au Loong-yu, *Hong Kong in revolt*, (Pluto Press, London, 2020), pages 8-14 and Sid Zoichi, "Umbrella revolution' not rained out yet', *Red Flag*, 9 October 2014: https://redflag.org.au/article/umbrella-revolution-not-rained-out-yet

Hong Kong to China, where courts have a 99 percent conviction rate.[132] The movement built slowly, but that year's Tiananmen Square commemoration on 4 June was the largest since 2012. Five days later, a million people marched against the proposed law, almost half of them under 30. The following week the numbers doubled to two million – out of a total population of 7.5 million. Hong Kong's Chief Executive promised to withdraw the bill, but the movement went on the offensive, uniting around five key demands (expressed in the slogan, 'Five demands, not one less!'):

- Withdraw the extradition bill
- Stop labelling protesters as rioters
- Drop all charges against protesters
- An independent enquiry into police behaviour
- For the resignation of the Chief Executive, and universal suffrage elections for her successor and the Legislative Council (the city council)

This was primarily a youth revolt, especially of the '1997 generation' (those born after Hong Kong's reversion). As veteran socialist Au Loong-Yu noted, they were:

> …an angry generation, because they were lied to, the promises made to them were not honoured, and when they asked questions, they were teargassed. It is a desperate generation, because they witnessed catastrophe after catastrophe, yet their calls for action were largely ignored by their parents until very late.[133]

But their anger evoked a much wider echo because of the stagnation of Hong Kong's economy, resulting in growing social

---

132 'China's 2022 Acquittal Rate Lowest in Two Decades', *Dui Hua Human Right Journal*, 12 September, 2023: https://www.duihuahrjournal. org/2023/09/chinas-2022-acquittal-rate-lowest-in.html

133 Au Loong-yu, *Hong Kong in revolt*, pages 44-45.

inequality and soaring housing costs. The demonstrations were met with increasing police brutality: beatings, tear gas and mass arrests. The young demonstrators – both university and school students – responded in kind:

> Across the city, students dug up the pavements and used the bricks as projectiles. Footpath fencing was stripped of tonnes of metal bars, and construction sites were constantly raided for materials to build barricades. While the black-clad and masked young militants in the relentless street clashes numbered only thousands or tens of thousands, a mass movement stood behind them, providing food, shelter, transportation, counselling and weaponry – baseball bats, golf clubs, petrol and alcohol for bombs and thousands of umbrellas to defend them against water cannons and shield them from prying police and media cameras.[134]

Though only a minority were willing to fight the police directly, the movement behind them, organised largely through social media platforms such as Telegram, worked inventively to support the movement. One journalist noted that:

> On demonstration nights, you can find outside local under-ground (MTR) stations piles of multi-coloured t-shirts, piles of travel tickets and loose change. The shirts are because demonstrators favour wearing black and then changing into other colours on leaving a demonstration to decrease the risk from the police or pro-Beijing thugs. The tickets and the money are freely available so that demonstrators do not have to use their travel cards and leave electronic record of their movements.[135]

---

134 Ben Hillier, *The art of rebellion*, (Spark Publishing, Melbourne, 2020), pages 9-10.

135 Colin Sparks, 'Mass mobilisation shakes Hong Kong', *rs21*, 5 August 2019: https://www.rs21.org.uk/2019/08/05/mass-mobilisation-shakes-hong-kong/

August saw a general strike called, with an estimated 350,000 strikers, which largely shut down the main airport. A second general strike in September was less successful, though both led to increases in union organisation. While the wider movement ebbed, student strikes and class boycotts spread, culminating in occupations in November at two major universities, and some of the most intense street-fighting to date. Both occupations were bloodily defeated, which led to further polarisation across the whole city. An October opinion survey found that 'about 50 percent of the population doesn't trust the police at all. Before the movement it was seven percent'.[136] District council elections held the same month also revealed the depths of popular anger. Pro-democracy candidates won 347 out of 452 seats contested, with pro-Beijing parties holding just 60 seats.

In 2020, the movement stalled in the face of both the government's intransigence and the sudden arrival of Covid, for which Hong Kong's authorities were completely unprepared. A healthworkers' strike won restrictions on border crossings from China as part of restricting the spread of Covid, and by the spring, Hong Kong was coping better with Covid than Britain. This was in large part because of memories of the 2003 SARS epidemic,[137] which had also spread from China, and had been badly mismanaged by Hong Kong's rulers.

The movement did revive, but on a much smaller scale than before. The CCP used the Covid crisis to postpone Hong Kong's elections and impose a draconian 'National Security Law', modelled on one introduced in China in 2015, which effectively outlawed all opposition. The jailings of activists and demonstrators have since multiplied, while in 2021 a number of major trade unions and other opposition groups dissolved themselves

---

136 Hillier, *The art of rebellion*, page 141.
137 For a brief history of the SARS epidemic see Mike Davis, *The monster at our door*, (The New Press, New York, NY, 2005), pages 69-80

in order to avoid further prosecutions.[138] The CCP beat the movement, but at the cost of further alienating a significant proportion of Hong Kong's population.

V Xi Jinping, repression and Covid

In the years since Xi Jinping came to power, China has become more repressive internally and more assertive internationally, especially around Taiwan and the South China Sea. For most Western commentators this was simply the CCP reverting to authoritarian type, but in reality, the shift towards a more aggressive economic nationalism was primarily a product of the 2008 crash. Although the internal economic conditions were very different, the CCP's strategy, as it gradually emerged, presaged the rise of right-wing populism and protectionism symbolised by figures such as Bolsonaro in Brazil and Trump in the USA.

Xi Jinping rose to power in 2012 representing a new consensus inside the CCP about how China should face the post-crash world. This 'new normal' approach involved accepting that economic growth would now fall below ten percent a year. Growth would now come through a combination of increased consumption, replacing imports with domestic production, and more state-directed investment overseas through the BRI. Increasing consumption mattered both for economic growth and winning greater popular support, and this has led to continuing increases in wages. Official figures show that average wages have doubled over the last decade,[139] though the rate of increase

---

138 See Au Loong-yu, 'The Annihilation of Hong Kong's Civil Society', *Made in China*, 8 March, 2022: https://madeinchinajournal.com/2022/03/08/the-annihilation-of-hong-kongs-civil-society/

139 'China's Average Wages – Trends and Implications for Businesses', *China Briefing*, August 15, 2023: https://www.china-briefing.com/news/average-salaries-in-china-trends-and-implications-for-businesses/

has slowed in recent years, and inflation meant that the real gains were rather less. Nevertheless, the CCP understands that retaining popular support depends above all on maintaining living standards.

This strategy has centred on restoring the power and authority of the central state over local officials and managers, as well as civil society, through attacks on official corruption, increased controls over private capital, and greater media censorship.

Corruption, private business and repression

There have been many previous campaigns against corruption inside the state and party machines, all of which fairly quickly fizzled out. Xi's campaign is very different, as one analyst noted:

> Since 2012, the authorities have investigated more than 2.7 million officials and punished more than 1.5 million others… In a party with 80 million members, once you exclude the tens of millions who are farmers, elderly and retired… that amounts to a generational clean-out.[140]

The anti-corruption campaign was driven by a number of different imperatives. It immediately helped clear Xi's path to power by removing several key rivals, in particular Bo Xilai, the neo-Maoist boss of Chongqing province. The campaign also had a populist edge, in seeming to respond to widespread popular anger about the abuses of local officials, as well as the palpable inequalities between rich and poor; by 2010 one percent of China's households owned one-third of the country's wealth, while the bottom 25 percent of households owned just one percent.[141] It also acted as a powerful disciplinary tool for

---

140 Richard McGregor, *Xi Jinping: the backlash*, (Penguin Books, Sydney, 2019), page 34.

141 Magnus, *Red flags*, page 73.

keeping officials obedient to Beijing's instructions, because almost all officials were vulnerable to accusations of corruption.

Corruption had become endemic amongst officials at all levels, as an inevitable if unintended consequence of the post-Mao market reforms, and grew exponentially as the economy grew. There are necessarily no exact figures for the sums involved, but the figures for the average bribe recovered in prosecutions give some sense of the scale. The average leapt from 54,000 yuan in 1995 to 273,000 in 2005.[142]

Nevertheless, as one study argued, corruption in the early years had stimulated economic growth:

> Because the new business activities created by reform created new opportunities for illicit gain, corrupt officials had personal and financial reasons to support reform rather than rally in defense of the old system... corruption may have arguably greased the wheels in the sense that the interests of corrupt officials were not at loggerheads with the profit-making interests of China's emerging class of traders, businessmen and entrepreneurs.[143]

This was true even though it was the 'wrong' form of corruption. The study quoted above distinguishes between 'developmental corruption' – where politicians and officials steal, but then use some of the money to bribe voters or otherwise invest it – and 'degenerative corruption', where they just keep or consume the proceeds. In Marxist terms, this is the difference between 'commodity circulation' and 'waste production'; the first contributes to further economic growth, while the second reduces society's stock of capital.

---

142 Andrew Wedeman, *Double paradox*, (Cornell University Press, Ithaca, NY, 2012), page 2. The 2005 figure was roughly equal to 15 years' worth of the average wage at that time.

143 As above, page 107-108.

However, by the time Xi came to power, such advantages had largely evaporated. The market was firmly established, and the central state's priority was now to reassert its authority by limiting local autonomy. Recouping lost funds wasn't the primary aim; on one estimate the campaign cost something over one percent of China's GDP in 2014 and 2015.[144] But in an era of declining growth and profit rates, the argument for frugality was an important political tool.

The reassertion of central authority also underpins greater state intervention in private businesses, especially the 'digital economy' corporations that emerged as internet and mobile phone coverage became ubiquitous across China: Huawei, Weibo, Alibaba and the like. Although the state still controls traditional core sectors of the economy,[145] most economic growth since 2008 has come in construction and services, which are dominated by private capital. Private investment overtook state investment in 2008, but by 2016 the gap was once again beginning to close.[146]

Restraints on private business have taken a number of forms, including boosting the powers of CCP committees within businesses, forcing companies to buy from Chinese suppliers, state interference with content on television and online platforms, and a number of high-profile arrests of executives. Private businesses have been only too ready to co-operate with the CCP, with the vast majority of China's dollar billionaires being either CCP members

---

144 Elizabeth Economy, *The third revolution*, (Oxford University Press, New York, NY, 2018), page 35.

145 In 2022, there were 136 Chinese companies on the Fortune Global 500 list of the world's biggest companies, over 70 percent of which were state-owned. 'Fortune Favors the State-Owned: Three Years of Chinese Dominance on the Global 500 List', *Centre for Strategic and International Studies*, 7 October, 2022: https://www.csis.org/blogs/trustee-china-hand/fortune-favors-state-owned-three-years-chinese-dominance-global-500-list

146 Nicholas R Lardy, *The state strikes back*, (Peterson Institute for International Economics, Washington, DC, 2019), pages 19-20.

or government officials.[147] In 2018 the 153 'super-rich' members of China's National People's Congress (the parliament that formally passes laws) had a net worth of US$650 billion, the equivalent of Switzerland's annual GDP.[148]

In 2015 China's stock markets crashed,[149] precipitating a huge flight of capital abroad following a currency readjustment. The government was forced to respond with greater controls on both stock market trading and capital exports. Although the stock markets recovered within a few months (at a huge cost to the state), it was a sign that the economic recovery following 2008 was built on shaky foundations. More importantly, as one analyst noted:

> What the stock market experience revealed was the deep contradiction that existed – and still exists – between wanting a 'decisive' role for markets and prices in resource allocation, and insisting on a dominant role for the state sector.[150]

Reasserting the power of the central state has also involved increased surveillance and repression of perceived threats to 'social harmony'. This has been most severe in Tibet, Xinjiang and Hong Kong, as detailed above. Elsewhere in China it has been more targeted, with strikes and demonstrations mostly

---

147 'China leads Hurun Global Rich List 2023 with 969 billionaires: report', *Global Times*, 23 March 2023 https://www.globaltimes.cn/page/202303/1287829.shtml

148 'China's Parliament Is a Growing Billionaires' Club', *New York Times*, 1 March, 2018: https://www.nytimes.com/2018/03/01/business/china-parliament-billionaires.html That's 153 out of 3,000 members – if all social groups were equally well represented, the NPC would have over 30 million members.

149 See my 'Bubbles, bounces and soft landings – China's stock market implodes' *rs21*, 15 July, 2015: https://www.rs21.org.uk/2015/07/15/bubbles-bounces-and-soft-landings-chinas-stock-market-implodes/

150 Magnus, *Red flags*, page 106.

tolerated, and repression reserved for those who try to organise outside the state's allowed limits.

Strikes and peasant protests have both declined since 2015. The CCP has also clamped down on grassroots organising, in particular targeting Chinese NGOs and small Maoist student groups organising support for migrant workers,[151] as well as many feminist organisations. The attacks on feminists have come in part because they have publicised just how widespread sexual harassment and sexual violence are inside China. They intensified after many groups connected with the international #MeToo movement in 2018:

> Feminist activists and thousands of students at dozens of Chinese universities defied heavy internet censorship and seized on the global momentum of #MeToo to demand an end to sexual harassment on campus. The swift mobilisation of over 8,000 students and alumni at around 70 universities… showed that China's young generation was 'enraged by the prevalence of gender inequality and repression'…[152]

But the feminist campaigns also reflected and amplified a wider discontent with the CCP's patriarchal authoritarianism and the growing stress on family and child-bearing. The protests led to top-level attacks on 'Western feminism' and the closing down and censorship of feminist apps and websites. This is, in turn, part of a much wider censorship of social media and online discussion, which has included the arrests of high-profile posters and even on occasion the cutting off of internet services in Xinjiang and in Tibetan areas of Sichuan.

However, the ubiquity of mobile phones and internet use has

---

151 See Ralf Ruckus, *The left in China*, (Pluto Press, London, 2023), pages 114-120.

152 Fincher, *Betraying Big Brother*, page 53.

also offered the CCP the opportunity to greatly increase mass surveillance, including the launch in 2015 of the Orwellian-sounding 'social credit' system which aims to:

> …monitor, rate and shape the behaviour of participants in a way that advances ethical behaviour… collect data on individual and corporate behaviour via the Internet and develop a rating system that will provide benefits for good behaviour and penalise bad behaviour, such as not repaying debts or traffic violations.[153]

The panoply of real-life and online controls available to the CCP, from CCTV cameras to tracking apps, cannot prevent protests from breaking out or spreading. In fact, the internet and social media have also become essential organising tools, as the struggle in Hong Kong in 2019-2020 demonstrated. But the CCP's enhanced surveillance capacities greatly raise the risks to individuals of stepping out of line, and they were to be invaluable social controls when Covid broke out in late 2019.

Covid – success, but at a heavy cost?

On the face of it, China coped well with the Covid pandemic. Both lockdowns were quickly implemented; the government was quick to provide additional healthcare and welfare facilities; the death toll per head of population was lower than many other countries; and China was the first major economy to recover. However, the reality is more complex.

When the first cases were reported in the city of Wuhan in late 2019, the immediate reaction of the city authorities was to cover it up, denying that it could be transmitted from person to person, and suppressing discussion. The Wuhan blogger Fang Fang, whose *Wuhan Diary* is an invaluable record of the pandemic in the city, quoted a doctor friend as saying '…they

---

153 Economy, *The third revolution*, page 79

all knew that this was a "contagious disease", but no-one dared speak out because they were being gagged.' The first doctor to raise the alarm was punished and forced to sign a confession.[154] The rapid spread forced the authorities to impose a quarantine in late January, but as Fang Fang recorded it came too late:

> …that was also when the period of true suffering arrived here in Wuhan – the number of people infected with the coronavirus exploded during the Lunar New Year. Because the local hospitals couldn't cope with the surge of new patients, the entire system was brought to the brink of collapse…[155]

By early February, the central government had taken charge, imposing an exclusion zone firstly on Wuhan and then on all of Hubei province. Across the country, cities and provinces shut down public transport and imposed movement restrictions, and also began massive programmes of health screening and hospital building. By the time Covid became a pandemic in the West, in China it was largely under control.

Western coverage of China's success emphasised the CCP's coercive ability to impose lockdowns, as well as mandatory testing and quarantines, but this was only part of their response. Equally important was their ability to mobilise huge amounts of both capital and labour to build hospitals in record time, though at great cost to workers' health and safety.[156] China also quickly become the world's supplier of PPE and medical technology.[157]

---

154 Fang Fang, *Wuhan Diary*, (HarperCollins, New York, NY, 2020), page 59.

155 As above, pages xii-xiii.

156 Hsiao-Hung Pai, 'Covid-19: The "China" narratives and Chinese workers', *rs21*, 6 April, 2020: https://www.rs21.org.uk/2020/04/06/covid-19-the-china-narratives-and-chinese-workers/

157 'China Dominates Medical Supplies, in This Outbreak and the Next', *New York Times*, 5 July, 2020: https://www.nytimes.com/2020/07/05/

The state's centralising focus also made it easier to discipline and direct private capital and to bring together millions of volunteers to organise food and other essential supplies, as well as checking on adherence to quarantine rules.

However, these were self-appointed groups rather than elected bodies, often revivals of the 'street committees' of Maoist China, which saw themselves as policing their neighbours and (in particular) those who didn't belong. As one study noted: '... in many places mutual aid efforts were successful not simply because of their cooperative character but instead because their inherent communitarianism entailed exclusion of outsiders.'[158] In Guangzhou that turned into open racism against African communities in the city,[159] while in Xinjiang and Tibet it became part of the Sinification offensive.

Whatever the limitations of the mutual aid groups, they showed both that China's 'Zero Covid' strategy at least initially had more strings to its bow than simple repression, and that a well-resourced state machine which reached deep into society and enjoyed a relatively high level of popular support could be effective in protecting public health. China wasn't alone in this – in east Asia, Singapore, South Korea, Taiwan and Vietnam all had similar successes with similar multi-pronged strategies. The relative successes of South Korea and Taiwan, not to mention Australia and New Zealand, rather undermined the idea that 'Zero Covid' was an impossible aim in a liberal democracy.

The economy, which contracted in spring 2020 for the first time since the aftermath of 1989, returned to growth by the end

---

business/china-medical-supplies.html

158 Chuang, *Social contagion and other material on microbiological class war in China*, (Charles H Kerr, Chicago, IL, 2021), pages 153-154.

159 'The coronavirus crisis has exposed China's long history of racism', *Guardian*, 25 April, 2020: https://www.theguardian.com/commentisfree/2020/apr/25/coronavirus-exposed-china-history-racism-africans-guangzhou

of the year. Unfortunately, that success led the state to rely more heavily on highly-policed lockdowns (including monitoring QR codes for negative tests on mobile phones), rather than a broader mix of health interventions such as continuous vaccination and booster programmes.

The early successes with quarantines and lockdowns also meant that the CCP was slow to respond as the virus mutated, continued to rely on Chinese-produced vaccines which were less effective against the Omicron variants, and failed to prioritise the elderly. In mid-2022, the *Lancet* quoted a health minister as saying that 'even though more than 87% of the population have received two doses of the vaccine, among those older than 80 years, just over half have had two doses and less than 20% have received a booster.'[160]

As outbreaks increased in 2022, local authorities imposed even harsher local lockdowns, which led to both growing social resentment and increased loss of life due to the heavy-handed implementation of lockdowns. According to one local activist interviewed for the Australian socialist newspaper *Red Flag:* 'During the Shanghai lockdown [which lasted over five months], which brought production and life to a halt, many more people died from the lockdown measures than from COVID-19 itself'.[161]

In October and November 2022, there were two outbreaks of worker unrest at the massive Foxconn campus in Zhengzhou, Henan province, which produces most of the world's iPhones and employs over 200,000 people. When management threatened to lock migrant workers into the factory following a local outbreak, thousands broke through roadblocks and started walking home,

---

160 Shawn Yuan, Zero COVID in China: what next?', the *Lancet*, Vol 399, Issue 10338, pages 1856-1857, 14 May, 2022: https://www.thelancet.com/journals/lancet/article/PIIS0140-6736(22)00873-X/fulltext

161 Quoted in Robert Narai, 'From crisis to catastrophe: COVID-19 engulfs China', *Red Flag*, 22 January, 2023: https://redflag.org.au/article/crisis-catastrophe-covid-19-engulfs-china

many reportedly given food and water by local residents near the plant. The following month, there was an even bigger revolt, when workers brought in to replace them demonstrated against their working and living conditions. They were first met with tear gas and police, then paid a significant bonus and sent home.[162]

That same month saw an announcement of significant easing of Covid rules, followed almost immediately by new lockdowns in most major cities as Covid cases increased. The day after the new lockdowns were announced, at least ten Uyghurs died in a fire at an apartment block in Urumqi, which had been under lockdown since August.

It quickly became known that they had died because they were locked in the building. This prompted several demonstrations in Urumqi, which brought together Han Chinese and Uyghurs in protest against the deaths. The following weekend, solidarity protests spread to Beijing, Shanghai, Wuhan, Guangzhou, Chengdu and many other towns and cities. Hundreds, and in some cases thousands, of protesters confronted police, removing quarantine barriers and on occasion chanting explicitly anti-government slogans. There were demonstrations at over 50 universities, and solidarity protests at several campuses in Hong Kong, the first oppositional activity there since the defeat of the 2019 revolt.

Unlike most protests, these were squarely aimed at the CCP and central government, and Xi Jinping in particular. They represented the biggest and most widespread upsurge from below of the Xi Jinping era. The chants against the CCP and Xi Jinping, even if confined to a minority of those protesting, were wholly unprecedented, and all the more

---

162 See Yige Dong, 'The Foxconn uprising in Zhengzhou', *Tempest*, 5 December, 2022: https://www.tempestmag.org/2022/12/the-foxconn-uprising-in-zhengzhou/ and Eli Friedman, 'Foxconn's great escape', *Asian Labour Review*, 8 November, 2022: https://labourreview.org/foxconns-great-escape/

threatening as they came soon after the CCP's 20th Congress, where Xi Jinping had cemented his absolute control over both party and government.

The protests were forced off the streets after just one week, but the CCP panicked. In December they simply removed almost all existing Covid restrictions (which private businesses had also been lobbying for), but without putting any new protective measures in place – this just as new infections were surging. The results were catastrophic. Official figures reported to the World Health Organisation recorded 144,000 cases of Covid and 354 deaths on 27 November; a month later they had soared to 40 million cases and 6,000 deaths.[163] A widely reported Beijing University study estimated that 900 million people, about two-thirds of the population, fell ill, including over 90 percent of the population of Gansu province.[164] The health system was briefly overwhelmed.

Though that immediate surge was the worst, there were further peaks in June, July, August and October 2023. China's official figures are gross understatements, with just under 122,000 Covid deaths reported to the World Health Organisation as of 28 January 2024 – but of course the same is true of almost every other country.

One 'excess mortality' study in the *Lancet* going up to the end of 2021 estimated a probable death total of almost 18,000 and a possible high of 30,000, compared to official figures of just under 5,000 deaths, almost all in Hubei province where the virus originated.[165] In February 2023, the *New York Times*

---

163 WHO COVID-19 dashboard, *World Health Organisation*: https://data. who.int/dashboards/covid19/deaths?n=c (accessed 14 February 2024)

164 'Covid cases in China touch 900 million – study', *BBC*, 13 January, 2023: https://www.bbc.co.uk/news/world-asia-china-64258799

165 'Estimating excess mortality due to the COVID-19 pandemic: a systematic analysis of COVID-19-related mortality, 2020–21', The *Lancet*. Vol 399, Issue 10334, pages 1513-1536, 16 April, 2022: https://

reported a number of studies suggesting that the real toll to that date could be between one and one and a half million deaths, taking into account the surge after restrictions were lifted.[166] These figures were in turn queried by other researchers, who estimated a more likely figure of between 620,000 and a million.[167]

It is worth stressing that even if the highest figures are true, China's deaths as a proportion of the population were lower than in the United States, Britain, Germany or Canada. The CCP's ability to mobilise huge amounts of capital, and deep roots in society, helped them to quickly react to the initial onset of Covid. However, they were unable to maintain that advantage as the virus mutated. The even more toxic mix of factory farming, the spread of urbanisation, unregulated markets and corrupt officials that created the conditions for the emergence of SARS and Covid remains as volatile as ever. The CCP's record in treating the symptoms stands up well against that of other ruling classes, but they are as complicit as other ruling classes in creating the conditions that will inevitably lead to the emergence of future pandemics.

---

www.thelancet.com/journals/lancet/article/PIIS0140-6736(21)02796-3/fulltext 'Excess mortality' (how many more deaths than the average for the previous five years) is of course a very rough proxy for Covid deaths, with Australia, New Zealand, Singapore and Taiwan having 'negative excess mortalities', meaning that the combination of health measures they adopted lowered the overall expected number of deaths.

166 'How deadly was China's Covid wave?', *New York Times*, February 15, 2023: https://www.nytimes.com/interactive/2023/02/15/world/asia/china-covid-death-estimates.html

167 John P. A. Ioannidis and others, 'What Really Happened During the Massive SARS-CoV-2 Omicron Wave in China?', *JAMA Internal Medicine*, 15 May, 2023: https://jamanetwork.com/journals/jamainternalmedicine/fullarticle/2804631

VI Conclusion

China's rise to becoming a world economic power was one of the most important developments of the last century, and it will profoundly shape this century. The sheer speed and scale of China's growth, unparalleled in the history of capitalism, is an extreme example of what Leon Trotsky called 'the law of uneven and combined development', where the growth of a world economy pulls the more backward parts of the world into its orbit. The processes of modernity and development are thus imposed from the outside, in an extremely uneven way that primarily benefits the major economic powers rather than the society thus impacted. As Trotsky put it:

> A backward country assimilates the material and intellectual conquests of the advanced countries. But this does not mean that it follows them slavishly, reproduces all the stages of their past... The privilege of historic backwardness – and such a privilege exists – permits, or rather compels, the adoption of whatever is ready in advance of any specified date, skipping a whole series of intermediate stages... From the universal law of unevenness thus derives ... the law of combined development – by which we mean a drawing together of the different stages of the journey, a combining of the separate steps, an amalgam of archaic with more contemporary forms.[168]

So, for example, Shenzhen could go from being a fishing village to a city of 12 million, one of the centres of world industry. But the faster China's economy grew, the faster all

---

168 Leon Trotsky, *History of the Russian Revolution*. (1932), Chapter One: https://www.marxists.org/archive/trotsky/1930/hrr/ch01.htm For an elaboration of the theory as applied to modern China, see Neil Davidson, *We cannot escape history*, (Haymarket, Chicago, IL, 2015), pages 175-188.

forms of inequality grew: gender inequality, income inequality, the gaps between country and city, rich and poor provinces, as well between different parts of the same province. As south-eastern China boomed, the former heavy industrial areas of the northeast stagnated, becoming 'rustbelts' like the American midwest or the north of England. And across western China, economic development became a key part of the process of marginalising and dispossessing Tibetans, Uyghurs and other ethnic minorities.

From 1991 to 2008 China was able to grow as a supplier of cheap manufactured goods to the West, and in particular the USA. But that model was unsustainable even before the economic crash, and since then China's rulers have had to hunt around for different pathways to growth, a process made all the more difficult because of China's new weight in the world economy, and the growth of economic protectionism in the West as a response to the post-2008 global economic slump.

The BRI, which was meant to boost the Chinese economy by stimulating growth abroad, has run into serious difficulties because of that slump. One recent report estimated that '…some 60 percent of all BRI loans lie with nations that are in financial distress, in large part because of BRI decisions.'[169]

The Covid pandemic only turned the screw further. Although China's economy recovered faster than most major economies, growth remains sluggish, with price deflation becoming a major worry for the authorities as consumer demand continues to slow. Additionally, foreign investors are increasingly wary, with foreign direct investment in China falling in 2024 to its

---

169 'Beijing Tries To Breathe New Life Into Its Belt And Road Initiative', *Forbes*, 6 November, 2023: https://www.forbes.com/sites/miltonezrati/2023/11/06/beijing-tries-to-breathe-new-life-into-its-belt-and-road-initiative/?sh=1e55eafa169d

lowest level since the 1990s.[170] The profound social and political consequences of Covid, combined with the deeper malaises of environmental degradation and demographic deficit, and the growing tensions between China and the West have prompted alarmist predictions of crisis in the Western media. The *Wall Street Journal* declared bluntly: 'China's 40-Year Boom Is Over. What Comes Next?'[171]

The end of the boom has been predicted for almost as long as it has lasted. A book called *The coming collapse of China* was published as long ago as 2001.[172] But as one more recent author noted: 'no crisis has been prophesied as repeatedly and for so long as the one that has so far failed to materialise in China'.[173] Another put it more succinctly: 'To read the history of modern China is to read the history of China collapse theories'.[174]

The challenges to China's rulers are multiplying both in the world economy and at home. While it is too soon to say that China's expansion is over, there is ample evidence that this particular phase of growth is coming to an end. However, this has happened before and China's rulers have successfully adapted. Deng Xiaoping's initial economic reforms after 1978 caused an economic crisis in 1988 that led to the political explosion in 1989; the rebooting of China's economy on the basis of cheap exports to the West after 1992 stuttered after the Asian economic crash of 1997 and came to a sudden end after the

---

170 'Foreign Capital Exodus from China Accelerates', *Australian Institute of International Affairs*, 30 September, 2024: https://www.internationalaffairs.org.au/australianoutlook/ foreign-capital-exodus-from-china-accelerates/
171 'China's 40-Year Boom Is Over. What Comes Next?', *Wall Street Journal*, 20 August, 2023: https://www.wsj.com/world/china/ china-economy-debt-slowdown-recession-622a3be4
172 C Gordon Chang, *The coming collapse of China*, (Random House, New York, NY, 2001).
173 McMahon, *China's great wall*, page xv.
174 Orlik, *China – the bubble that never pops*, page 194.

2008 crash; and the most recent phase of massive state investment and attempts to increase domestic consumption resulted in over-investment in infrastructure and a consequent spiralling of debt, both of which have proved to be unsustainable. As one analyst summarised:

> In each case, a successful policy generated a decade of growth but ultimately ran into its limits... the cycle ended in crisis, but that crisis proved a trigger for far-reaching reforms that – combined with the economy's underlying strengths – catalyzed the next decade of growth.[175]

In assessing the prospects for the future, it is crucial to bear in mind that the successive challenges that the CCP has faced have been products of economic success. It would be unwise to completely rule out a new period of expansion. However, both the internal and external environments are far less favourable than in the past. While past developmental strategies benefitted from what Trotsky called 'the privilege of historical backwardness', the speed and scale of China's expansion have left far fewer openings in the world economy for further expansion. And the consolidation of political power in Xi Jinping's hands raises the question of what happens after him.

As Ho-fung Hung argued:

> The current leadership believes that it can survive an economic downturn by tightening its control over society, eradicating autonomous elite factions, and adopting a more assertive posture on the international stage amid rising geopolitical tension – even if such measures serve to aggravate its developmental problems...

---

175 As above, page 202. Orlik sees 1997 as marking the end of one such period, but the expansion of export industries carried on well into this century – I would argue 2008 was the more decisive turning point.

The current weakening of the economy and hardening of author-itarianism are not easily reversible trends. They are, in fact, the logical outcome of China's uneven development and capital accumulation over the last four decades. This means they are here to stay.[176]

The events of 1989 were a political and economic water-shed, but it bears repeating that the repression did not stifle all opposition from below, but rather set parameters for how far protests are allowed to go, parameters which have been set both by activity from below as well as by the state. The CCP's stress on the need for a 'harmonious society' reflects its concerns that growing inequality and workers' confidence to protest could spill over into wider future conflicts.

The spread of new technology has enabled even closer monitoring of the population but, as the 2022 anti-lockdown protests showed, such surveillance cannot predict when something might erupt. As Louisa Lim argued:

> Could a mass movement like Tiananmen happen again? Yes, it could. Rapacious land seizures, widespread official corruption and choking environmental problems are creating pockets of discontent among people who feel they have little left to lose.

She added the important caution that 'As long as these [protests] remain localised, the likelihood of a mass movement is diluted.'[177] However, the volatility of strikes and protests means that the possibility of moving beyond the purely localised is never entirely absent. The very success of sustaining growth over decades has created expectations of continuing prosperity,

---

176 Ho-fung Hung, 'Zombie economy', *Sidecar (New Left Review)*, 4 August, 2023: https://newleftreview.org/sidecar/posts/zombie-economy

177 Louisa Lim, *The republic of amnesia*, page 210.

which may prove increasingly difficult to meet. This may well be 'China's century' but for the CCP it promises to be a remarkably unstable one. Despite its defeat, the 1989 movement continues to cast a long shadow.

Charlie Hore, 2025

On 1 october 1949 Mao Zedong stood on a platform overlooking Tiananmen Square in the heart of Beijing and announced the birth of the People's Republic of China, declaring: 'The Chinese people have stood up!' Forty years later, when millions of Chinese workers and students stood up for their rights in the same square, they were crushed by the very army that had brought Mao to power. The sheer brutality of the repression shocked the world, particularly when contrasted with the largely peaceful collapse of the Eastern European regimes that followed soon after. How could the liberation of 1949 have turned into the oppression of 1989?

The revolution of 1949 was one of the most momentous and influential events of this century. The old order, dominated by warlords, police terror and the rivalries of Japanese and Western imperialism, was overthrown by a millions-strong army. For a quarter of the human race, the way seemed open to eradicate poverty, misery and famine, and build a better society. For millions more around the world it seemed a powerful example to follow.

China's impact was to be even greater in the political explosion of the 1960s. As students and workers across the industrialised world fought their rulers, Mao's teachings became the inspiration for many socialists. In the 'Third World' those ideas were even more powerful, promising as they did national liberation and an end to imperialist domination.

Few socialists today look to China for inspiration. The illusions of Maoism have been shattered by Mao's successors, who have systematically ditched everything that was distinctive about Mao's strategy for economic development. The Cultural Revolution is now – rightly – described as a major disaster. And the new rulers' quest for foreign investment has led them to embrace the world system Mao once seemed to want to overthrow.

Yet if few socialists today will defend China, fewer still have attempted to explain what happened to the hopes of 1949. The right wing have a simple answer: all revolutions turn inevitably to tyranny. It is an explanation that has become widely accepted on the left today, as past illusions have been shattered by the events of the 1980s.

Yet there is an alternative explanation, one that starts with understanding the real nature of 1949. Mao's revolution was not socialist but nationalist: the aim was to build a strong and independent national economy that could compete on equal terms with the world economy. The needs and aspirations of China's workers and peasants were always subordinated to that aim. The 'modernisers' around Deng Xiaoping abandoned Mao's strategy because it failed, but their aims remained the same. The revolt of 1989 fundamentally threatened their rule. Granting the movement's demands would have led to an even greater explosion from below which the ruling class could not hope to control, and so they chose the only other option: brute force.

This book is not yet another history of China in the 20th century, but rather an attempt to provide a socialist explanation of that history, and in particular to explain the economic and social changes in the decade after Mao's death that led to the revolt of 1989.

Although 1989 ended in defeat, it remains a fundamental turning-point in Chinese history. For the first time since 1927, it raised the possibility of real socialist change brought about by the collective power of the working class. That taste of power will not soon be forgotten. This book is dedicated to those who fought and died in Beijing and elsewhere, in the hope that it can contribute to the building of a movement which will one day avenge them.

The road to Tiananmen Square

CHAPTER 1

The first Chinese revolution

The story of Mao's rise to power-from head of a ragged army of fewer than a thousand guerrillas in 1927 to his victory in 1949-became one of the great myths of this century. From the beginning, it was claimed, Mao had a distinctive strategy for overthrowing capitalism and imperialism in China-building strong 'Red bases' among the peasantry from which to conquer the towns and cities. This led him to break with Stalin's domination of world communism, and fundamentally reshape Marxism to make it fit the realities of the Third World.

The truth is very different. Mao's rise to power began with the defeat of the first, working-class, revolution of 1925-27. The disastrous strategy which Stalin imposed on the young Chinese Communist Party (CCP), a strategy Mao entirely endorsed, made certain the revolution's defeat.

The origins of that revolution lay in the devastating impact of imperialism on China. That impact began with the Opium Wars of the 1840s, fought by Britain for the right to import opium into China from India. The attraction of China as a limitless market for consumer goods quickly pulled others in Britain's wake. By the turn of the century every major imperialist power had its claws deep into China:

...the Powers either appropriated or laid claim to much of the area along the coast, which was more accessible and more easily exploited than the interior, from the Southwest (France), through the Yangzi Valley (England) and the Shandong peninsula (England and Germany) to the Northeast (Russia and Japan)... Great Britain controlled the Kaiping coalfields, Japan the Fushun coal mines and the Anshan iron mines. Nearly every new railroad brought European and Japanese capitalists an opportunity for direct investments or lucrative loans.[1]

As China was pulled deeper into the world economy, enormous changes took place in parts of the countryside which had never seen a foreigner. Cheap mass-produced imports ruined the old handicraft industries and shifting patterns of trade devastated many areas that had become dependent on a single crop.

The most far-reaching upheavals, however, took place in and around the cities. Foreign 'concession' or 'settlements' were set up in most major cities, policed exclusively by the powers. In Shanghai, the main park along the waterfront had a sign at its gates reading 'No dogs or Chinese allowed.' Around the concessions new factories, mills, shipyards, mines and railways mushroomed, drawing in dispossessed peasants from the countryside, to work long hours in the most appalling conditions.

The old imperial government in Beijing was utterly incapable of resisting the spread of imperialism, losing even its powers of taxation. In 1911 an aborted nationalist rising led to the fall of the empire. A nominal Republican government replaced it, but real power across the country passed into the hands of local warlords. Famine, civil wars and banditry became endemic, while ruinous taxation and the demands of the

---

1   Lucien Bianco, *Origins of the Chinese revolution* (Stanford University Press, Stanford, CA, 1971), page 7.

warlords pushed the mass of the peasantry into unimaginable destitution. The stream of peasants into the cities became a millions-strong flood.

The First World War accelerated the growth of the cities. The increased demand for food and clothing fuelled a 40 percent increase in exports between 1913 and 1919, while in the absence of Western competition Chinese and Japanese capitalists flourished as never before. Imports of industrial machinery increased thirteen-fold between 1915 and 1921, and the industrial working class grew correspondingly. By the end of the war some 1.5 million industrial workers were concentrated into China's major cities, linked by family and village ties to millions more artisans, transport workers and unemployed.

The end of the war sparked off the first protests which were to lead to the revolution of 1925-27. Intellectuals had been debating how to 'save China' since the late 19th century, and the anarchy prevailing after the fall of the empire gave their searching new urgency. Increasingly the younger and more militant ones looked to the West for inspiration, arguing that China's old traditions were the main obstacle to progress, and that only 'Science' and 'Democracy' could save China. College students, whose numbers expanded greatly during the first years of this century, were at the forefront of this movement. Many had studied abroad; all had been exposed to a variety of Western influences and teaching. This made them both better able to understand the depths of China's crisis, and to see the possibilities that modernisation offered.

In 1915 Japan had annexed the German concessions in Shandong province, to the fury of Chinese nationalists. The war's end was greeted with joy, arousing hopes that the Versailles Peace Conference of 1919 would return the occupied territories to China. Students and teachers, as one historian noted, 'believed that the Allied victory was a real one of democracy over despotism and militarism, and of the workers and plain people over their oppressors.'[2]

But the Versailles Conference decided that Japan should keep its conquests, and the Chinese delegation agreed without protest. The contrast between the freedom and self-determination that the Western powers had promised, and the imperialist carve-up that they in fact delivered, aroused a deep sense of betrayal among those who had looked to 'Westernisation' as China's salvation. On 4 May more than 3,000 students assembled in Tiananmen Square in the heart of Beijing, in the first nationalist demonstration ever seen in China, aimed both at the Western powers and the Chinese government's sell-out of China's interests. Their example led to a nationwide protest movement.

By the middle of June students and school-students had organised strikes in more than 200 cities and towns. The movement's very existence was a fundamental challenge to many of the ingrained customs and habits of Chinese society. For youth publicly to challenge their elders' decisions was an open attack on youth's traditional deference to their parents. In the same way, the central role played by women students struck at old beliefs about women's deference to men.

Most important of all, the students worked from the outset to bring the previously voiceless masses of the cities into the movement. Their street agitation succeeded in drawing workers and the unemployed, as well as merchants and officials, into action, united around the demand for a total boycott of Japanese goods. And when the government cracked down in Beijing, arresting hundreds of students, they provoked a furious backlash.

In Shanghai, the major industrial centre of China, there was a one-day commercial shutdown. Immediately afterwards, between 60,000 and 90,000 workers went on strike for the release of the students. According to one historian:

---

2   Chow Tse-Tung, *The May Fourth Movement* (Stanford University Press, Stanford, CA, 1967), page 85.

The movement had such a thorough influence at the grass roots of society that even the beggars, thieves, prostitutes and singsong girls went on strike. Later on, the postal clerks, policemen and firemen also threatened that they would stop work if the government maintained its attitude towards the students.[3]

This one strike alone involved roughly five times the total number of strikers in 1918 and the Shanghai workers were not alone. Railway workers, dockers, seamen, rickshaw pullers, miners and printers all joined in the agitation, forcing the government to back down. The arrested students were released, and three pro-Japanese ministers dismissed.

The May 4th Movement was above all a nationalist one, uniting all urban classes in opposition to imperialism, and to the government's refusal to defend Chinese interests. But it marked a fundamental break in Chinese nationalist politics, from small groups of conspirators to open mass organisation. Above all, it brought the Chinese working class as an organised force into the struggle, giving them a first taste of their power.

The rise of the workers' movement

The workers' successes both pushed the student movement into seeing the working class as a powerful ally, and stimulated union organisation and a series of successful wages strikes. Between 1919 and 1921 wages rose by 10 to 15 percent in Shanghai's cotton mills, and by 10 to 40 percent among Guangzhou (Canton) mechanics. One Shanghai tobacco company was forced to pay for importing rice from southern China to settle a strike![4] New trade unions sprang up among previously unorganised workers, and established unions grew rapidly.

---

3   As above, page 158.
4   Jean Chesneaux, *The Chinese labour movement 1919-1927* (Stanford University Press Stanford, CA, 1968), page 157.

The impact of the Russian revolution of 1917 was even more important to the movement's evolution. At first it was simply seen as a successful example of a national revolution against imperialism. And when the new Soviet government simply gave up all its claims on Chinese territory, their prestige was greatly increased. But by the early 1920s, a number of Lenin's works had been translated into Chinese, and a minority among the movement's leaders began to see the connections between capitalism and imperialism, and to understand the central importance of the workers' movement. This led to the foundation of the CCP in 1921.

The CCP's founding members were all intellectuals, but within months it was spreading its influence among the working class. Its members threw themselves into union-organising, and played a major part in organising the first All-China Labour Congress, which met in May 1922 with delegates from a dozen cities representing some 300,000 workers.

As workers' strikes spread from foreign-owned companies to those run by Chinese capitalists, they ran into increasing hostility from the warlords. In February 1923 that hostility turned into murderous repression when troops were sent to break a strike on the main north-south railway line. Thirty-five strikers were killed and many more seriously wounded in attacks on three railway stations. At Jiangan, just north of the city of Wuhan, the union branch secretary (a CCP member) was beheaded in front of the strikers for refusing to tell them to resume work.[5]

Sympathy strikes and protests spread across southern China, but throughout 1923 the repression increased. This coincided with a slump in the economy, which threw hundreds of thousands out of work. The numbers of strikes dropped to half that of 1922, and by the end of the year the labour movement

---

5   As above, page 209.

and the CCP were effectively illegal in most areas. The one exception to this was the area around Guangzhou, where a nationalist government had come to office in 1923.

The Guomindang (Nationalist Party) had led the abortive revolution of 1911, but soon afterwards fell apart. From 1919 onwards it began to regroup, helped by an alliance with the minor warlord who ruled Guangzhou. Though it was primarily a collection of intellectuals with a passive mass base, it was the most vigorous nationalist force in China.

The Second Congress of the CCP agreed to cooperate with the Guomindang on agreed common aims, but insisted that:

> ...if the proletariat extends a hand to promote the democratic revolution, this does not mean that the proletariat should capitulate to the bourgeoisie... Within the democratic alliance, the workers must not become an appendage of the petty bourgeoisie but must continue to fight for their own interests.[6]

This position – support for nationalist struggles, but recognising that the working class needed an independent party to fight for its interests *against* bourgeois nationalists-followed the general position adopted by the Communist International in 1920, which spoke of:

> ...the need for a determined struggle against attempts to give a communist colouring to bourgeois-democratic liberation trends in the backward countries... The Communist International should enter into a temporary alliance with bourgeois democracy in the colonial and backward countries, but should not merge with it, and should under all circumstances uphold the

---

6   Quoted in Benjamin Schwartz, *Chinese communism and the rise of Mao*, (Harvard University Press, Cambridge, MA, 1979), page 40.

independence of the proletarian movement even if it is in its most embryonic form.[7]

Yet as early as 1922 Comintern representatives were pressing the CCP to give a 'communist colouring' to the Guomindang. In August 1922 CCP leaders agreed under pressure to join the Guomindang as individual members. One CCP historian, writing in the 1930s, noted that:

> ...while the party central committee respected the motion of the Internationale, most of the comrades had only approved a democratic revolutionary united front and were quite doubtful about entering the Guomindang.[8]

By 1924 Russian advisors were helping to reorganise the Guomindang into a mass party, and to train its armed forces. CCP members worked, not as an independent force, but as the most active elements of the Guomindang, building it on the ground. How could such a transformation – from independent workers' party to a subordinate wing of nationalism – have come about so quickly?

The answer lies in the changes taking place inside the Comintern, which mirrored those happening inside the Soviet Union itself. The civil war of 1917-21 had been won by the revolution, but at a terrible cost. Famine and disease were rampant, both in the countryside and the cities, and industrial production had fallen to a fraction of its pre-war levels. The working class who made the revolution had, by the early 1920s, been largely dispersed. Many of the most committed revolutionaries had

---

7   *Theses, manifestos and resolutions of the first four congresses of the Communist International*, (InkLinks, London, 1983), page 80. [Available online at: https://www.marxists.org/archive/lenin/works/1920/jun/05.htm]

8   Quoted in Schwartz, *Chinese communism and the rise of Mao*, page 41.

fallen in the civil war; many more workers had simply deserted the hungry cities for their native villages. Others had joined the ranks of the ever-growing bureaucracy, who operated without any democratic control from below.

That bureaucracy had quickly come to identify their own survival with that of the revolution, and consequently to confuse the survival of the Soviet state with the interests of the world revolution. It was only a short step from this to basing the Comintern's strategy on Soviet foreign policy. A nationalist revolution in China would greatly weaken the imperialist powers threatening the Soviet state. The CCP was too small to wage a successful struggle for socialism; therefore, the Guomindang was the revolutionary force in China.

Whatever the doubts about this strategy in the ranks of the CCP – and there were constant protests about its consequences – two factors combined to ensure that it was carried out. The first was the absolute prestige of the Soviet leaders of the Comintern. The second was the fact that, from mid-1924 onwards, it seemed to be achieving great results.

The repression of 1923 had set back the Chinese workers' movement, but it had not crushed it. On May Day 1924 200,000 workers in Guangzhou and 100,000 in Shanghai marched demanding the eight-hour working day, and there were numerous demonstrations in other cities. Their leaflets reflected the regained confidence of the movement:

> Eight hours of work, eight hours of education and recreation, eight hours of rest – how reasonable this programme is! For 40 years the working class has poured out its blood for its realisation. The time is past when the workers are but cannon fodder for the bosses. They will not cede but to Revolution? Then they shall have it![9]

---

9   Quoted in Harold Isaacs, *The tragedy of the Chinese revolution* [Haymarket, Chicago, IL, 2010 – this is a reprint of the original (1938)

That summer there was a British-backed attempt by local warlords to oust the Guomindang, which was defeated by Soviet-trained troops and workers' militias. In early 1925 the warlords attacked again but were beaten off by a peasant rising in the surrounding countryside. For the first time, the Guomindang was fully in control of Guangzhou and the surrounding province.

Once again there was an upsurge of strikes and union organisation, around a mixture of economic and anti-imperialist demands. This new wave drew many groups of workers and many cities into the struggle for the first time. But it was in Shanghai that the strikes reached their height. And it was a massacre of demonstrating workers in Shanghai that transformed the strike wave into the beginnings of a revolution.

The revolution breaks

In May 1925 wages strikes spread through Japanese textile mills across Shanghai. In picket-line fighting, security guards killed a young worker, and a protest march on 30 May drew several thousand workers and students. Outside a police station in the international settlement, British police fired into the demonstration, killing twelve people and wounding many more. Two days later a general strike began in all foreign-owned factories and on the waterfront, organised by the Shanghai General Union, a CCP-led coordinating body.

By 13 June nearly 160,000 workers were out. Though the CCP tried to limit the strikes to foreign-owned companies, to keep the support of the Chinese bourgeoisie, among the first strikers were:

---

edition], page 52. [Some passages – including this one – are worded slightly differently to those quoted in the original edition of this book, and I have changed the quotes accordingly.]

...about 2900 male and female operatives of the Hung Foong Cotton mill, a Chinese company. Contrary to CCP policy, workers in other Chinese concerns also struck spontaneously, but by 11 June those Chinese businesses and industries thus affected were, *with a few exceptions*, working on a normal basis again.[10]

Even where workers in Chinese-owned factories stayed at work, they pressed for the removal of foreign-made machinery. The protest movement that erupted in the weeks following the massacre drew more workers into action than ever before. The May 30th Movement (as the protests came to be known) marked a decisive shift in the fight against imperialism. The working class were no longer simply a part of the movement; they were now leading it, and the other classes were for the moment forced to follow in their wake. Nowhere was this clearer than in Guangzhou and Hong Kong, where another massacre led to a sixteen-month general strike.

On 23 June British and French troops shot into a demonstration in Guangzhou, killing 52 people and injuring more than a hundred. A general strike was called in Hong Kong, and by the end of the month more than 50,000 workers had left the colony. The running of the strike showed the extent to which workers' organisations had developed:

Central control was maintained not only by a strike committee consisting of thirteen persons, but also by a 'Strikers Delegate Congress' comprising over 800 delegates (one for every 50 strikers), which was a kind of workers' parliament. It met three times a week, thus ensuring constant contact with the rank and file... The responsibilities of the strike committee went far beyond the normal field of activities dealing with a work stoppage.

---

10   Richard W Rigby, *The May 30th Movement* (Dawson and Sons, London, 1980), page 42 (my emphasis).

During the summer of 1925 the committee became, in fact, a kind of workers' government – and indeed the name applied to it by both its friends and its enemies was 'Government No 2.'... The committee had at its disposal an armed force of several thousand men... Anyone infringing the [blockade] regulations was brought before a court set up by the strike committee, which had appointed the judges; and this court imposed either fines or prison sentences that were served out in jails belonging to the committee.[11]

As the strike went on, the strike committee extended its power along the coast of Guangdong and into Guangzhou city. The centre of British power in China came to a near-standstill. According to the Chamber of Commerce, from August to December 1924, between 160 and 240 British steamers a month entered Guangzhou harbour; in the same period in 1925, the numbers dropped to between twenty-seven and two![12]

The general strike enabled the Guomindang to extend its control to the provinces bordering Guangdong, and to declare themselves the national government. At the same time, however, it posed them a fundamental dilemma. They needed the mass movement to defend and extend their power, and if they were to force any concessions at all from imperialism. Yet the growth in workers' organisation and confidence threatened their rule and their profits just as much as it threatened imperialism.

The nationalist bourgeoisie were sincere in wanting an end to imperialist domination over China. But they wanted this in order to become a ruling class in their own right, and to claim the maximum possible profits from industry and agriculture for themselves. They could compromise over their share of the profits with imperialism, particularly as the nationalist fervour sweeping the cities was forcing

---

11   Chesneaux, *The Chinese labour movement 1919-1927*, pages 292-293.
12   Isaacs, *The tragedy of the Chinese revolution*, page 58.

the foreign powers to negotiate with them. No such compromise was possible with the risen workers.

As Leon Trotsky argued in 1927:

> The struggle against imperialism, precisely because of its economic and military power, demands a powerful exertion of forces from the very depths of the Chinese people. Really to arouse the workers and peasants against imperialism is possible only by connecting their basic and most profound life interests with the cause of the country's liberation. A workers' strike – large or small – an agrarian rebellion, an uprising of the oppressed sections in city and country against the usurer, against the local military satraps, all that arouses the multitudes, that welds them together, that educates, steels, is a real step forward... But everything that brings the oppressed and exploited masses of the toilers to their feet inevitably pushes the national bourgeoisie into an open bloc with the imperialists. The class struggle between the bourgeoisie and the masses of workers and peasants is not weakened, but, on the contrary, it is sharpened by imperialist oppression, to the point of bloody civil war at every serious conflict.[13]

During the winter of 1925-6 the bourgeoisie still needed to ride on the back of the mass movement. They were divided on how best to respond to their dilemma, and those divisions were reflected in increasing factional splits within the Guomindang. On the surface the 'unity of all classes' was maintained, with even the Guangzhou Chamber of Commerce ending its manifestoes 'Long live the World Revolution'.[14] But in secret Guomindang leaders, businessmen and Western diplomats began to seek each other out and to affirm common interests.

---

13   Leon Trotsky, *On China* (Monad Press, New York, NY, 1976) page 161.
14   Isaacs, *The tragedy of the Chinese revolution*, page 72.

In March 1926 Chiang Kaishek, a leader of the Guomindang's right-wing, carried out a bloodless coup in Guangzhou. Many CCP members were arrested, and the Hong Kong strike committee headquarters was raided. Those arrested were quickly released with apologies for the 'excesses' of junior officers, but this show of force worked. Chiang became undisputed leader of the Guomindang, forcing both his factional rivals and the CCP to back his assumption of power. He quickly pressed his advantage, placing major restrictions on the CCP's freedom of action and bringing the Guomindang's armies under his command.

In July he launched the Northern Expedition, which aimed to bring the whole of southern China under nationalist rule. This carried the revolution into the countryside and raised the class tensions inside the nationalist movement to breaking point.

With very few exceptions, the peasantry had remained apart from the agitation of the 1920s. Their enemies remained those they had faced for generations – the moneylenders, the landlords and the warlords – and the agitation in the cities promised them no real change. But in the summer of 1926, as the nationalist armies swept across southern China, the villages exploded into revolt:

> 'Down with the unequal treaties!' said the Guomindang, The only unequal treaties the Hunan peasants knew about were the tenancy agreements under which they were compelled to surrender to the landlord up to 70 percent of their crops... The slogan for 'abolition of the unequal treaties' meant to the Hunan peasant abolition of thraldom on the land... When the masses started moving and the Left Guomindang proved unwilling or unable to give point to these mild planks in its own programme, the momentum of their awakening caried the peasants with swift, direct logic to the slogan 'All Land to the Tillers!'[15]

---

15   As above, page 194. The wording of this quote is slightly different to that used in the original.

In many villages the peasants followed the seizure of the land with a revolution in village society, smashing many of the old customs that had kept them downtrodden. Women and children were no longer sold into prostitution; opium-smoking and costly religious rituals were banned; and the centuries-old practice of binding women's feet was abolished. The moneylenders were driven out of the villages along with the landlords, and many peasants simply stopped paying rents and land taxes.

The rural risings drove the Guomindang leaders and the bourgeoisie to absolute fury. Many were themselves absentee landlords – all had family or clan connections with the landlords. As the dispossessed landlords arrived in the cities with lurid and wildly exaggerated tales of mass killings, the Guomindang demanded the immediate suppression of the peasant revolution.

National revolution or workers' power?

Stalin, who was now in effective control of the Comintern, echoed their demands. In October 1926 he sent a telegram to the CCP ordering restraint of the peasantry.[16] The telegram was withdrawn as an 'error', but replaced by instructions that the peasant revolt must be led by the Guomindang – the very people it was directed against! CCP leaders did their best to carry out these contradictory instructions, appealing for land confiscations to be restricted to 'bad' landlords, and for the land of Guomindang members to be left alone.

This was an impossible position. The landlords simply joined the Guomindang as soon as they felt threatened. For their part, the peasants could not understand the distinction between 'good' and 'bad' landlords – the only distinction they made was that between the bad landlords, who they simply dispossessed, and the worst, who they killed.

---

16   Robert C North, *Moscow and Chinese communists* (Stanford University Press, Stanford, CA, 1963), page 90.

The contradictions in this two-faced position were vividly spelt out in an argument between CCP and Guomindang leaders in early 1927, when they were discussing legalising the land takeovers:

> On behalf of the Communists, Tan Pingshan timidly suggested that only the land of the counterrevolutionary landlords be confiscated. Wang Jingwei [Guomindang government leader] leaped into the breach... 'If the peasants in any given district are strong enough, they consider every landlord to be counter-revolutionary in order to expropriate his land. Under political confiscation there is no criterion. Where the peasants are strong, they go straight ahead to economic confiscation. Where they are weaker... they fall first on the small landlords who thus suffer before anyone else, and we want to keep the small landlords on our side.'[17]

The question of the land laid bare the class divisions within the nationalist revolution. Victory was only possible with the fullest mobilisation of the workers and peasantry – but this had to involve an open break with the Guomindang, who would sooner concede to imperialism than lose their power and privileges. Yet the more the Guomindang moved to the right, the greater the Comintern's insistence that the CCP must subordinate themselves to Chiang Kaishek.

Stalin defined the Guomindang as a 'revolutionary bloc of four classes' in which the task of workers and the CCP was 'to push it to the left'. In March 1926, the Guomindang was even admitted as a sympathising member of the Comintern, and Chiang Kaishek voted onto its Presidium, with only Trotsky voting against. The same month, the Comintern representative in China told protesting CCP members that: 'The present period

---

17   Quoted in Isaacs, *The tragedy of the Chinese revolution*, page 215.

is one in which the Communists should do coolie service for the Guomindang.'[18]

The CCP had grown enormously during the revolution. From fewer than a thousand members at the beginning of 1926, it had by early 1927 grown to more than 30,000. It was CCP members, acting as advance scouts for the Northern Expedition, who inspired the peasants to revolt. But their influence was strongest among the working class, and that influence spread rapidly as the revolution moved northwards. As the Guomindang took the cities of central China in the autumn and winter of 1926, the workers' movements in those cities grew both in size and influence.

By early 1927, there were some 393,000 union members in Hubei province and more than 400,000 in Hunan, and it was their militancy which enabled the Guomindang armies to take the cities with barely a shot being fired. The Guomindang government was transferred from Guangzhou to Wuhan in November 1926. In January 1927 workers' action forced the British to abandon their concessions in Hangzhou (a district of Wuhan) and Jiujiang (Jiangxi province) – the first time this had happened since the Opium Wars of the 1840s. As one historian recorded:

> The unions of Hubei and Hunan were, in fact, becoming a 'workers' government' to an even greater extent than those of Guangzhou had been during the Hong Kong strike and boycott. They controlled large funds obtained not only from dues… but also from contributions paid after successful settlement of a wage dispute… They also had armed and carefully trained bands of pickets… In April 1927 the Wuhan textile union had a corps of 500 men, of who 60 were always on duty on a three-month rotation; they were paid by the mills through the union

18   Quoted in above, page 87.

intermediaries. The militias intervened to ensure the success of strikes, especially in foreign-owned enterprises in the region.[19]

Most tellingly, he also noted that:

From the fall [of 1926] on, the unions had acted in the interests of the proletariat as a class, which meant that Chinese and foreign enterprises in the liberated areas had been given the same treatment.[20]

In retaliation, both Chinese and foreign capitalists began to organise a flight of capital from Wuhan and to demand that Chiang Kaishek put down the workers' movement. By the spring of 1927 he was ready to respond. From its conquests in central China the Northern Expedition began to converge on Shanghai. In mid-February the Shanghai unions called a mass strike and armed rising to welcome Chiang Kaishek, then only 45 miles from the city. The Guomindang armies halted 25 miles from the city while the warlords put down the rising with extreme ferocity, killing several hundred workers and crushing the strikes. Chiang's hopes that this would be sufficient to crush Shanghai's workers were misplaced, as the rising of 21 March showed.

That day, as the Guomindang armies entered the outskirts of Shanghai, between 600,000 and 800,000 workers went on strike, and a well-trained workers' militia took over the strategic points throughout the city. Police and foreign troops held out in one district but were overwhelmed by the following day. Though a city government was set up, real power was held by the workers' militias in the streets. In the days following the rising, some 75 new trade unions sprang up, and practically every employer in

---

19   Chesneaux, *The Chinese labour movement 1919-1927*, page 325.
20   As above, page 329.

the city faced demands for wage increases, union recognition and better working conditions.

Five days later Chiang entered Shanghai to welcoming demonstrations organised by the CCP. He began immediately a series of meetings with the leaders of Shanghai's capitalists and underworld gangs to put together a reliable force to use against the workers. There was no secret about these meetings. Equally, it was widely known that as the Guomindang armies advanced down the Yangtse they had murdered workers and broken unions in town after town. A senior Comintern delegation followed Chiang's armies down the Yangtse, witnessing the terror. One of them later admitted that they 'had the experience of actual street fighting being suspended during our visit while leaders of both sides talked to us.'[21]

Yet as late as 5 April, Stalin could cynically argue:

> The peasant needs a worn-out old jade so long as she is necessary. He does not drive her away. So it is with us. When the Right is of no more use to us, we will drive it away... It has capable people, who still direct the army and lead it against the imperialists... Also, they have connections with the rich merchants and can raise money from them. So they have to be utilised to the end, squeezed out like a lemon and then thrown away.[22]

The speech was never officially published, for just a week later the Guomindang 'squeezed and threw away' the Shanghai workers. Underworld thugs launched dawn raids on union offices across the city, and between four and seven hundred people were murdered in the course of the day. The unions had almost nothing to fight back with, having buried or surrendered almost all their arms on the CCP's instructions.

---

21   Quoted in Isaacs, *The tragedy of the Chinese revolution*, page 134.
22   Quoted in North, *Moscow and Chinese communists*, page 96.

The reign of terror quickly spread to all the towns and cities under Chiang's control, and over the following months claimed tens of thousands of lives. The trade unions, peasant associations and the CCP were crushed. Chiang Kaishek rode to power on the back of the workers' movement, then destroyed it in order to safeguard the power of the nationalist bourgeoisie – and it was Stalin's subordination of working-class interests to the myth of 'nationalist unity' which made the defeat possible. As Trotsky later argued:

> The national bourgeoisie sent its Chiang Kaisheks and Wang Jingweis as envoys to Moscow, and through its Hu Hanmins knocked at the door of the Comintern, precisely because it was hopelessly weak in the face of the revolutionary masses; it realised its weakness and sought to ensure itself. Neither the workers nor the peasants would have followed the national bourgeoisie if we ourselves had not dragged them by a rope.[23]

---

23 Trotsky, *On China*, pages 305-306.

CHAPTER 2

The road to power

T he Shanghai massacre utterly destroyed the workers' movement across eastern China and was a crushing blow to the revolution, from which it never recovered. It was such a mortal blow because it was delivered by Chiang Kaishek, the very man whom Stalin and the CCP had built up as the leader of the revolution. The CCP had delivered the workers' movement to him, bound hand and foot. The Guomindang were able to impose their terror so effectively because the CCP had disarmed, both physically and politically, the workers' organisations.

Yet elsewhere the revolution was still on the rise. In the central provinces of Hubei, Hunan and Jiangxi, the peasant associations were still growing, while the workers' movement in Wuhan remained as strong as ever. The Wuhan government was forced to break from Chiang Kaishek after the massacre, but the region's landlords and capitalists took heart from it. In Wuhan there were mass lockouts and a flight of capital, while in the countryside the landlords began a particularly vicious repression.

In Moscow, Trotsky hammered away at Stalin's criminal policy, arguing that only a decisive change of course could save the revolution and in particular that it was now necessary to organise workers' and peasants' soviets (councils) openly to challenge the Guomindang:

> The victory over foreign imperialism can only be won by means of the toilers of town and country driving it out of China. For this, the masses must really rise millions strong. They cannot rise under the bare slogan of national liberation, but only in direct struggle against the big landlords, the military satraps, the usurers… only this road, that is, the deeper mass sweep, the greater social radicalism of the programme, the unfurled banner of workers' and peasants' soviets, can seriously preserve the revolution from military defeats from without.[1]

Trotsky's argument was rooted in the experience of the Russian revolution, and in the theory of 'permanent revolution' he had drawn from that experience. After the abortive 1905 revolution, Trotsky had argued that the backward conditions of Russia meant that the bourgeoisie could not be relied on to lead the revolution against Tsarism, and that only the working class was able to take the fight to the finish. In such a situation, the specific interests and demands of the working class would come to the fore, demands directed against both Tsarism and capitalism. A successful revolution was only possible if workers took power into their own hands. But it could not stop there. Either the revolution moved forward to extend workers' power and begin to build socialism, or there would be a vicious and bloody counter-revolution.

The revolutions of 1917 proved him right. Lenin and the Bolshevik Party accepted after the February revolution the necessity of taking the revolution forward to socialism. Trotsky, in his writings on China, insisted time and time again on the relevance of the Russian experience to what was happening in China.

---

1   Trotsky, *On China*, pages 207-8.

Stalin's response was precisely the opposite. He argued that the Wuhan government now represented the authentic revolutionary Guomindang, and that the CCP's task was to strengthen it. Two CCP members joined the Wuhan government as Ministers of Labour and Agriculture, with orders to restrain 'excesses' in order to preserve unity.

The day after the ministers took office the counter-revolution in central China began in earnest. The ruling warlord in the city of Changsha closed down the unions and peasant organisations, and began mass executions which eventually claimed more than 20,000 victims. From Changsha the massacres spread throughout Hunan, with hundreds being murdered in village after village to wipe out the last vestiges of the peasant revolution. Within days the repression had spread into Jiangxi and Hubei.

Local leaders mobilised a peasant army of several thousands to march on Changsha. They were stopped by the CCP, who sent a telegram on 27 May ordering a retreat:

> To the Provincial Peasant Association and the Provincial Labour Union, care of the Xiangtan and Xiangxiang unions: The Central Government has appointed a committee of five which left here this morning for the settlement of the Changsha incident. Please notify all peasant and labor comrades of the province to be patient and wait for the government officials in order to avoid further friction.[2]

By the middle of June the massacres had reached the outskirts of Wuhan. One peasant official wrote that:

> Even ten li [three miles] from Hanyang the tuhao [landlords] are surrounding and killing the peasants. There used to be 54 xian [counties] with peasant associations. But last week there were

---

2   Quoted in Isaacs, *The tragedy of the Chinese revolution*, page 210.

only 23. According to our estimate the day before yesterday, of these 23 xian there were only four in which the peasants were holding their own. Today not one xian is left.[3]

Here and there isolated groups of peasant activists fought back as best they could. But the CCP's failure to organise resistance demoralised the movement and made a general fight-back impossible. In Wuhan itself, they went so far as to persuade the unions to hand over their arms to the government. But the more they retreated, the stronger the reaction grew. In July the Wuhan government joined the attack. By the end of the month all unions and peasant associations were illegal, and thousands more lay dead.

With the counter-revolution now completely dominating both the cities and the villages, and the CCP reduced to a fraction of its former strength, Stalin's response was to announce… a new revolutionary upsurge! He ordered a series of revolts, known as the 'Autumn Harvest Uprisings', in which peasant armies were to attack strategic towns from which they would launch a national offensive. It was suicidal lunacy and led to the near-extinction of the remnants of the CCP.

Mao Zedong led one of those armies. Up to this point, he had been an uncritical supporter of the alliance with the Guomindang and had obediently followed all the twists and turns of Stalin's policies. He now survived because he disobeyed his orders. His army of 2,000 men were ordered to attack the city of Changsha, but after a battle in which half of them were killed he fled to the Jinggang Mountains, a desolate and backward area on the borders of Hunan and Jiangxi. A few other units managed to escape, but most of them were quickly wiped out. They won no support in the areas they passed through, the local peasants often informing on them to government or warlord forces.

---

3   Quoted in above, page 225

Stalin had one final, unbelievably cynical, card left to play. The disaster in China, together with foreign policy setbacks elsewhere, had greatly weakened his authority in the Soviet Union and confirmed the criticisms made by Trotsky and the Left Opposition of his strategy. According to one historian:

> Reports of heightened opposition activity came one after the other from various cities and from entire provinces – Leningrad, the Ukraine, Transcaucasia, Siberia, the Urals and of course Moscow… There was a steadily growing number of illegal and semilegal meetings attended by industrial workers and young people. The influence of the opposition in a number of large party units became quite substantial… The army was also strongly affected by opposition activity.[4]

Stalin needed a victory in China to silence his critics, so he manufactured one. The Fifteenth Congress of the Russian Communist Party was held in December 1927. The day the congress opened, the 'Canton Commune' rising broke out in Guangzhou, the last city in China where the CCP had any real forces. Several thousand CCP members launched an attack on the city centre, to the amazement of the general population. It was a desperate adventure without any possibility of success, launched in complete isolation from the working class of the city. Within two days they had been crushed, and yet another reign of terror began in the city.

This 'desperate frontal attack foredoomed by every single circumstance, objective and subjective, to defeat'[5] served its purpose. Stalin was able to use the lie of a 'spontaneous insurrection' to

---

4   Michael Reiman, *The birth of Stalinism* (I B Tauris, London, 1987), pages 27-28.

5   Isaacs, *The tragedy of the Chinese revolution*. page 264 [This is a different quote to that used in the original edition].

defeat and expel the opposition and take absolute power inside the Communist Party. The consequences of the Chinese defeat ran around the world. It was the last of the revolutionary upheavals sparked off by the Russian revolution, and its outcome confirmed to millions of communists around the world that 'socialism in one country' was the only possible way forward. Stalin secured his absolute power, both in Russia and in the Comintern, on the corpses of untold numbers of Chinese workers and peasants.

In the wilderness

The 'Canton Commune' finally broke forever the links between the CCP and the Chinese working class. An internal circular of November 1928 admitted that 'Unfortunately, our union organisations have been reduced to a minimum, our party units in the cities have been pulverised and isolated. Nowhere in China can we find one solid industrial cell.'[6]

Though the few leaders left in the cities kept calling for the rebuilding of the CCP among urban workers, the reality was that the only forces left were the troops around Mao in the countryside. Mao was joined by two other surviving bands in 1928, and had some 10,000 troops (of whom fewer than 2,000 were armed). The 'Red Bases' they founded led a precarious existence for the next six years, moving several times but gradually extending the territory under their control. The government was called a soviet, though it had nothing in common with workers' councils beyond the name. In the early 1930s similar bases were established in the provinces of Anhui and Hunan, and in Shaanxi and Gansu in the north-west.

Mao's forces could survive only because of the utter chaos prevailing in China in the 1930s. Though the Guomindang had achieved their aim of forming a national government, it was a pyrrhic victory. Their writ extended only to the areas around

6   Quoted in Schwartz, *Chinese communism and the rise of Mao*, page 128.

the major cities, and to any territory occupied by their troops. The rest of China was ruled by rival warlords, many of whose territories covered only a few dozen square miles. Areas where the local warlords were weak, or where the land was so poor that there was no profit to be made out of it, had long been 'bandit country' where it was possible to escape from both local officials and the warlords.

The Jinggang mountains, and the areas Mao's 'Red Army' later moved to, fitted all these criteria. The original bases were set up in territory disputed among three rival warlords, and those disputes made it possible to survive despite initial peasant hostility. As Mao admitted in 1928:

> The prolonged splits and wars within the White regime provide a condition for the emergence and persistence of one or more small Red areas... amidst the encirclement of the White regime.[7]

The Red Army were essentially bandits, with some degree of political motivation. Banditry was endemic in China: in 1925 there were half a million in Henan province alone, and a full million in Shandong in 1930.[8] Mao's writings of this period are littered with attacks on 'mountain-top mentality', 'localism', and 'roving rebel bands', showing the constant tendency to fall into banditry pure and simple. As the areas controlled by the CCP grew, the peasantry came to accept them as the new local power, welcome because they placed some restrictions on the powers of the local landlords.

By 1932 they had become a serious enough threat for the Guomindang to take them seriously. From 1932 to 1934, five

---

7   Mao Zedong, *Selected Works*, volume 1 (Foreign Languages Press, Beijing, 1965), page 65.
8   Elizabeth J Perry, *Rebels and revolutionaries in north China 1845-1945* (Stanford University Press, Stanford, CA), page 154.

offensives were launched against the Red Arm's central base in Jiangxi, and many smaller bases were overrun. Though the first four offensives were beaten back, by October 1934 the core of the 'liberated areas' was under severe threat. It was in response to this threat that the famous 'Long March' was launched.

Contrary to the myths, Mao did not plan the Long March as part of a conscious strategy. He had been removed from all real power inside the CCP and was not even told about the plans until they were fixed.[9] Nor did anyone else consciously plan what was to happen. One historian writing after Mao had died related that: 'One of the most careful Chinese Communist historians confessed: "Where and when the decision to start the Long March was made we can't find out."'[10]

The Long March was a desperate solution to a desperate problem. The base area was about to be overrun by the Guomindang, and the only chance of survival was to make a break for it and resettle somewhere more secure: no fixed destination was set. As the Red Army was continually harried by Guomindang and warlord forces, it was forced deeper and deeper into the wilds of western China, until the only option left was to head for the 'Soviet areas' in Shaanxi. It was Mao's insistence on this strategy that brought him to become undisputed leader of the CCP.

For those who survived it, the Long March was an epic of human endurance. Between 80,000 and 90,000 people began it in October 1934; about 4,000 completed it a year later. Some were left along the way to start up new guerrilla bases, but more than 50,000 died. The survivors had travelled between 6,000 and 7,000 miles, fighting on average a battle every other day.

What could possibly have inspired people to endure such hardships? The answer lies in the conditions in the Chinese

---

9   See Harrison Salisbury, *The long march* (Pan, London, 1986) pages 9-12.
10   As above, page 52.

countryside in the 1930s. Famine, drought, floods, epidemics and wars were constant features of everyday life: between 1926 and 1931 they killed one-third of the population of Gansu alone. As tens of millions of peasants left their homes all over the country to search for food or to avoid devastation, the old were abandoned to die on the roadside, and children were sold as servants – and even occasionally eaten.

Even without such disasters, most peasants lived lives of desperate poverty, trapped between the landlords, moneylenders and tax collectors, sliding deeper and deeper into poverty every year. Even death merely transferred debt to the next generation. As the rural rich were also the local magistrates, their word was literally law. One of the few authoritative studies of peasant life in the 1930s estimated that '…between 40 and 50 percent of the peasant families in China have land insufficient… to provide them with food, apart from all their other requirements.'[11]

The author concluded that:

> There are districts in which the position of the rural population is that of a man standing permanently up to the neck in water, so that even a ripple is sufficient to drown him. The loss of life caused by the major disasters is less significant than the light which they throw on the condition prevailing even in normal times over considerable regions… Famine is, in short, the last stage of a disease which, though not always conspicuous, is always present.[12]

The Red Army promised an end to the power of the landlords and tax collectors, and that the land would be given to the peasantry. The simple fact that they treated the peasants

---

11 R H Tawney, *Land and labour in China* (Allen and Unwin, London, 1932) page 71.

12 As above, page 77.

as human beings, in contrast to the casual brutality of all other Chinese armies, made it possible for the peasants to believe them. Not that the landlords were ever dispossessed in the 'Soviet areas' – but even there the Red Army enforced lower rents than before.

The war against Japan

When the remnants of the Red Army arrived in the northwest, they added another cause to fight for: liberation from Japanese imperialism. Japan had invaded China in 1931, annexing the northeastern provinces, in which they set up a puppet kingdom. Since then, they had steadily encroached on northern China, and struck as far south as Shanghai, in an undeclared war. The Guomindang had not fought back at all, preferring to concentrate on wiping out the Red Armies. The only armed opposition the Japanese faced was from the guerrillas in Shaanxi; but in Beijing a powerful nationalist movement erupted among students, mobilising greater numbers than the May 4th Movement of 1919, which spread rapidly to campuses through eastern China.

Mao began agitating for a 'United Front' with the Guomindang against Japan, demanding an end to fighting between the two armies and joint operations against Japan. This had a great resonance both among the students and among junior Guomindang officers – unity with other Chinese to fight a foreign invader sounded to them like a good definition of the role of a nationalist party.

In December 1936 Chiang Kaishek was kidnapped by some of his junior officers and forced to sign a peace treaty with the CCP. (The officers wanted to kill him, and he was saved only by the intervention of Zhou Enlai, Mao's envoy.) The butcher of the Shanghai workers in 1927 now became 'the leader of the nation's anti-Japanese unity'. In return for the peace treaty, 'the Communist Party announced the abolition of the

worker-peasant democratic dictatorship'.[13] All talk of dispossessing the landlords was dropped, and the sole focus became
'patriotic unity against Japan'.

The following year Japan attacked in earnest, and by 1938
occupied practically all of eastern China. Though individual
units fought back, the Guomindang army as a whole was incapable of any real resistance, and the government was forced to flee
to Sichuan. The Guomindang's only real attempt to stem the
Japanese advance was yet another massacre, one of their worst
war crimes ever. They dynamited the banks of the Yellow River
in Henan, causing one of the most devastating floods of the 20th
century. Nearly a million peasants were killed and almost four
million made homeless. In one province alone, more than three
million acres of farmland were lost as the river moved south.[14]

The Red Army and its associated guerrilla forces provided
the only effective opposition to Japan, and it was the war against
Japan which transformed the CCP into a force capable of
challenging for power. In 1937 they had some 30,000 members
and the Red Army was 40,000-strong. By 1940 these figures
had risen to 800,000 and 500,000 respectively, with hundreds
of thousands more peasants organised in local guerrilla bands.
The lessons in guerrilla warfare learnt so painfully on the Long
March were brilliantly applied on the north China plain and
in the hills. The Japanese controlled the towns and the railway
lines, the Red Army the countryside in between.

The CCP built its power base on mass peasant nationalism; but that nationalism was itself a creation of the war.
The students who flocked into the hills of Shaanxi to become
the Red Army's officers came from an established nationalist

---

13 Mao Zedong, *Selected Works*, volume 2, (Foreign Languages Press,
    Beijing, 1965), page 41.
14 Perry, *Rebels and revolutionaries in north China 1845-1945*, pages 15 and
    183-184.

tradition; there was no such tradition among the peasantry. One historian argued that:

> Prior to 1937, the population of north China was more willing than the Chinese of other areas to countenance a Japanese-sponsored government; the Japanese actually possessed such a potential for popular support in the rural areas that... they could have succeeded if they had only taken the trouble to shoot a few hundred of their own officers![15]

He went on to note that 'the peasantry, on the eve of war, was no more opposed to the Japanese *than it was to other authorities*.'[16] There were even villages where the Japanese were welcomed with food, gifts and firecrackers – partly on the pragmatic assumption that it was better to give the food than to have it plundered, but partly on the assumption that nothing could be worse that the Guomindang army.

Two things combined to change this and create a mass nationalism. The first was the actions of the Japanese army. Like any invading imperialist army, they treated the entire population as actual or potential enemies. Each raid into the countryside convinced the villagers that neutrality was impossible, and that the invaders ought to be fought. As the rural elites had fled to the cities almost to a man, the only force capable of organising the defence of the villages was the Red Army.

The second was the fact that the Red Army broke the absolute power of the old masters in the villages. Mao spoke of 'the dual policy of requiring the landlords to reduce rent and interest and of stipulating that the peasants should pay this

---

15   Chalmers A Johnson, *Peasant nationalism and Communist power* (Stanford University Press, Stanford, CA, 1962) page 31.

16   As above, page 69 (my emphasis).

reduced rent and interest.'[17] This was in no sense a policy based on the interests of the poor peasantry – the maximum rent allowed was still a quarter of the crop! But neither was it based solely on the landlords' interests. Even when the Red Army enforced the payment of rent and debts, this was done without the customary brutality of the old masters' hired thugs. The CCP stood as a force above all rural classes, acting in their own interests as a future ruling class – but in the process they treated poor peasants and the rich alike.

The 'United Front' with the Guomindang coincided with the general strategy of Popular Fronts in Europe – the unity of the Western Communist parties, on Stalin's orders, with the 'progressive bourgeoisie' against fascism. But Mao's policy was in no sense based on a slavish obedience to Moscow. The CCP was an independent nationalist force, able to follow its own path because Moscow knew little or nothing of what was happening in China. One of the first mentions of Mao in Comintern documents was a long obituary published in March 1930, which alleged that he had died of consumption![18] On the Long March all contact with Moscow was lost. The meeting in 1934 at which Mao became CCP leader was marked by:

Mao's desire at this time to avoid any political rift with Moscow, and to maintain the fiction of the conformity of his proceedings with the prescriptions of Comintern... After the session Mao sent an envoy to Moscow to report on the proceedings; but the envoy did not reach his destination until after the seventh congress of Comintern in August [1935], and, having to travel through hostile territory, carried no documents. The text...

17   Mao Zedong, *Selected Works*, volume 3, (Foreign Languages Press, Beijing, 1965), pages 14-15. In north China, where most peasants lived off a combination of a small plot of land they owned and rented land, the questions of rent and interest on debts were equally important.

18   Schwartz, *Chinese communism and the rise of Mao*, page 136.

is said to have been communicated to [the Comintern] only in 1939.[19]

Thus, while Mao's writings of the period echo the rhetoric of Popular Frontism, in reality he was carrying out a very different strategy – one which involved the CCP becoming the ruling class, rather than accommodating to the existing rulers as was the case in Europe. The United Front strategy strengthened the CCP, rather than weakening it. One reason for this was that it was based on the empirical lesson Mao had learned from 1927 – 'Hold on to your guns'. As one historian of the period argued: 'Perhaps the most important thing about this revolutionary movement is not that it was armed with a doctrine and strategy, but that it was armed.'[20]

But a more important reason was that the United Front allowed the CCP to take on the Guomindang on their own ground – and win. If a government cannot defend the territorial integrity of its own state, it loses all legitimacy. The Guomindang, corrupt to the core and riven by factionalism, was incapable of defending China's 'national interests' against Japanese imperialism. Only the CCP was capable of this task. They thus staked their claim to become the rulers of post-war China. The Guomindang's corruption and factionalism were not just the failings of individuals. They reflected the inability of the old ruling classes to solve any of China's fundamental problems – imperialism, warlordism and the land question. The Guomindang represented classes which had lost any confidence in their own future.

By 1945 more than 10 percent of China was in the hands of the Red Army, and CCP guerrillas were operating over much

---

19 EH Carr, *The twilight of the Comintern 1930-1935* (Macmillan, London, 1982), pages 373-374.
20 Bianco, *Origins of the Chinese revolution*, page 203.

larger areas. The civil war which broke out almost immediately after the victory over Japan was from the beginning a completely unequal affair. Though the United States pumped vast quantities of arms into the Guomindang forces, these steadily lost ground, with hundreds of thousands of their soldiers deserting to the Red Army in battle after battle.

The civil war was not fought as a guerrilla war, but as a series of set-piece battles between two regular armies, with the mass of the population mere spectators. But there was a fundamental difference between the two armies. The Red Armies were motivated by the belief that they were fighting for a better life. The Guomindang armies were made up of half-starved unwilling conscripts kept in line only by terror, and led by corrupt and cowardly officers who had no confidence in their ability to survive, let alone win. Often the armies existed only on paper, with their commanders inventing whole battalions whose pay and rations they simply pocketed. Time and time again the Guomindang lost critical battles when such non-existent forces failed to appear.

In the cities, shortages and inflation – reaching an extreme 50,000 percent in Shanghai in 1948 – made everyday life unbearable for all but the tiny minority who were lining their pockets. The gap between rich and poor widened to an extent never seen before, and the vast majority of the middle classes were thrown into desperate poverty. Most of them came to hope for the Red Arm's victory as the only way out of their plight.

The war dragged on for four years, largely because of the immense distances which the Red Army had to cover, but the outcome was never seriously in doubt. In 1949 Chiang Kaishek finally admitted defeat and fled to Taiwan. The CCP were masters of China.

CHAPTER 3

1949: A socialist revolution?

1949 was a genuine revolution, in which a million-strong peasant army smashed forever the old ruling classes, broke the power of Western imperialism and laid the basis for a new social order. But it was in no sense a socialist revolution.

For Marx, as for Lenin, socialism was necessarily the self-emancipation of the working class. In 1949:

> …the proletariat played a negligible role in the last and decisive phase of the revolution. Neither major strikes nor urban uprisings paved the way for the Red Army as they had twenty years earlier for Chiang Kaishek in Shanghai. There were very few workers in the triumphant Red Army; it was composed essentially of peasants and officered by other peasants and intellectuals.[1]

By the time the Red Armies reached the major cities of eastern China the decisive battles had already been won. And as they entered the cities, the workers were merely passive spectators. 'Liberation' was brought to them from outside. This was not because Chinese workers were incapable of fighting. The years from 1945 to 1949 saw

---

1   Bianco, *Origins of the Chinese revolution*, pages 83-84.

a steadily rising number of strikes as the workers fought to defend themselves against hyperinflation. In 1949 the cities went quiet on explicit instructions from the CCP. As the Red Army neared the cities, the CCP sent ahead orders that:

> …workers and employees in all trades will continue to work and that business will operate as usual… officials of the Guomindang [other officials and] police personnel… are to stay at their posts, obey the orders of the People's Liberation Army and the People's Government.[2]

One sympathetic American journalist recorded it was '… noteworthy that the Communists are not trying to curry favour with the city workers by paying excessively high wages, and that in private factories they give the last word on production to management.'[3]

These policies were no accident, but rather necessary consequences of the struggle waged by the CCP. For the revolution was above all a nationalist one: their aim was to build a strong and independent national economy. Armed revolution was necessary to overthrow the old ruling classes, but it was to be strictly controlled from above.

Leon Trotsky had argued, in developing his theory of 'permanent revolution', that in countries such as China the national bourgeoisie were unable to carry out the equivalent of Europe's bourgeois revolutions through waging a successful struggle against imperialism and the power of the landlords. This was both because of their myriad social and economic ties as a class to the landlords and to world capitalism; and, more important,

2   *New China News Agency*, 3 May 1949, quoted in Tony Cliff, 'Permanent revolution', *International Socialism* 1:12, 1963: https://www.marxists.org/archive/cliff/works/1963/xx/permrev.htm [Reference updated]

3   Jack Belden, *China shakes the world* (Penguin, London, 1973) page 616.

because the threat to their power from the struggles of workers and peasants was greater than that of imperialism. The experience of 1927 had decisively confirmed Trotsky's argument.

One of the most persistent Stalinist arguments against the theory was that Trotsky 'underestimated the revolutionary potential of the peasantry'. This was a complete distortion: for Trotsky, the participation of the peasantry was essential for victory. But, he argued, they were incapable of leading the revolution:

> Without the decisive significance of the agrarian question for the life of the whole of society and without the great depth and gigantic sweep of the peasant revolution there could not even be any talk of the proletarian dictatorship... But the fact that the agrarian revolution created the conditions for the dictatorship of the proletariat grew out of the inability of the peasantry to solve its own historical problem with its own forces and under its own leadership.[4]

Therefore, he argued, the national revolution could only be successful if led by the urban working class. This meant that the national and the socialist revolutions would be fused into a single 'uninterrupted' or 'permanent' process:

> The dictatorship of the proletariat which has risen to power as the leader of the democratic revolution is inevitably and very quickly confronted with tasks, the fulfilment of which is bound up with deep inroads into the rights of bourgeois property. The democratic revolution grows over directly into the socialist revolution and thereby becomes a permanent revolution.[5]

---

4   Leon Trotsky, *The permanent revolution* (Pathfinder, New York, 1969) page 194. Emphasis in original.

5   As above, page 278.

The events of 1949 proved Trotsky right on every point except the last two – the most important parts of his analysis. For they rested on the assumption that the working class was capable of providing such leadership. The massacres of 1927 had crushed the revolutionary spirit in China's cities, and the conscious withdrawal of the CCP from the cities had left a political vacuum. (Small groups of Trotskyists had fought courageously in the cities from the early 1930s, but they were too small, and too often hit by Guomindang repression, to fill the vacuum.[6])

Yet in the absence of a revolutionary working class the potential for revolution remained. A section of the urban intelligentsia, who were able to break completely with the old ruling classes, had proved capable of filling that vacuum of leadership, building a mass armed movement of the peasantry under their strict control. The 'permanent revolution' which Trotsky had envisaged now became deflected in a purely nationalist direction.

This process was not peculiar to China. In many other underdeveloped countries – Vietnam in 1945 and Cuba in 1959, to name but two – similar revolutions took place. In all of them an old, corrupt ruling class, or a greatly weakened colonial power, was overthrown by peasant armies led by nationalist forces drawn from the urban middle classes. Those classes felt most keenly the oppression of the old system, which gave them a superior status to the mass of the population but deprived them of any hope of advancement. They also benefitted from an education, which both brought home to them their nation's backwardness and opened up the possibility of overcoming it. Their nationalism was at the same time a rejection of Western

---

6   The definitive history of Chinese Trotskyism is Gregor Benton (ed),
     Prophets unarmed (Haymarket, Chicago, IL, 2017). For a short
     introduction, see my 'Trotskyism in China', *International Socialist Review
     111*, Winter 2016/2-17: https://isreview.org/issue/111/trotskyism-china/
     [References updated]

imperialism and a desire to emulate its economic development.[7]

The CCP's victory thus achieved the old desire of Chinese nationalism for a strong and independent country which could begin the process of independent economic development – but the decisive agency of change would be the new state, not the old bourgeolsie The CCP had come to power as a force in their own right, standing above all the classes of the old society. Yet they were not free to act as they wished. It was the existence of a competitive and hostile world economy that dictated the need for a strong national economy, and the imperative of beginning to compete with that world economy thus dictated the new state's economic priorities.

State capitalism

The vast majority of the Chinese people – even large numbers of capitalists – welcomed the revolution. Mao's victory promised an end to the backwardness and misery that had been China's lot for centuries. By the time the government had consolidated their hold over the whole country in 1952, they had delivered on their promises to a significant extent. In the countryside the landlords were dispossessed and their land given to the peasantry. In the cities runaway inflation, mass unemployment and the constant shortages had been curbed. In the years that followed, there were also impressive improvements in literacy, education, health care and living standards, which gave rise to a major leap in life expectancy. The new Marriage Law of 1952 broke the absolute power of husbands and their families over women's lives. Child mortality was vastly reduced, while a rudimentary system of food distribution made famine seem a thing of the past.

Yet the CCP's economic strategy was not centred on improving living standards, but rather on the accumulation of capital from China's meagre resources to begin the construction of an

---

7   For an elaboration of this explanation see Cliff, 'Permanent revolution'.

industrial base. The elimination of the landlords, moneylenders, warlords and all the other parasites of the old order made possible the more efficient exploitation of workers and peasants, for which an increase in living standards was essential. The imposition of accumulation as the central dynamic of the economy, and the consequent social divisions of labour this gave rise to, created a form of capitalism – bureaucratic state capitalism – in which the economy was not run by individual capitalists but by the ruling state bureaucracy. This process of accumulation created and drew together a class of top bureaucrats, factory managers, military leaders and so on, drawn overwhelmingly from the top ranks of the CCP. They were bound together as a class both by their control over the priorities of the economy, and by their inevitably antagonistic relationship to the mass of workers and peasants. For if the accumulation of capital was the central goal, then the fulfilment of basic human needs clearly had to be subordinated to it.

In China that contradiction was particularly acute, because of the extreme backwardness of industry. Compared to India in 1949-50 (by no means an advanced industrial economy) China produced less than half the amount of electricity; had half the number of cloth spindles; a quarter the number of looms; and less than one-third the extent of railway tracks. Output in every major category of industry was less than it had been in Russia in 1913.[8]

The CCP thus needed extremely high rates of accumulation, which would get higher as the 1950s went on. According to Mao: 'The ratio of our country's accumulated capital to national income was 27 percent in 1957, 36 percent in 1958 and 42 percent in 1959.'[9]

---

8   Ygael Glückstein (Tony Cliff), *Mao's China* (Allen and Unwin, London, 1957), pages 24-26.

9   Quoted in Nigel Harris, *The mandate of heaven*, (Haymarket, Chicago, IL, 2015), page 209. [All references to this title have been updated.] The 1958-9 figures are almost certainly overestimates (because of the chaos

The overwhelming majority of this went into spending on heavy industry and arms. In the first Five-Year Plan (1953-8), for instance, 58 percent of planned investment went to industry, with most of the rest going to defence, transport and communications. Agriculture got only eight percent.[10] At the same time, living standards rose by only two percent a year during the early 1950s (and would drop severely between 1959 and 1961).

The contradiction between accumulation and human need also led to the establishment of a powerful system of state control, from the secret police down to officials in the villages, which could contain any protest from below. The potential for such protests was shown as early as 1957, in the 'Hundred Flowers' campaign. Mao called for greater freedom of speech for intellectuals in order to tie them more closely to the CCP, by making them feel that they had a stake in the new society. The government was overwhelmed by a torrent of criticisms and accusations, many of them daring to attack Mao himself. More seriously:

> The circle of complainers broadened rapidly. Urban workers began to express dissatisfaction by means of strikes, demands for better work conditions, slowdowns and phoney sick calls; peasants withdrew from the new collectives or tried to withhold taxes, claiming that the government was extracting more than landlords had ever done.[11]

The CCP quickly abandoned the campaign. In the repression that followed (organised by Deng Xiaoping, then CCP general secretary) thousands of intellectuals were jailed, and more than 200,000 people were expelled to the countryside.

---

caused by the Great Leap) but they give some idea of what the ruling class were aiming at.

10 As above, page 45.

11 Jonathan Spence, *The gate of heavenly peace* (Penguin, London, 1982) page 379.

Initially the pattern of industrialisation in China was closely modelled on Stalin's Russia – in particular the all-embracing Five-Year Plan which controlled all aspects of economic development. But while China's first Five-Year Plan did develop an industrial base, it did not do so fast enough for the needs of the ruling class. In the early 1950s the Chinese economy grew at a faster rate than at any previous time this century. Yet by comparison with the rest of the world economy, then in the middle of the most sustained boom in the history of capitalism, it was falling further behind.

The demands of military competition put further pressure on the strategy. To the east and the south, China was ringed by hostile regimes heavily armed by the United States. The remnants of the Guomindang regime on Taiwan, in particular, posed a constant threat. Their stated aim of reclaiming China was backed by vast quantities of American aid and direct American threats to intervene in any war between them and China. The Korean War of 1950 proved that the threats were not idle ones. Drawn into the war by the prospect of a direct American invasion, the Chinese army suffered more than a million casualties and was heavily defeated.

The enormous concentration of capital into heavy industry, and the top-heavy bureaucracy needed to run such concentrations, led to very high levels of waste and inefficiency throughout the system. That waste was greatly added to by an enormous squandering of scarce resources on arms spending. One writer, working from official figures, estimated that the production of the atom bomb in 1964 cost between a quarter and a half of that year's total electricity output.[12]

Far from trying to reduce the tensions, the CCP deliberately exaggerated the atmosphere of siege, using it to demand even greater sacrifices from workers and peasants. The threat of the

---

12   Michael Kidron, *Capitalism and theory* (Pluto, London, 1974) page 122.

Guomindang's return was still real enough to those who remembered conditions before 1949 for this to exert a moral pressure which officials could use against anyone who protested. Mao's strategy ran quickly into the material barriers of China's poverty, and the contradiction between that poverty and the needs of competition and accumulation. As early as 1956, growth was slowing down. Yet he pushed for an even faster pace of growth:

> [Steel] output this year will be over four million tons... the United States... can produce 100 million tons... Given 50 or 60 years, we certainly ought to overtake the United States. This is an obligation. You have such a big population, such a vast territory and such rich resources... if after working at it for 50 or 60 years you are still unable to overtake the United States, what a sorry figure you will cut! You should be read off the face of the Earth. Therefore to overtake the United States is not only possible, but absolutely necessary and obligatory.[13]

The Great Leap Forward

Mao attempted to overcome this contradiction by a series of 'mass campaigns', in which the lacking capital and resources were replaced by greatly increasing the exploitation of the mass of the population. The first of these was the 'Great Leap Forward' of 1958-60. Grossly inflated targets were set for both industrial and agricultural

---

13   Mao Zedong, *Selected Works*, volume 5 (Foreign Languages Press, Beijing, 1977), page 315. Compare this with Stalin's famous speech of 1931: 'No, comrades, the pace must not be slackened. On the contrary we must quicken it as much as within our powers and possibilities... To slacken the pace would be to lag behind, and those who lag behind are beaten... We are 50 or 100 years behind the advanced countries. We must make good this lag in ten years.' (Quoted in Isaac Deutscher, *Stalin* (Penguin, London, 1966) page 328.) Mao's longer time-scale reflects both the fact that he was speaking during the long boom of the 1950s, and the fact that the gap between China and the USA was far greater than the gap between Russia and the Western powers in 1931.

production (steel output was to overtake America in four years, for instance), and new work disciplines were enforced. Factory managers tried to dragoon their workers into meeting the targets by abolishing meal-breaks, instituting 18 or 24-hour shifts and abandoning all safe working practices. When these failed, they simply lied, causing further havoc as other factories' targets were raised to use these (mythical) increases in production.

In the cities the Great Leap soon collapsed under the weight of its own contradictions. Workers could be forced once or twice to work an 18-hour shift; but this could not become the normal working day. Machinery run at twice its normal speeds simply wore out twice as fast. And much of the real increase in output was wasted, as the imbalances between different sectors of industry meant that it could not be used

If in the cities the Great Leap was a fiasco, in the country-side it was a disaster. In 1952 an all-encompassing land reform had redistributed land from rich peasants and landlords to the poorer peasants, giving most families enough land to live on. Since then, the CCP had moved cautiously to introduce various forms of collective working, in order to increase production while using as little state investment as possible. Progress had been for the most part slow and wary, as the state sought to gain peasant consent for each stage.

But in 1958 all caution was thrown to the winds. The peasant cooperatives were merged into 'People's Communes', new economic structures covering on average 25,000 people. The land was forci-bly collectivised, and the peasants organised into large-scale work teams to meet the high production targets. Primitive communal kitchens and nurseries were set up, not to free women from the drudgery of housework, but to force them full-time into the fields. Thousands of small-scale rural factories were set up, using such capital as the commune possessed, to reduce even further the need for state investment in the countryside.

The factories were inevitably a drain on the rural economy

– the 'backyard' furnaces set up in thousands of villages used more industrial-grade steel than they produced. But the worst effects were felt on the land itself. Peasants angered by the loss of their land refused to work or did as little as possible. The local officials did everything they could to meet the impossible targets, and then resorted to lying on a grand scale. The 1958 grain harvest, originally claimed to be 375 million tonnes, in fact turned out to be 250 million, and the target for 1959 was cut from 525 to 275 million.[14]

1958 was a particularly good harvest. The next three were not. By 1961 famine – supposedly eliminated by the revolution of 1949 – had returned to large parts of north China. Western demographers, working from Chinese figures, have estimated that between 27 and 30 million people died of hunger in those years.[15] In Fengyang country, northern Anhui province, where particularly detailed records survived, one in four people starved to death – in some communes, that figure rose to one in three.[16]

Northern Anhui was traditionally one of the poorest areas of China, but even on the outskirts of Beijing there was enormous suffering. An intellectual who had been exiled to the countryside spelt out what it meant in stark terms:

The press was reporting on the excellent situation, how good and glorious things were. The catchword was 'The situation is very good and becoming better and better.' There was no food to eat in the village. The peasants were eating the leaves of trees, boiling leaves in water, mixing them with a little cornflour to make the leaves stick together... We intellectuals were lucky. We

14 Harris, *Mandate of heaven*, page 59.
15 Anne Thurston, *Enemies of the people* (Harvard University Press, Cambridge, MA, 1988) page 80. [More recent research, such as Yang Jiasheng, *Tombstone*, (Allen Lane, London, 2017), suggests that the real death toll was significantly higher.]
16 Yang Jiasheng, *Tombstone*, page 275. [Reference and figures updated.]

were eating sweet potato leaves. The best are the leaves of the sweet potato. Then the leaves of the plum. The worst are willow leaves. The peasants were eating willow.[17]

In the far west more than 20,000 people crossed the border from Xinjiang into Russia, and there were armed rebellions in at least two, and possibly five, provinces: 'In [Henan], and in Shandong to the east of it, members of the militia stole weapons, set up roadblocks, seized stocks of grain and engaged in widespread armed robbery.'[18]

Far from expanding the economy as Mao had hoped, the Great Leap cost almost ten years of economic development. Not until 1965 did total production (though not output per head) regain the levels reached in 1957.[19] The disasters caused by Mao's policies were aggravated by the departure of practically all Russian advisors in 1959-60, which halted more than a hundred major construction projects.

The split between China and Russia, which became an open break in 1961, was to be the inspiration for the growth of Maoism as a major revolutionary current in the late 1960s. But its real roots lay in the very different ambitions of the two ruling classes. While Russia supplied China with much-needed technology and technicians, the price asked was a high one. The Russian bureaucracy wanted to treat China as it then treated its Eastern European satellites – as a source of plunder. The ruling classes of Eastern Europe had little choice about this – their power rested on Russian tanks, as the 1956 invasion of Hungary had reminded them only recently.

Mao, by contrast, had come to power not only independently

---

17   Thurston, *Enemies of the people*, page 78.

18   Edward Rice, *Mao's way* (University of California Press, Berkeley, CA, 1974), page 179.

19   As above, page 181.

of Stalin but in spite of him. Stalin never believed that the Red Army could take power; in 1944 he dismissed them in talks with America's ambassador as 'margarine Communists'. Right up to Mao's victory, Russia had remained a supporter of the Guomindang. In January 1949, when the Guomindang government was forced to flee their capital in Nanjing, the Russian ambassador was the only one to accompany them![20]

In 1945 Russian troops had looted much of the heavy industry of northeastern China, claiming it as 'war reparations' from Japan (Stalin had declared war on Japan just nine days before the war ended.). Tensions between the two ruling classes diminished during the early 1950s, as China needed Russian technology and investment too much to worry about the price. But when increased Russian demands coincided with a reduction in the amounts of aid and investment given to China, as a consequence of Khrushchev's moves to extend Russian influence in Asia and Africa, the CCP had an independent power base from which to defy the Russians.

Though Mao was the prime mover behind the 1961 split, he had by that time lost all real control over the running of the Chinese economy. The disasters of the Great Leap had originally been blamed on 'overenthusiastic' local officials, but at a summit meeting of the CCP leadership in 1959, Mao took the blame and gave up most of his official positions. Isolated inside the ruling class, he probably did so in order to avoid a public split. But the effect of the move was to deepen his isolation.

Economic policy swung sharply in the opposite direction. Though most communes remained as administrative structures, control over agricultural production returned to village level. Targets were cut sharply, and private plots were given back to the peasants to boost output. In many areas this effectively meant returning to private agriculture. By 1962, '...the private

---

20   Gluckstein, *Mao's China*, pages 394 and 401.

grain harvest in Yunnan was larger than the collective harvest, and private cultivated land rose to 50 percent of the total. In Guizhou and Sichuan there was, even as late as 1964, more private than collective tilling.'[21]

In the cities a similar liberalisation took place. Productivity bonuses and piecework came into the factories, and factory managers were given greater control over their operations. Private markets reappeared and foreign trade – in particular grain imports – was increased. This was not a fundamentally different strategy from that pursued by Mao, as was later claimed; rather it was a necessary response to economic devastation.

But while the new policies eased the immediate crisis, they did nothing to resolve the deeper dilemmas facing the ruling class. Far from catching up with the advanced economies, China was falling even further behind. At the same time, the Sino-Soviet split meant that the external military threat was greatly increased. Mao's enemies inside the ruling class had managed to tum him into a ceremonial figurehead for the moment; but they had no alternative strategy for the Chinese economy as a whole.

---

21   E L Wheelwright and Bruce McFarlane, *The Chinese road to socialism,* (Penguin, London, 1973) page 70.

CHAPTER 4

'It is right to rebel' – the Cultural Revolution

The 'Cultural Revolution'… was responsible for the most severe setback and the heaviest losses suffered by the party, the state and the people since the founding of the People's Republic. It was initiated and led by Comrade Mao Zedong.[1]

This assessment, made by Mao's heirs in 1981, would in the 1960s have been heresy to most revolutionaries. The 'Great Proletarian Cultural Revolution' was seen as an integral part of the wave of protests and rebellions that swept the world in the late 1960s, and even as an inspiration for that rebellion. Students in Beijing and Shanghai, like their counterparts in Paris, Berlin and elsewhere, were on the march against conservatism and bureaucracy. Their revolt seemed clear proof that China could avoid the degeneration of revolutionary ideals that had occurred in Russia.

In reality, the Cultural Revolution was a vicious and bloody power struggle inside the ruling class, in which tens of millions were persecuted and jailed, and around 1.6 million people killed,

---

1   *Resolution on CPC history 1949-81* (Foreign Languages Press, Beijing, 1981) page 32.

the vast majority by the army or police.[2] Mao took the struggle to the streets for one simple reason: if it had been confined to the ruling class, he would have lost. The only 'cultural' aspect of the Cultural Revolution was its pretext.

In 1961 a play was staged in Beijing about Hai Jui, a sixteenth century official who attacked the emperor for his cruelty and indifference to the peasants' poverty, and was sacked for speaking out. The allusion to Mao was obvious and reflected widespread feeling in the ruling class – the playwright was deputy mayor of Beijing. In late 1965 Mao decided to counter-attack and found that no newspaper in Beijing would print his article. It finally appeared in an obscure Shanghai literary journal. On this flimsy basis, he ordered the start of a new propaganda campaign.

His opponents could not simply ignore this, so they took over the campaign to render it harmless. In doing so, they fell into Mao's trap. In May 1966, he savaged their management of the campaign and called for a nationwide attack on 'those persons in power taking the capitalist road'. In a slogan that rang around China, he declared: 'It is right to rebel!' (The irony of this – that rebellion is justified when the ruler says so – was lost on most people at the time.)

At bottom the argument was about the division of power inside the ruling class. Was Mao to be a dictator over the ruling class as a whole, or simply one of its senior members? His opponents had been trying to diminish his authority ever since the Great Leap, by turning him into a figurehead without any real control over the day-to-day running of society. But in doing so they built up Mao's moral authority as the leader of the revolution, an authority which he was able to turn against them. In addition, since the early 1960s Mao had been building a

---

2   [These are significantly higher figures than quoted in the original, taken from Andrew Walder, *Agents of disorder*, Harvard University Press, Cambridge, MA, 2019), pages 187-194.]

group of loyalists at the head of the armed forces, whose support was to be invaluable.

In Beijing, Mao got what he wanted – the removal of his enemies from their positions of power – almost at once. But to repeat this in the provinces it was necessary to take the battle onto the streets. This was the real role of the famous 'Red Guards'.

From August 1966 Red Guard groups were set up among students and school-students, first in Beijing and then spreading across the country. Trapped in a demeaning and stifling education system that denied all individual expression, Mao's appeal to rebellion struck a chord with them – and with many others. One man who was a school-student at the time told a researcher:

> When people tell you that they were always opposed to the Cultural Revolution, that they never supported it… you must not believe them. You must ask them more. Because when the Cultural Revolution began, everyone supported it. 90 percent of the people, 99 percent of the people, supported it – even those who were accused, even those who came under attack.[3]

The students moved quickly from attacking their teachers to the local bureaucracy. Unpopular officials (and in the cities there was no shortage of them) were dragged out of their offices and forced to confess their 'crimes' in front of mass kangaroo courts. The terror quickly widened to take in far wider targets. Anything which represented 'bourgeois' or 'feudal' culture was to be destroyed. Libraries were burnt down, and temples and museums ransacked. Anyone who had received a Western education or owned anything that betrayed 'bourgeois influences' – translations of foreign novels, busts of Beethoven,

---

3   Thurston, *Enemies of the people*, page 154.

pianos – became an 'object of struggle'.[4] In Tibet, this xenophobia turned into open and violent racism:

> There were killings and people hounded into suicide. People were physically attacked in the streets for wearing Tibetan dress or having non-Han [Chinese] hair styles. All but a handful of monasteries… were destroyed, many taken down brick by brick until not a trace was left.[5]

Mao's personality cult was taken to extremes that even outdid Stalin's Russia:

> O supremely beloved Chairman Mao, ten thousand songs of praise would not be enough to sing of the boundless love which revolutionary fighting men feel for you. Ten thousand red pens could never finish describing the boundless trust which these revolutionary combatants put in you, ten thousand ocean waves would not suffice to extol the limitless adoration which revolutionary combatants have for you, the infinite expanses of space would not be sufficient to contain the feelings of boundless loyalty…[6]

Every family was expected to begin the day by bowing to his portrait, just as they used to bow to the family gods; being unable to recite selections from his 'Little Red Book' on

---

4   Most memoirs of the Cultural Revolution were written by such intellectuals. Two of the most harrowing examples are Nien Chieng, *Life and death in Shanghai* (Grafton, London, 1986) and Yue Daiyuan and Carolyn Wakeman, *To the storm* (University of California Press, Berkeley, CA, 1985).

5   A Torn Grunfield, *The making of modern Tibet* (Zed Books, London, 1987) page 181.

6   Quoted in Simon Leys, *The Chairman's new clothes* (Allison and Busby, London, 1977) page 130.

command was taken as clear proof of disloyalty. The worship of Mao invaded even the most trivial aspects of everyday life. One intellectual remembered:

> Once I went into a store to buy a new shirt. The salesperson was standing there, and when I walked in, he said, 'Long live Chairman Mao.' Long live Chairman Mao? Not 'Hello, good morning.' So I said 'Long live Chairman Mao, I would like to buy a shirt.' So he sold me a shirt.[7]

The education system ground to a halt as millions of students headed for Beijing in the hope of catching a glimpse of Mao or set off on imitation 'long marches' across country to 'revolutionary shrines'. When Mao allegedly swam the Yangzi River (in a time four times as fast as the then world record) hundreds died trying to emulate him. All this was often described at the time as 'mass lunacy', yet there was a rational core to it. Mao and his supporters needed to whip the Red Guards into a frenzy to guarantee their unquestioning obedience. One oath revealingly pledged to '..follow step by step, to apply sentence by sentence each of Chairman Mao's directives, even if at first we do not understand them... so that the thoughts of Mao may form the substance of our soul and control all our movements.[8]

Civil war

By late 1966 the disruption had gone so far that Mao had to try to wind the movement down. This proved impossible – the situation had gone completely beyond anyone's control. For the local bureaucrats had not taken the attacks lying down. The reforms of the early 1960s had given them much greater powers than before, and they were not about to hand these back without a

---

7   Quoted in Thurston, *Enemies of the people*, page 100.
8   Quoted in Leys, *The Chairman's new clothes*, page 98.

fight. A few could defy the Red Guards openly. In Xinjiang, the CCP secretary – who was also provincial governor and political commissar of the garrison – had demonstrating students gunned down in the streets.[9] Two years later he was appointed head of the 'revolutionary committee' set up to mark the 'victory' of the Cultural Revolution.

Most local officials, however, responded by declaring their undying loyalty to Mao, organising their own groups of Red Guards and accusing those who opposed them of being 'counter-revolutionaries'. Warring gangs of hundreds and sometimes thousands began to multiply, each professing to be the only true Maoists. In Wuhan there were at least 54 such gangs; one battle between them left at least 250 dead and more than 1500 wounded.[10] At Beijing's prestigious Qinghua University, battles were fought to the death with spears, home-made rifles and mortars. As the fighting intensified, the gangs began to raid army barracks for tanks, artillery and anything else they could lay their hands on. In the heart of the city of Changsha:

> ...members of the Changsha Youth Organisation... levelled anti-aircraft missiles at the Xiang Embroidery Building in an attack on the Workers' Alliance. The entire block-long four-storey building had burned to the ground.[11]

By the summer of 1967 large parts of China were spiralling towards all-out civil war. In Sichuan, '...a crazy quilt of Army and Red Guard factions were engaged in battles throughout [the province]. Some had formed into guerrilla bands fighting in the hills and mountains.'[12]

---

9   Stanley Karnow, *Mao and China* (Penguin, London, 1984) pages 251-2.

10   Leys, *The Chairman's new clothes*, page 77.

11   Liang Heng and Judith Shapiro, *Son of the revolution* (Fontana, London, 1983) page 137.

12   Karnow, *Mao and China*, page 386.

One former Red Guard described the situation in Changsha as:

> ...absolutely terrifying. Bullets whistled in the streets, and the roar of a motorcycle or the wail of a siren meant violence and tragedy. The gateways of many units [workplaces] had broad white lines drawn across them, and armed guards waited on the other side to shoot anyone who stepped across without permission. There was a 9pm curfew and no one wanted to go out during the day unless he had to; there were many reports of the deaths of innocent vegetable buyers by stray bullets. People crisscrossed their windows with tape to prevent their shattering as the city shook with explosions and gunfire, and at night the sky flashed light and then dark with the passing of rockets.[13]

Alongside the outbreak of civil war, another threat had emerged to the ruling class: the reappearance of the working class as a political force. Many of the Red Guard groups set up by local bureaucrats to attack the students were composed of workers. From the end of 1966 some of them began to stage strikes and demonstrations for their own demands – better wages, working conditions and hours, and an end to managerial privileges. The strikes began in Shanghai in November 1966, and by the following January there was almost a general strike in the city. One foreign teacher described what followed:

> Up to this time, the party had refused... to meet the demands of certain workers. One of the main bones of contention was that 'temporary' employees did not receive the same pay and welfare benefits as 'permanent' workers... Now the cadres suddenly capitulated. As a result, vast sums were withdrawn from the banks; thousands of workers left Shanghai to 'make revolutionary

---

13   Liang Heng and Shapiro, *Son of the revolution*, page 133.

liaison', and those who stayed behind had a field day converting their windfalls into furniture and household goods.[14]

In the spring and summer of 1967 the strike wave spread across the country, sometimes through railworkers (who were at the head of the movement from the beginning), but more often as a local response to appalling conditions and the power vacuum. Most strikes were short-lived and successful, with workers going back when they had won their demands, and there were few reports of any real co-ordination. Yet as one group of workers went back, others would come out.

With both CCP and state machines paralysed, the only force that could be counted on to restore order was the army. Yet while the army would break strikes (as they did across Shanghai) and shoot down demonstrators, they would not necessarily take orders from Mao's allies. Many local commanders had close ties with the officials who had been attacked by the Red Guards, and they were loath to take orders from the people who they held responsible for the chaos of the previous eighteen months.

The extent of this disaffection was demonstrated in July 1967 when the army command in Wuhan mutinied. Two senior Cultural Revolution officials, sent from Beijing to arbitrate a particularly bloody Red Guard feud, were kidnapped by the local army chiefs, who were on the opposite side of the feud to the Beijing officials. Mao ringed the city with paratroopers and sent gunboats up the Yangzi, and a major shooting war was narrowly averted by negotiations. Yet the local commanders were simply relieved of their posts, while three months later one of the officials was disgraced and publicly denounced.[15]

The reasoning behind this was simple. The paramount need

---

14   Neale Hunter, *Shanghai journal* (Oxford University Press, Oxford, 1988), page 216.

15   For a fuller account see Leys, *The Chairman's new clothes*, pages 76-81.

was now to restore order, and to do that Mao needed the armed forces, even if that meant reinstating many of his opponents. From mid-1967 the army began to take control of local governments, factories and colleges, and enforce an end to the fighting. As they consolidated their authority, 'Revolutionary Committees' were set up to mark the end of the Cultural Revolution in each province. These were dominated by the military, but also relied on the recently-disgraced officials. Red Guard involvement was either token or non-existent.

The response of many Red Guards was to assume that there were a lot more 'capitalist-roaders' than they had thought, and to step up the fighting. For most of them, this meant simply descending further into gangsterism or banditry. But others moved sharply to the left, and at least one group began to develop a class analysis of China, arguing that the problem was not individuals, but rather the whole 'Red capitalist class'.

Shengwulian, as the group became known, achieved national fame in March 1968 with their manifesto *Whither China?* They argued that:

> …the basic social contradictions that gave rise to the great prole-
> tarian cultural revolution are contradictions between the rule of
> the new bureaucratic bourgeoisie and the mass of the people. The
> development and intensification of these contradictions decides
> that society needs a more thorough change – overthrow of the
> bureaucratic bourgeoisie, thorough smashing of the old state
> machinery, realisation of a distribution of assets and power, and
> establishment of a new society – People's Commune of China.[16]

---

16 Quoted from extracts published in *International Socialism* 1:37, June/
    July 1969, page 27. The document can be found in full in The Seventies
    (editors) *The revolution is dead-long live the revolution* (Black Rose,
    Montreal, Canada 1977) pages 153-70. (The Seventies were a group of
    libertarian ex-Red Guards based in Hong Kong.) [A fuller history of

Shengwulian, who had an important influence at least across their home province of Hunan, went on to draw the conclusion that the new 'Revolutionary Committees' were a sham, that the army had become a force for counter-revolution, and that the immediate task was arming the workers.

The ruling class' response to this increasing disorder was to step up the repression. From the end of 1968 young people were deported wholesale to the countryside in order to break the Red Guards. On official figures, between twelve and eighteen million people were sent to the countryside by the mid-1970s – that is up to one in ten of the urban population.[17] And there were worse things than deportations. In the southern province of Guangxi the repression caused some 100,000 deaths and destroyed most of the town of Wuzhou.[18] Similar massacres took place in a number of other provinces, in particular Guangdong and Inner Mongolia.

The Cultural Revolution was formally wound up at the CCP's Ninth Congress in April 1969. Skirmishes with Russian troops on the northern border the previous month seem to have been the final straw that caused the various factions to call a halt. But serious disorders continued for some time in outlying provinces, and it was not until 1971 that the ruling class re-established complete control.

The extent of the rebellions was shown in an order sent to Shanxi province in July 1969. This explicitly forbade: hiding, exchanging or transporting arms; using state workshops to

---

Shengwulian is in Yiching Wu, *The cultural revolution at the margins*, (Harvard University Press, Cambridge, MA, 2014), pages 142-189.]

17 Several different figures have been quoted for the numbers sent to the countryside. This figure is taken from the government propaganda magazine *Beijing Review*, 27 September 1982, which stated that: 'In… 1977-81, a total of 37 million people were assigned jobs in China's cities and towns. About half were people who had been sent to the countryside during the Cultural Revolution.'

18 Leys, *The Chairman's new clothes*, page 205; Karnow, *Mao and China*, page 438.

make arms for personal use; sabotaging road or rail commu-nications; looting banks; and organising strikes. Strikers were given guarantees that there would be no victimisations if they returned to work within a month.[19] Clearly it was impossible for the ruling class to break all strikes by force.

Clearly, too, the violent opposition to the ruling class was not the work of a 'handful of bad elements', but rather a mass activity. Though their fear of opposition from below could temporarily unite all factions inside the ruling class, the destruc-tion caused by the Cultural Revolution, and the fact that it had solved none of the divisions, meant that the faction-fighting was simply postponed to another day.

Waiting for someone to die

In the aftermath of the Cultural Revolution, the ruling class faced two fundamental problems. Both posed major challenges to the victors of the Cultural Revolution.

The first was the task of rebuilding the party and state machines. Restoring the shattered confidence of the army of lower officials was an uphill task. Mao's strategy of keeping them on their toes through constant – and contradictory – campaigns would be directly counter-productive. What the officials now returning to their offices wanted was peace and quiet, and a leadership in Beijing that knew its own mind two years running.

The second problem was the economy. Although the Cultural Revolution had barely affected the countryside, industry had been badly hit. It could be generally agreed that a period of liberal economic policies was needed to repair the ravages of the past few years, as after the Great Leap. But to a section of the ruling class – represented first by Zhou Enlai and then Deng Xiaoping – a more fundamental change of direction was necessary.

---

19 Quoted in Leys, *The Chairman's new clothes*, pages 192-5.

The development of Chinese science and technology had come to a complete halt during the Cultural Revolution. In four years not one student had graduated, while the vast majority of scientists had been exiled to the countryside to clean out pigsties or plant rice. Mao's dream of catching up with the rest of the world economy through developing as a siege economy was now clearly unworkable.

Yet the onset of crisis in the world economy in the early 1970s, and the real threat of a war with Russia, made the pressure to compete greater than ever before. Now, it was argued, this could only be done through an opening to Western capitalism, in particular America and Japan. This was not a new argument – it had been pushed by many of those who had been disgraced during the Cultural Revolution. Because of this, it was bound to arouse the opposition of those who had inherited their positions. The victors were themselves divided into a number of competing factions.

Above all the warring groups stood the enigmatic and devious figure of Mao, increasingly senile and dying of Parkinson's disease, but still capable of playing the factions off against each other to maximise his power. It was obvious that he had no real strategy for this new situation – but it was equally obvious that no faction could impose their own until he died.

The next six years were to see a series of vicious and complex power battles, whose methods seemed more drawn from the Medici court or prohibition-era Chicago than any Maoist notion of 'mass democracy'. The first victims were the senior military leaders allied to Lin Biao, Mao's chosen successor. They disappeared from public life in late 1970, and for the next two years there was a deafening silence about their fate. This was broken with the announcement that they had plotted to kill Mao and carry out a military coup. On being discovered, Lin Biao and family had fled to Russia in a plane which conveniently crashed in Mongolia, killing all aboard.

The official account was of course nonsense. To accuse Mao's chosen successor and the main architect of the Red Army's guerrilla strategy during the 1930s and 1940s of representing 'the interests of the overthrown landlord and capitalist classes and the desire of those overthrown reactionaries to topple the dictatorship of the proletariat and restore the dictatorship of the bureaucracy'[20] was to accuse the entire ruling class of unbelievable stupidity in allowing such a traitor to remain undiscovered for 40 years. It was also to cast doubts on everyone else – if Mao's chosen successor could be a traitor, so could every other member of the ruling class.

Lin Biao's exact fate is still unknown – what is clear is that he was eliminated in a faction fight, in a manner that did the regime no credit whatsoever.[21] The issue which got him killed was most probably the establishment of diplomatic relations with the USA and the start of small-scale imports of foreign plant and technology. These events, combined with Chinese support for the suppression of popular revolts in Bangladesh (then East Pakistan) and Sri Lanka, were a direct reversal of the international stance which Lin Biao had pioneered since 1966, and the first in a series of moves to bring China into a closer relationship with the world economy.

But while Mao was prepared to approve a limited opening to the world economy, he was not prepared to dismantle the siege economy entirely. His reservations limited the power of the 'modernising' faction and strengthened that of the 'Gang

---

20 Yao Wenyuan, *On the social basis of the Lin Biao anti-party clique* (Foreign Languages Press, Beijing, 1975) page 2.

21 Simon Leys, *Chinese shadows* (Penguin, London, 1978), page 180 quotes 'more recent [1974] and reliable reports that he was assassinated in Beidahe' (the top bureaucracy's summer resort). A later work - Yao Mingle, *The conspiracy and murder of Mao's heir* (Collins, London, 1983) - asserted that he was gunned down in an ambush after leaving a banquet in Beijing.

of Four', now the main inheritors of the Cultural Revolution.[22]

Lin Biao's removal only increased the tensions between the survivors. The only secure figures were Mao himself and Zhou Enlai, who served as a protector for the modernisers. While these two lived, neither faction could eliminate its rivals. But as both were close to death, the succession seemed to hinge on which of them would die first.

The Gang of Four took over the campaign to vilify Lin Biao, turning it into a campaign to 'Criticise Lin Biao, criticise Confucius'. This unlikely combination in fact masked an attack on Zhou Enlai and his economic policies. Economic events strengthened their hand. China had re-entered the world market just as the recession was starting to bite. The imports of technology coincided with a decline in exports, causing a balance of payments deficit for 1974 of US$1.1 billion (in 1969 the total value of foreign trade had been only US$3.4 billion). The Gang of Four forced through a drastic reduction in imports and turned economic policy back decisively to the siege model.[23]

They further pushed their advantage with a campaign to cut back 'bourgeois rights', by which they meant overtime payments, bonuses and piecework in the factories. This classic attempt to ease economic difficulties by cutting wages provoked numerous strikes and disturbances, culminating in a near-general strike in Hangzhou in spring 1975. After the Gang of Four had failed to get a return to work, Deng Xiaoping (who had come back into the leadership in late 1973) broke the strikes by sending 10,000 troops into the factories.[24]

---

22 The four were: Jiang Qing, Mao's third wife; Yao Wenyuan, a thug journalist who became Mao's main ideological hit-man; Zhang Chunqiao, CCP secretary in Shanghai; and Wang Hongwen, formerly a works policeman in Shanghai, promoted as a 'model worker'.
23 Bill Brugger, *China: radicalism to revisionism 1962-79* (Croom Helm, London, 1981) pages 185-6.
24 Harris, *Mandate of heaven*, pages 141-143

This resurgence of workers' struggles swung the pendulum back towards the modernisers, and imposed a brief truce on the various factions. But this was broken in early 1976 when Zhou Enlai died. Though the Gang of Four were not able to put their own man in his place, they were strong enough to block Deng Xiaoping's promotion and install a compromise candidate. They then launched the snappily-titled 'campaign to beat back the right-deviationist attempt to reverse correct verdicts', aimed openly at Deng Xiaoping.

Though all these campaigns were restricted to the media, for fear that any 'mass mobilisations' would get out of hand, they nevertheless meant further rounds of arrests, denunciations and repression across the country. The increasing absurdity of the campaigns, combined with steadily lowering living standards, produced a simmering bitterness and anger in the cities.

In April 1976 that accumulated hatred exploded in the most important challenge to the regime since its inception – the 'April 5th movement' Tiananmen riots, which involved well over 100,000 people in Beijing alone.

The riots were sparked when police removed wreaths commemorating Zhou Enlai (revered as the only person with the authority to mitigate the excesses of Mao and the Gang of Four) which had been placed at a memorial at the heart of Tiananmen Square. The wreaths had been placed on the Chinese Qing Ming (Spring) festival, on which the dead are traditionally honoured, and Deng Xiaoping's supporters used it to organise open demonstrations against the Gang of Four. These drew tens of thousands of people, often coming in contingents organised by junior officials. One group of workers from a heavy machinery factory took all day to carry a 1,000-pound metal wreath into the square.[25]

One participant recorded in a Hong Kong journal:

---

25   Thurston, *Enemies of the people*, page 14.

At 7.45am, more than 50,000 people had gathered on the square… at 9am there spread from the masses at the square the words that 'The wreaths were inside the Great Hall of the People.' Calling out the name of Zhou Enlai, the masses rushed towards the Great Hall only to be barred by the army… [the militia] wanted to lay down an ambush in front of the Great Hall but before they reached the main gate, they were broken up into sections. Another chaotic skirmish started in which a hundred or more militiamen were wounded, twelve seriously.[26]

The riot lasted all day: police stations and cars were burnt, soldiers attacked and militia barracks wrecked. It was not until late in the evening that the police regained control, beating to death several thousand of those left in the square. Similar disturbances were reported in Hangzhou, Nanjing, Zhengzhou, Kunming and Guiyang, and in Anhui and Guangxi provinces.[27]

The extent of the panic among the ruling class can only be guessed at. The riots took place only yards from the Forbidden City where the top bureaucracy lived – and where Mao lay on his deathbed. The rulers closed ranks at once against this threat from the streets. Deng Xiaoping was blamed for the riots and instantly disgraced, and a massive repression began, which led to more than 100,000 arrests in Beijing alone.

Although the Gang of Four had now removed their main rival, their victory was to be short-lived. For the main conclusion the bureaucracy as a whole drew from the riots was that the

---

26 *Minus Eight* (Hong Kong) June/July 1976, pages 10-11. *Minus Eight* was published by The Seventies (see note 15 above); the title was a countdown to 1984.

27 According to *China News Analysis* (CNA),4 June 1976, drawing together various provincial radio broadcasts. CNA was a right-wing but generally authoritative magazine published in Hong Kong. The reports were confirmed in *Peking Review* [renamed *Beijing Review* in 1979], 24 November 1978.

Gang now threatened to drag them all down. Their insistence on continuing the campaign against Deng through the Tangshan earthquake disaster of July – the second worst in recorded history, which killed over 600,000 people – only worsened their isolation. Deeply unpopular even with other hard-line Maoists in the CCP leadership, they clung to power only through Mao's protection. And on 9 September 1976 Mao died.

After a month of uncertainty, the succession was settled by the Gang's arrest at gunpoint. The by now ritual denunciations followed: they had been for years agents of imperialism, implacably opposed to Mao and all he stood for, yet responsible for all the crimes of the Cultural Revolution. The propaganda machine they had built up and used to such effect on their enemies now turned exactly the same torrent of lies and abuse on them. As one Canadian Maoist, *defending* their arrest, admitted:

> …the official People's Daily used the same language to describe the Four and their 'crimes' as it had used to condemn Deng Xiaoping not many months before. One could be forgiven for thinking that sometimes the articles were simply reruns with appropriate name changes made to take care of new circumstances.[28]

With Mao dead and his closest supporters behind bars, the stage was clear for the modernising faction to establish their dominance over the ruling class as a whole. By 1978 Deng Xiaoping had removed all remaining effective opposition and set about systematically demolishing Mao's economic strategy. The siege economy was to be abandoned in favour of an opening to Western capitalism and the development of 'market socialism', as the only way to pull China out of the poverty and stagnation that was Mao's legacy.

---

28   Neil Burton, 'In defense of the new regime', in Charles Bettelheim and
      Neil Burton, *China after Mao* (Monthly Review Press, New York, 1978),
      page 11.

CHAPTER 5

'The socialist market' – China's economy after Mao

I n 1978 Deng Xiaoping announced a complete change of economic direction with the 'Four Modernisations' (of industry, agriculture, science and technology, and defence). The new strategy had two major components: importing modem plant and technology to develop export-orientated industries; and the introduction of 'market relations' to replace central state control over much of industry, and practically all of agriculture.

Mao's previous economic strategy was attacked by the modernisers as having led to economic decay and impoverishment. They revealed that per-capita calorie intake was lower in 1978 than it had been in 1957, and that 10 percent of the rural population were as poor as they had been in 1949.[1] The attacks focussed on Mao's voluntarist campaigns, in particular the Great Leap and the Cultural Revolution. But it is important to remember that the campaigns were launched in response to economic stagnation. Even without the destruction they caused, Mao's strategy could not have worked. His successors shared

---

1   Michael Yahuda, *China's foreign policy after Mao* (Macmillan, London, 1983) page 133.

the aim of building a strong industrialised economy capable of competing with the world economy; they ditched his strategy because it had failed.

The opening to the world economy did not work in the way the ruling class hoped it would. The initially ambitious plans to import large quantities of modem technology greatly diminished in importance. This was partly because the ruling class discovered that they simply couldn't afford them. In 1979-80, 1983 and 1985 there were major cutbacks in purchases from abroad. Each round of cuts left a number of projects abandoned half-built, and made Western investors wary of such projects.

But it also proved far more difficult to integrate high-technology plants into the economy than had been thought. The history of the Baoshan steelworks north of Shanghai, the showpiece of this strategy, was a salutary lesson. It was intended to be the largest steelworks in the world, employing more than 40,000 workers and using state-of-the-art Japanese and German technology. But:

> ...the swampy ground could not bear the weight of the huge blast furnaces... and enormous amounts of precious foreign exchange had to be spent importing iron pilings to reinforce the foundations. The Japanese blast furnaces were found to require a higher grade of iron ore than China produces, so Australian ore has had to be imported... the 100,000-ton carriers bringing the ore from Australia were blocked from the Yangzi pier by a sand bar in the estuary, and the only solution was to build a new port and storage facilities 130 miles to the south.[2]

Baoshan illustrated a general trend that was to upset the ruling class' plans time and again. Each move towards greater integration into the world market drew the ruling class in deeper than they had intended. The more they attracted trade and

2   Lynn Pan, *The new Chinese revolution* (Sphere, London, 1988) page 85.

investment, they less they could control the pace or direction of its development.

Another crucial component of the strategy was the drive to attract foreign investment. Special Economic Zones were set up, later expanded to take in some twenty coastal cities, offering all manner of tax concessions, free land and buildings – and low wages. The governor of Fujian province announced in 1980 that:

> We are now studying the wage rates of Hong Kong, Singapore and South Korea. We believe that our wage rates will be lower than these places. In order to protect the investors' profitability, the wage rate cannot be too high.[3]

Direct foreign investment failed to materialise on the scale desired. Most of the investment which took place was been in offices, hotels and processing industries, rather than the high-tech industries hoped for. The majority of it came from Hong Kong, typically invested in small-scale projects. As of 1988, Hong Kong had invested US$2.1 billion, almost four times the amount from Japan.[4] That figure included an unknown amount of what was actually Chinese money, invested through 'shell companies':

> …a business in China sets up a front company in Hong Kong. The Hong Kong shell then invests in China, technically as a foreign investor. As a result, the business in China is transformed into a foreign joint-venture and is entitled to benefits denied local enterprises.[5]

---

3   *Far Eastern Economic Review* (hereafter *FEER*), 18 January 1980. [*FEER* was a weekly business magazine published in Hong Kong. From the late 1970s onwards, it was one of the best sources for information on the Chinese economy, but unfortunately it has not been preserved online.]
4   *FEER*, 29 March 1990.
5   *FEER*, 23 June 1988.

Although foreign trade increased enormously since 1978, that too became a source of major problems. While China became a major exporter of oil, coal, textiles, armaments and minerals, imports rose far more steeply. Between 1979 and 1990, there were trade deficits in all but two years, which had to be financed by short-term loans.

All the industries targeted for development as major exporters were hit by severe fluctuations in world prices – oil by the price slump of 1985-6, armaments by the end of the Iran-Iraq war, and minerals by different Chinese provinces undercutting each other in commodities markets. At the same time, industrial growth and the growing independence of local officials meant a growth in imports which the central state could not control. The ruling class lost control over the results and consequences of its turn to the world economy, while reaping few of the benefits which it hoped for.

While the opening to the world market did not deliver all it promised, the Chinese economy was nevertheless transformed since 1978, growing at a faster rate than at any time in Chinese history. Overall economic growth averaged over 10 percent a year throughout the 1980s, one of the highest rates of growth anywhere in the world. The main cause of this was the second part of the 'modernisation' strategy: a radical restructuring of the internal economy, greatly reducing central state control over investment and production targets. Yet the very success of this reform programme led to major economic difficulties that fuelled the 1989 explosion.

Agriculture

The first reforms took place in the countryside. Between 1979 and 1981, the communal fields were broken up into individual family plots. Peasants were allowed to grow what they wanted, paying a fixed sum in taxes and guaranteeing to sell a proportion of their crop to the state – everything else was theirs to eat or sell on the open market.

The initial results were spectacular. By the mid-1980s output had risen by more than 60 percent since 1978, while one survey suggested that real incomes had on average doubled in the years 1978-84.[6] The World Bank estimated that the proportion of the rural population living below the poverty line had declined from 31 percent in 1979 to 13 percent in 1983, and argued that 'the speed and scale of the improvement is probably unprecedented in world history.'[7]

The rise in output was mostly due to peasants working far harder than before. While purchase prices for most crops rose sharply, state investment dropped to almost nothing, on the assumption that peasants would reinvest much of their new wealth. But given the small size of their plots (one or two acres) such investment was simply not profitable. The area of land ploughed or sown by machine steadily declined, as did the area irrigated. The early rates of growth could not be sustained for any length of time.

The other side of the reforms was a sharp decline in social provision. As the communes lost practically all their income the minimal services they provided soon disappeared. Almost all health care, for example, was privatised, at enormous cost to those who fell seriously ill. In 1990 a stay in the county hospital could cost more than 300 yuan – about six months of a peasant's average income – and a serious illness treated at home 100 yuan.[8]

The decline in rural education, as children were taken out of school to work the family plot, was staggering – secondary school enrolment dropped from 46 percent in 1978 to 30 percent

---

6   Quoted in Stephan Feuchtwang, Athar Hussain and Thierry Pairault, *Transforming China's economy in the Eighties*, volume 1, (Zed Books, London, 1988) page 88.

7   World Bank, *China: long-term development issues and options* (Johns Hopkins University Press, Baltimore, MD, 1985) page 30.

8   *FEER*, 26 July 1990.

in 1983[9] – and of course enrolment figures were higher than the numbers actually attending. Girls in particular were taken out of school as early as possible. In 1981, in one school studied in Shaanxi, girls made up 62 percent of first-year primary students, but only 30 percent of the third year of middle school.[10]

These figures show just one aspect of an enormous deterioration in the status of women. Under the old system of working the fields collectively, although women's work was only paid at 80-90 percent of men's, women had in theory an independent income (though it was often paid to the husband or eldest son). Now even the theory had gone. One researcher argued that:

> ...the new economic arrangements in the countryside are returning women to their pre-Liberation position in relation to the means of production. Now instead of reporting to the team leader for job assignments... a woman will be under the supervision of the male head of her household. He will decide when she works, what she does, and whether she can take time off.[11]

The government's attempts to reduce population growth by limiting each family to one child, which began in 1979, made their position still worse. This led to some 300,000 cases of female infanticide in 1983 and 345,000 in 1984.[12] The explanation for the reappearance of this old tragedy was all too simple. Children are required by law as well as by custom to look after their parents in old age. But women's duty is to their husband's parents, not to their own. The communes provided only minimal care for the elderly, and with the privatisation of the land even that minimal care has effectively gone. As the peasants saw it

9   World Bank, *China: long-term development issues and option*, page 30.
10 Margery Wolf, *Revolution postponed*, (Methuen, London, 1987), page 129.
11 As above, pages 268-269.
12 Quoted in *National Abortion Campaign News*, (London), summer 1986, page 14.

(and they were right) no male child meant no security in old age. So if the state insists that you can only have one child, it had to be a boy.

Infanticide was a minority response even in the poorest areas – much more common was simple disobedience. In 1983 first children comprised only 56 percent of rural births, while almost 20 percent were third or subsequent children.[13] Village officials had little power to stop this, other than by imposing fines, and the government had to first modify the policy – conceding that couples whose first-born was a girl could try again – and then effectively drop it. Yet the stigma on girl children remained.

While the agricultural reforms did initially increase living standards, they also increased inequalities in the countryside, by depending on peasants working harder with less state investment. In naturally fertile areas with a high population density this worked; in more backward areas it did not. The proportion of the rural population earning less than 200 yuan a year dropped from 73 percent in 1979 to 28 percent in 1982. But in Jiangsu the figure was less than 17 percent, while in the north-western province of Gansu it was over 46 percent.[14] Even these provincial figures hid wider disparities between different areas.

In themselves the disparities were not new. What changed during the 1980s was that such wide gaps in living standards could be found within the villages. While it remained broadly true that in poor areas everyone was poor, the reverse was not true. In those areas which prospered, large pockets of poverty remained. Such inequalities are the most worrying for the state, because they stared the peasants in the face. It was not news in Gansu that people a thousand miles away in Jiangsu were far richer than they were. But peasants in the same village who had

---

13 *FEER*, 26 November 1985.
14 World Bank, *China: long-term development issues and options*, page 29.

seen no rise in their living standards, while others had, resented the fact bitterly.

One Chinese journalist, returning to his home village in a prosperous part of Jiangsu province, illustrated the extent of those inequalities:

> An old classmate... now a village doctor, has become a 'ten thousand dollar man' – the Chinese equivalent of a millionaire. As he is the only doctor in the village, the peasants have no alternative medical care within seventeen kilometres... One peasant, Chang Liang, used to receive subsidies and allowances from the state, and the commune provided a small hut for him to live in. After the introduction of the new system the subsidies were withdrawn. His life became so difficult that he died at the age of 45, largely because he could not afford the hospital treatment. His wife and children have subsequently had to turn periodically each year to begging simply in order to survive.[15]

Private wage-labour, both in the fields and in village industries, returned on a large scale. The government initially allowed each enterprise to employ only eight people, but that quickly became a dead letter. Formally, since all land remained state property, this did not mean a return to landlordism – but to those who had to work for the newly-rich farm managers, it would have been hard to tell the difference. The ruling class welcomed these growing inequalities. In a major survey of the economy, one senior government minister argued that:

> Achieving common prosperity does not mean becoming well-off simultaneously or enjoying the same level of affluence. Historical

---

15 Ni Er, 'The irresponsibility system', in *Inside Asia*, April-May 1986.

lessons tell us that seeking equal prosperity for all at the same time will only engender egalitarianism and common poverty.[16]

What did worry the ruling class were the effects of the changes in agriculture on urban prices, and thus on wage levels. The combination of increased production – which meant that workers could spend their wages instead of having to save them because the shops were empty – and the growth of the market led to endemic inflation after decades of virtually stable prices. By 1985 inflation in the cities was into double figures.

1985 also saw a major drop in the grain harvest. While the official explanation was 'natural disasters', the figures for cash crops belied it – sugar production increased by 19 percent and tobacco by 29 percent.[17] The real explanation lay in the logic of the market system. Almost every other crop could be traded on the free market, but grain prices were fixed by the state as a political necessity. Grain production was thus far less profitable, and the peasantry used their freedom to grow what they liked to raise more profitable crops. On official figures, more than four million hectares (ten million acres) of land were taken out of gram production in 1985.[18]

One solution briefly considered was a major shift in consumption patterns away from grain towards meat and dairy products. But the cost of this would have been even greater than the grain subsidies and it would have taken decades to bring about. Moreover, the World Bank warned that it was a political mistake even to try:

One possibility of particular concern would be an increase of per capita consumption of animal products to a level that could

---

16   *Beijing Review*, 10 February 1986.
17   *FEER*, 16 January 1986.
18   *Beijing Review*, 21 April 1986.

not be sustained… international experience suggests that the cutback in meat consumption that would then be required could cause acute social problems.[19]

Once they get a taste for it…

The more serious response was to offer incentives to persuade peasants to switch back to grain production. The packages included extended credit, higher prices, and substantial discounts on fertiliser and diesel oil, as well as allowing a higher proportion of the crop to be sold on the free market.

Yet in 1986 the amount of land planted with grain declined again in ten provinces, while the gap between grain prices and those for other crops remained as wide as ever. Though the harvests increased from the low point of 1980, grain output per head of population declined for the rest of the 1980s – and the increased amount of grain available on the free market led some peasants to give up even growing their own supply.

The aim of withdrawing state controls from agriculture and allowing the free market to increase agricultural production proved to be impossible. Precisely because of the workings of the market, the state was from the mid-1980s onwards forced to pump more and more cash into the countryside simply to slow down the decline in food production.

Industry

If the central problem in agriculture was stagnation, in industry it was just the opposite. From 1981 onwards, the urban reforms allowed factory managers to keep hold of the enterprise's profit (paying only a fixed proportion in taxes) to reinvest as they saw fit. They were also allowed to buy raw materials and components, and to sell their output, on the free market. Though central state control still operated over key sectors of industry (power,

---

19   World Bank, *China: long-term development issues and options*, page 51.

transport and armaments) practically all consumer industries, and most heavy industry, operated on this basis. Provincial and local officials were also given broader economic powers than before, in particular to negotiate foreign loans and investment.

As in agriculture, these reforms led to some of the highest rates of growth ever seen in China. Between 1983 and 1985 the increase in China's industrial output was greater than the total industrial output of South Korea.[20] By 1985 industry had achieved an annual growth rate of 18 percent, more than double the planned target of eight percent. The result, according to one senior minister, was:

> ...inflation of credit funds, soaring consumption funds, a shortage of energy and raw materials and a strain on communication facilities. Maintaining the speed of growth has required the import of large quantities of raw materials and machine parts... the amount of distribution has outstripped the allowances of the national economy...[21]

The CCP's response to this 'overheating' was to limit enterprises' rights to trade independently, and to reassert central state controls over investment. Initially it seemed that the state's attempts to slow the economy down were working in 1986. Yet as the year went on their worry became that the economy was going into recession. Economic policy went quickly into reverse. But by early 1987, state controls were tightened once again as the same problems reappeared. That pattern of increased control followed by relaxation followed by new controls continued. Both growth and investment ran well above planned levels until late 1989, and it proved impossible for the central state to regain its control. This anarchy had two fundamental causes.

---

20   *FEER*, 5 June 1986.
21   *Beijing Review*, 10 February 1986.

The first was that the sector which grew fastest – the new village industries – was entirely outside traditional state controls. These were essentially small sweatshops processing crops or turning out components for the state sector. Set up in the early 1980s to employ peasants who had no land after the agricultural reforms, they grew at breakneck speed. The sheer scale of the transformation of parts of the Chinese countryside was staggering. By 1985 there were some fourteen million such plants, which:

> ...employed 70 million people, 19 percent of the rural labour force, and generated 19 percent of China's total industrial output by value. They were responsible for 29 percent of the country's coal output, half its garment production, 53 percent of all building materials supplies and earned US$4 billion in exports.[22]

By 1988 the value of the output from these village industries was greater than the total value of agricultural output,[23] and one peasant in five had abandoned the fields to become a factory worker.[24] Their growth was highly uneven across the country, however. The vast majority of the new rural industries were located in the prosperous southern coastal provinces.

Their very success was at the heart of the dilemma facing the Chinese ruling class. On the one hand, they seemed proof positive that 'market socialism' could promote economic growth. The Chinese press lauded them as a Thatcherite dream – small businesses founded by entrepreneurs with enterprise and initiative (paying Thatcherite dream wages), able to respond flexibly to changing market conditions. And in soaking up tens of millions

---

22 John Gittings, *China changes face*, (Oxford University Press, Oxford, 1990), page 140.

23 *FEER*, 2 March 1989.

24 *Beijing Review*, 18 January 1989.

of peasants left landless by the agricultural reforms, they helped the state avoid a population explosion in the cities.

On the other hand, their growth was largely at the expense of older established industries. Shanghai and the northeast, the heartlands of heavy industry, stagnated from the mid-1980s onwards as the new village industries ate into their markets, both inside China and abroad. Because they grew up outside the state plan, their use of raw materials and energy made the shortages far worse. They could also simply ignore state directions to slow down (although they were to be the most vulnerable to the credit squeezes imposed from 1988 onwards.)

But they were not alone in defying the central state's directives. The new powers of local managers and officials led to a fundamental redistribution of power inside the ruling class. By 1985, centrally planned state investment was less than half of all investment. Most of the rest came not from private capital, but from locally controlled parts of the state sector. The people controlling that investment were making decisions on the basis of their own particular (and conflicting) interests, rather than in the interests of the ruling class as a whole.

That contradiction found its sharpest expression in the epidemic of 'economic crimes' – illegal business practices – that gripped the mass of lower-level officials from the early 1980s onwards. A minority of such cases were simple personal greed, such as the electricity company manager who cut off a local theatre for refusing him free tickets, the Beijing gas official who ran a private supply off the company mains, or the railways minister who for three years ran a bribery ring selling scarce capacity to the highest bidder.

But the vast majority were organised creative applications of 'market socialism' – the primacy of the profit motive taken to its logical conclusion. One 1985 case showed how far it was now possible to go. A factory in Beijing got hold of foreign currency to import foreign equipment. The draft was cashed in neighbouring Hebei province, and the cash (some US$41 million) sent 2,000 miles south to Hainan island, where local officials used it to import colour TV kits to be assembled in an empty factory they owned, which were to be sold by a sales network extending across most of southern China. Their only mistake was failing to pay off the local customs officers.[25]

Many smaller and less flamboyant schemes operated success-fully for years-and continue to operate. If the rate of return on illegally importing colour TV sets was higher than on producing electrical goods (and it was) then managers who thought they could get away with it would do so, irrespective of technicalities such as the law (or the 'national interest'). The logic was impec-cable. Yet it was a logic the central state had to fight if it was to retain any real control over the economy.

From the early 1980s onwards there were periodic crack-downs on local officials, with spates of highly publicised executions. But all these could do was put a temporary lid on the problem. Factory managers were indeed scared off for a while – but so scared that they avoided any innovation lest it turn out to be an 'economic crime'. For the dividing line between such crimes and extending the market reforms was impossible to draw in practice – the first was a necessary function of the second. What the periodic scares really pointed to was the fact that the central bureaucracy had lost control over the army of lower officials who actually ran the economy.

The attacks necessarily petered out: while the central state could no longer trust its local officials, it could even less afford to alienate them. The crucial changes needed to make the Chinese economy competitive in world terms – raising productivity and lowering labour costs – could not be carried out by central fiat, but only by those local officials.

The scale of the cutbacks deemed necessary was enormous. By the mid-1980s it was estimated that some 20 percent of all

25 *Beijing Review*, 24 February 1986.

enterprises were running at a loss, at an annual cost of some two billion yuan.[26] Because of disguised unemployment, practically every major factory was heavily overmanned by world standards. One estimate of the scale of this was given by a government minister who said in 1986 that 'fifteen million people will become surplus labour at state-owned enterprises during the next five years'[27] – that is, one in six of the urban workforce. Yet the real level of attacks on wages and working conditions, before the recession of 1989, was very modest indeed. The ruling class knew only too well the dangers involved, and moved cautiously. For instance, they talked in the early 1980s of extending the 'household responsibility system' in agriculture to all factory workers – essentially moving from hourly rates to Measured Day Work (without the carrots). Yet by the end of the decade they had only succeeded in imposing it on new workers entering the state sector.

They showed a similar caution in closing down 'uneconomic' enterprises. In 1986 a draft bankruptcy law was introduced in one northeastern city, threatening the worst performers with closure inside a year. One factory – employing all of 72 people – finally closed, and it then took two years for the law to be extended nationally. The major result of the law was that tax payments to the city authorities leapt by 50 percent in 1985[28] – suggesting either that the figures for the number of factories in debt were far too high, or that managers engaged in asset-stripping to massage the figures. Either way, it was clear that large parts of industry's operations were being hidden from even the local state.

Ending the 'social wage' paid through state price subsidies and the subsidies given by state enterprises was similarly seen as essential in opening up the labour market to 'the discipline of

---

26 *FEER*, 3 April 1986.
27 *Xinhua Daily News Bulletin* (Beijing), 7 May 1986
28 *Beijing Review*, 3 March 1986.

market forces'. Those subsidies – on food, clothing, housing and transport costs – were seen as a key restraint on local managers' abilities to control wage costs. One study estimated that in 1983 such subsidies were worth 1,000 yuan a year per worker - greater than the average annual wage of 830 yuan.[29] To abolish or even cut back those subsidies noticeably without replacing them with some form of welfare provision would have been to invite widespread discontent among workers.

Inflation and the onset of crisis

By 1986 real wages were being cut, not through any planned attacks on living standards but by runaway inflation. In 1987 an official spokesman admitted that the real income of one in five urban residents was falling because of inflation and that one in twenty 'had real difficulties'.[30]

For the ruling class this was a decidedly mixed blessing. The *Financial Times* nicely summed up their dilemma:

> In some respects inflation is actually desirable as it is one way to introduce the necessary wage cuts which are needed in many industrial sectors where labour costs are rising dangerously through the payment of bonuses, irrespective of productivity or profitability which are often not increasing at all.

But, the paper went on to argue:

> China's rulers are all too well aware that it was ultimately the hyperinflation of the 1940s which was the key factor in the fall of the Guomindang government. The prospect of a similar fate

---

29   Nicholas Lardy, 'Consumption and living standards in China 1978-83', *China Quarterly*, issue 100, December 1984; http://www.jstor.org/stable/653656

30   *Financial Times*, 18 July 1987.

probably acts as the speediest brake of all. Nor does the public reaction to food price rises in Eastern Europe go unnoticed.[31]

It was not a dilemma they could easily resolve. After years of suppressed inflation, when the state fixed artificially low prices, the loosening of controls unleashed a prices explosion. The extreme unevenness of industrial growth – rapid booms followed by slumps as raw-material and energy shortages began to bite – meant periodic and unpredictable shortages of certain basic commodities, while surpluses of others were wasted. Energy shortages, in particular, meant that most southern cities suffered daily power cuts by 1986, while a shortage of transport capacity meant that much of what was produced rotted or rusted in goods yards. The combination of the two added a further degree of chaos to industrial planning. Those who controlled the goods in short supply naturally cashed in, fuelling the inflationary spiral.

The decision to allow two levels of prices for most raw materials – one set by the state, the other by the market – further aggravated the problem. Uncertainties about supply meant that it was the market price that in practice predominated. Even when state bodies supplied the goods, the demand meant that they could get away with charging the market price. When the market was glutted, the uncertainty of future supply led prices to fall by less than they had risen.

But it was not just shortages which made inflation endemic. An equally important factor was the expansion of the financial and banking sector, and the consequent expansion of credit. Before 1978 the banking system was fairly rudimentary, existing largely to accumulate personal savings (high because of the shortage of consumer goods) which the state could use as a reservoir of capital.

---

31 *Financial Times*, 18 December 1987.

Part of the process of industrial reform involved ending factories' dependence on the state budget for funds, and using instead the banking system to channel funds for investment. It worked only too well. As one study noted:

> Between 1979 and 1984 there was indeed a major diversification of sources of industrial finance and considerable decentralisation of financial decision-making: power flowed to individual economic departments, local governments, industrial enterprises, rural coops, specialised banks, local bank branches, investment trusts, individuals (in joint-stock ventures) and foreign interests. The proliferation of 'extra-budgetary funds' (EBF) from these sources created what has been called a 'second budget' or an 'unorganised capital market'. As a proportion of state budgetary funds, EBF rose from 4 percent in 1953 to around 60 percent in 1981... The state lost a good deal of its ability to control the money supply in general and the expansion of investment funds in particular.[32]

The combination of all these economic ills, and in particular the sense that the central state was steadily losing control over the economy, led to major differences opening up inside the ranks of the 'modernisers' as early as 1981. At stake was a fundamental argument about the nature, pace and direction of the whole strategy. But it was not a split between two clear and well-defined opposing factions; rather it was a reflection of the basic contradiction in the modernising strategy.

For the 'conservatives', as Deng Xiaoping's opponents came to be known, the pace of development had to reflect Chinese backwardness, with state planning focussed on developing key areas of the

---

32 Stephan Feuchtwang, Athar Hussain and Thierry Pairault, *Transforming China's economy in the Eighties*, volume 2, (Zed Books, London, 1988), page 13.

economy; the speed of growth had to be such that the ruling class retained its overall control over the direction and development of the economy. The other side pointed instead to the primacy of competing in the world market. Years of centralised state control had left China falling behind the competition, rather than catching up. Only greater decentralisation and further expansion of the market could give the economy the necessary dynamism. Losing a degree of control over the economy was an unfortunate side-effect which had to be endured.

The first group were saying, in effect, that China had to learn to walk before it could run. To which the second group responded that running now was the only way to catch up, even if this meant constantly falling over. The argument could not be decided one way or another, because both groups were right in pointing to material constraints on their actions. The contradiction between the capacities of the Chinese economy and the demands placed on it by world competition was irreconcilable.

Since 1982, the emphasis of economic policy thus shifted from decentralisation to planning and back again, according to whether the priority was perceived as regaining control or stimulating growth. As the CCP's central control weakened, and the choices became harder, their splits became far deeper. These first surfaced publicly in late 1985, when the veteran economist Chen Yun attacked Deng Xiaoping over chaos in the economy, rampant corruption among lower officials, widespread disaffection among younger workers and Japan's growing influence, arguing that:

In terms of the country as a whole, the planned economy's primacy and the subordinate role of market regulation are still necessary... Only by doing a good job of macro-economic control can we stimulate the micro-economy and make it dynamic but not chaotic.[33]

---

33 *Xinhua Daily News Bulletin*, 24 September 1985.

That open split, which was to surface several times in the following years, greatly exacerbated the tensions inside the economy. The increased efforts to regain control mostly failed to work. But the return of constantly contradictory orders from above had one of two effects on the lower levels: managers and local officials either waited for orders from on high, afraid to take an initiative lest it be wrong; or they simply ignored all such orders.

These open divisions and lack of direction were also major factors in opening up a greater space for opposition from below than ever before.

CHAPTER 6

Waiting for reforms – opposition 1978-88

I n the aftermath of the Tiananmen Square massacre of June 1989, it was widely argued that it happened because China had undergone *perestroika* without *glasnost*[1] – economic restructuring without political reforms – and that Deng Xiaoping had simply instituted a system of 'economic Stalinism.' The same argument was used to explain the economic crisis: without political reforms that would properly open up the system, the economic reforms would necessarily be distorted or stillborn. A free-market economy could prosper, it was said, only in a free political atmosphere (for which read bourgeois democracy).

The last proposition can be easily disproved by looking at China's immediate neighbours, the 'miracle economies' of South-East Asia. Taiwan was ruled for 38 years under martial law; Singapore is in effect a one-party state; while South Korea was run from its inception until the mid-1980s by a succession of civilian and military dictators. Hong Kong – then possibly the nearest approximation to a classical free-market economy anywhere in the world – was run

---

1   [Russian terms for 'economic reform' and 'political reform', popularised by Mikhail Gorbachev in the mid-1980s.]

for more than 150 years as a colonial administration, without even the flimsiest trappings of democracy.

But the argument's basic premise was wrong. While the process of political and social change took a very different form in China from Gorbachev's Russia, and its evolution was much more uneven, nevertheless the political changes were enormous. In many respects, what happened was much more like the initial de-Stalinisation of Russia under Khrushchev. As late as 1976:

> Although the cult of Mao was shorn of some of its more ridic-
> ulous excesses, it was still maintained at a very high level of
> intensity... Airports, railway stations, main roads, and major
> intersections had murals depicting the Chairman in one role
> or another... Millions upon millions of walls and billboards
> displayed his Thought... On the radio day after day there were
> dramas in which the power of his thought brought salvation to
> some community.[2]

The 'modernisers' as the faction around Deng Xiaoping were known were determined to scrap Mao's economic strategy. This necessarily meant that they had to reject much of Mao's political heritage. The party machine, and the relationship between the party and the mass of the population, had to be fundamentally transformed. Reform from above was necessary both to reinvigorate the economy, and to stave off further revolts from below.

Tony Cliff's explanation of the roots of de-Stalinisation in Russia fits closely the situation in China in 1978:

> First, arbitrariness and excesses of the terror became. an
> impediment to economic rationality, for which regularity,

---

2   Roger Garside, *Coming alive: China after Mao* (New American Library, New York, NY, 1981), pages 91-92.

security, predictability as regards the hierarchical relations in the economy are essential.

Secondly, beyond a certain point, terror may not lead to increasing effort on the part of actual or potential victims, but on the contrary, to the paralysis of all faculties except that of simulation, to avoiding any decision that could lead to trouble, to passing the buck.

…Finally, the ruling class for its own sake needs relaxation. Its members want to live to enjoy their privileges. One of the paradoxes of Stalin's regime was that even the socially privileged bureaucrats were not at one with it. Too often the secret police, besides arresting workers and peasants, laid its hand on them.[3]

But the process of reform was more difficult in China than in Russia, for a number of reasons. When Khrushchev denounced Stalin in 1956 the worst of the terror had been over for almost twenty years and living standards were rising, albeit slowly. In 1978 the horrors of the Cultural Revolution were only too fresh in people's minds, and the majority of Chinese were no better off than they had been in the mid-1950s.

Khrushchev and those around him had kept silent under Stalin's rule. Mao's successors, in contrast, were people who had fought him in the past and suffered for it. They therefore aroused greater popular expectations for change. As one chronicler of the Democracy Wall movement put it:

The majority of the leaders had been victims of the Cultural Revolution… they had seen at close quarters the reality of Maoism, and learnt how much those deprived of democracy and the rule of law suffer. Now that they had regained power, they

---

3   Tony Cliff, *Russia: A Marxist analysis* (International Socialism, London, 1964) page 202: https://www.marxists.org/archive/cliff/works/1964/russia/ch10.htm#s7

would therefore be disposed to establish democracy and the rule of law.[4]

Thirdly, there were powerful limits to the extent to which Mao could be rejected. The legitimacy of the state itself was founded on Mao's military victory in 1949, and the senior military leaders whose support had aided Deng Xiaoping's rise to power would not let him forget it. Most important of all, Khrushchev had come to power in the middle of the long boom in the world economy. In 1978, the Chinese ruling class faced far greater economic pressure from the outside world on a much weaker economy.

In short, their need to modernise the economy and relax the state's control over society was much more urgent, but they had far less room for manoeuvre.

Their first target was the Cultural Revolution. From 1978 onwards the new leadership admitted that it was a major disaster in which horrendous crimes had been committed. A process of compensating the victims began, and more than three million people who had been jailed or persecuted were freed and rehabilitated.[5]

Mao's responsibility for the Cultural Revolution was delicately skirted round. In late 1980 the Gang of Four were put on trial in an attempt to blame them for all the evils of the Cultural Revolution, while absolving Mao of anything more than making mistakes. This involved denying that the Gang

---

4   Christian Bourgeois (editor) *Un bol de nids d'hirondelles ne fait pas le printemps de Pekin* (One bowl of swallows-nest soup doesn't make a Beijing spring), (10/18, Paris, 1980) pages 9-10 (my translation).

5   Andrew J Nathan, *Chinese democracy* (I B Tauris, London, 1986) page 7. By 1983 this process had extended to some 25 million people who had been persecuted in various campaigns in the 1950s and early 1960s. Hu Yaobang's responsibility for this campaign contributed greatly to his reputation as a liberal reformer.

had been promoted under Mao's personal protection: one writer compared the argument to 'crediting the ass whose jaw Sampson borrowed in battle with the ability to destroy the Philistines'.[6]

It was a show trial in every sense of the word, designed to reassure Western investors that the Cultural Revolution was finally over and that Deng Xiaoping was securely in charge. The proceedings were rigged from start to finish – when Jiang Qing showed signs of departing from the script at one point she was simply removed from the court.

Mao's new status was best summed up by one of Deng Xiaoping's mouthpieces in 1981:

> [Mao's] mistakes are opposed to scientific Mao Zedong Thought and therefore Comrade Mao Zedong's thinking in his late years should not be confused with Mao Zedong Thought. Mao Zedong Thought is a scientific theory which does not embrace Comrade Mao Zedong's mistakes.[7]

Black cat, white cat

Deng Xiaoping's famous maxim 'It doesn't matter whether the cat is black or white, so long as it catches mice' announced the end of the domination of Maoist ideology, not just over the economy, but over many other spheres of academic, scientific and cultural life. In part this was prompted by the ruling class' need to present a radically different image of themselves to the outside world.

But there were equally pressing internal reasons for relaxing the state's controls over everyday life. If the truth were to be told about the real state of the Chinese economy, and if Chinese science and technology were to catch up to world standards,

---

6   Simon Leys, *Broken images* (Allison and Busby, London, 1979) pages 77-78.

7   *Beijing Review*, 15 June 1981.

then academics had to be free to speak their minds without worrying about the local party secretary looking over their shoulders. Equally, if popular support for the regime was to be rebuilt, then the state had both to admit past mistakes, and be seen correcting them.

The economic reforms also demanded a major relaxation of state controls. Free markets could only work if they were not regulated by local officials; dismantling the communes necessarily meant doing away with most of the state's day-to-day controls over the lives of the peasants; and in the cities the spread of self-employment and small businesses to soak up youth unemployment involved an easing of the tight policing of the streets.

Liberalisation went furthest in the cultural field, as the greatest need was to win back the active or passive support of urban intellectuals. The limited freedom to speak out about the realities of the Cultural Revolution led to a torrent of short stories, novels, poems and films. Initially much of the literature simply repeated the style of Maoist propaganda, with the evil landlord or capitalist-roader replaced by the follower of the 'Gang of Four', and a simplistic moral being drawn at the finish.

But by the early 1980s genuinely interesting cultural works were being produced, tackling such previously taboo subjects as prison life, sexuality, corruption, the backwardness of the countryside and even the Red Army of the 1930s.[8] The same

---

8   Among the most interesting novels and short stories published in English from this period are: Bei Dao, *Waves* (Heinemann, London, 1987); Lu Wenfu, *The gourmet* (Readers International, London, 1987); Wang Anyi, *Baotown* (Penguin, London, 1990); Yu Luojin, *A Chinese winter's tale* (Renditions, Hong Kong, 1986); Zhang Jie, *As long as nothing happens, nothing will* (Virago, London, 1988); and Zhang Xianliang, *Half of man is woman* (Penguin, London, 1989). Very little contemporary Chinese poetry was translated – one of the best volumes available was Bei Dao, *The August sleepwalker* (Anvil, London, 1988). *Seeds of fire*, edited by Geremie

expansion took place throughout the media. At the end of 1986, there were more than 5,000 magazines and newspapers being published in China; by contrast, in 1973 only 64 were available in Beijing – all of which said exactly the same thing.[9] The vast majority of the new publications were devoted to apolitical subjects, but even the official media became far more outspoken than before.

In part this was a necessary measure for winning back a degree of popular support. The Maoist propaganda sheets were both unreadable and unbelievable; if the media was to convince anyone of anything, it had to reflect the realities of everyday life, and thus had to talk about economic and political problems.

But it also reflected a certain breakdown of the state's control over society at large. Running an authoritarian police state is relatively straightforward. But when some things that the state has not initiated are nevertheless permitted, the tasks of the censors become far more complex. The bounds of what is permissible come under constant challenge.

There was still a substantial amount of censorship; novels, films and papers simply disappeared or were sent back for reworking before they appeared. But the sheer volume of cultural production meant that much of the censorship came after publication, and uncertainties about the new rules meant that censors preferred to pass the buck to higher authorities. One

---

Barme and John Minford (Bloodaxe, Newcastle, 1989) is a valuable if uneven collection of the more openly dissident writings.

A large number of 'fifth generation' Chinese films were shown in Britain in the 1980s and 1990s, though at the time many did not get beyond the London art houses and film festivals. Among the best are *Yellow earth, Red sorghum, The last day of winter, Swan song, Horse thief,* and *King of the children.* The best contemporary introduction to 'fifth generation' Chinese cinema was Chen Kaige and Tony Rayns, *King of the children and the new Chinese cinema* (Faber, London, 1989).

9   The figures are from Orville Schell, *Discos and democracy* (Pantheon, New York, NY, 1988) page 89. and Nathan, *Chinese democracy*, page 157.

film critical of the invasion of Vietnam, for instance, went all the way to the Politburo for a decision. After it was shown, Deng Xiaoping reportedly broke a long silence by remarking that it would do well in Hanoi, and the film was never seen again. But the director carried on working.[10]

None of this meant that China's new leaders were ever sincere democrats, or that they were once interested in increasing popular freedom. The myth of Deng Xiaoping as the great liberaliser, assiduously promoted by the vast majority of the Western press and politicians, was to die a bloody death in Tiananmen Square in 1989. The political and social changes carried out since 1978 were introduced to enlarge the CCP's social base, so that they could win popular consent for harsh economic restructuring.

But what Chris Harman and Andy Zebrowski wrote of Gorbachev's Russia was equally true of China:

> Glasnost from above has extended the fight over future policy from the top leadership of the party into the ranks of those who control the levers of intellectual life... But once arguments begin to occur in such milieus they cannot be restricted to the issues laid down by the rival leadership factions. Glasnost from above opens the door for something much more profound – glasnost from below.[11]

Democracy wall

The first such explosion was the Democracy Wall movement of 1978-81. The movement began with small groups of dissidents who came together after the 1976 riots, some of whom had connections with older groups of former Red Guards. It found a

---

10 Chen and Rayns, *King of the children and the new Chinese cinema*, page 45.
11 Chris Harman and Andy Zebrowski, 'Glasnost – before the storm'
    International Socialism 2:39, summer 1988, pages 26-27.

mass base in the youth sent down to the countryside, who from 1977 onwards began flooding back into the cities.

The activists had no fully developed political analysis, and the differences among them were great, though rarely openly expressed. They built the movement around a set of general demands: for greater democracy, the release and rehabilitation of the Cultural Revolution's victims, an end to censorship, and the sacking of those responsible for the suppression of the 1976 riots.

They unreservedly backed Deng Xiaoping against the remaining Maoist hardliners in the CCP, as did most of the population. By promising economic reforms and jailing the Gang of Four, the government made itself more popular than any time since the early 1950s. Tens of millions had suffered in the Cultural Revolution and the campaigns of the early 1980s. Even if they didn't believe that Jiang Qing and her cohorts had been entirely responsible for all their ills, they were nevertheless delighted to see them publicly humiliated.

But while the activists were prepared to back Deng, they wanted far greater change than was on offer. From early 1978 onwards numbers of wallposters appeared in Beijing and other cities, demanding a speed-up of democratisation, the release of those arrested in 1976 and punishment for those who had suppressed the riots.

Deng Xiaoping had used the 1976 riots to weaken the Gang of Four's position; he now used this new ferment to confirm his leadership. A central committee work conference in October 1978 (which lasted five weeks instead of the planned three days) demoted four of his main rivals to purely symbolic functions. Three of them were removed for having directed the suppression of the 1976 riots, which were declared to have been 'exemplary revolutionary actions'.

The numbers of wallposters had naturally multiplied during the meeting. Following the news that the meeting had declared the 1976 riots 'justified', the movement began to focus on a street in west-central Beijing, where a long wall became covered with posters. It became an arena for non-stop debates on politics, art and culture, and for the sale of the first dissident journals. Mass meetings began, and on 25 November more than 10,000 people gathered to hear a number of speakers. One gave an account of an interview given by Deng Xiaoping to an American journalist, in which he said: 'Democracy Wall is a good thing. The people are free.' The same month, the authors of a 1973 wallposter which had attacked the Gang of Four, and which was seen as the founding statement of the movement, were released from jail in Guangzhou. The message seemed clear – the new authorities not only tolerated but supported the movement.[12]

The freedom to speak out without fear of arrest, the thirst for new ideas, and the burning need to tell the long-suppressed truth about the last ten years quickly outgrew the medium of wall-posters. By January 1979 dozens of hand-printed journals were circulating in and between every major city. One study recorded 55 such magazines in Beijing alone, and another 88 in 22 other cities across China – there is no doubt that the real figure was much higher.[13] Speakers as well as journals spread from city to city – in late November activists from Beijing addressed meetings of up to 150,000 in Shanghai.

Many of the activists were content simply to enjoy the victories they had won, and not push their luck too far. This was particularly true of the cultural side of the movement. Many of the unofficial journals were entirely devoted to short stories and poems, and all carried them regularly. Artists, sculptors and

---

12   This account of the movement is drawn from the introduction to Bourgeois, *Un bol de nids d'hirondelles ne fait pas le printemps de Pékin*, and from Nathan, *Chinese democracy*, pages 3-44.

13   Claude Widor, *The* samizdat *press in China's provinces 1979-81: an annotated guide* (Hoover Institute, Stanford, CA, 1987). Nathan, *Chinese democracy*, (page 24) recorded 127 titles in 26 cities, as well as at least 45 campus publications.

engravers organised unofficial exhibitions, and a new spirit of experiment crept even into the official media. Though practically all the art was directly political, this was the least threatening side of the movement, and consequently survived the longest, though under constant threat of arbitrary censorship.

But the movement as a whole had too powerful a dynamic to be contained in this form. The experience of the past few months had taught the activists that they could win if they fought. Every extension of freedom of speech, every new issue of a journal, brought to light new injustices.

The rehabilitation of some Cultural Revolution victims and the return of some expelled students from the countryside provoked a flood of demands for justice from those in similar positions. By late 1978 there were 10,000 such people in Beijing alone, sleeping rough and living by begging, prostitution or theft.[14] Hundreds of thousands of students and other petitioners descended on cities across the country. The students could not simply return home, as they lacked the necessary documents to claim rations and the right to live in the city. All too often their parents refused to take them back for fear of the police. Official rehabilitation was essential if they were to resume their normal lives.

As the government refused to move on the issue, the demonstrations became larger and more militant, and spread to other cities. Deng Xiaoping's reaction was to demand that the movement cease 'creating disturbances' and restrict itself to discussing subjects allowed by the government.

In reply, Wei Jingsheng, editor of a journal called Explorations and one of the movement's most outspoken leaders, attacked Deng openly:

14 Gregor Benton, *Wild lilies, poisonous weeds* (Pluto Press, London, 1982) pages 33-4.

Does Deng Xiaoping want democracy? No, he does not. He is unwilling to comprehend the misery of the common people. He describes the struggle for democratic rights... as the actions of troublemakers who must be repressed. To resort to such measures to deal with people who criticise mistaken social policies and demand social development shows that the government is very afraid of this popular movement.[15]

Two weeks later he was arrested, and soon afterwards others protesting about his arrest were themselves jailed. The repression increased throughout 1979, at first accompanied by announcements that the movement would be tolerated if it kept within set limits.

The repression was undoubtedly linked to the Chinese invasion of Vietnam in February 1979. The invasion had two main aims: to 'punish' Vietnam for its invasion of Cambodia, which had removed the Chinese ally Pol Pot; and to warn that China would use military force to defend 'their' offshore oilfields, which lay in waters disputed by Vietnam. Though only a minority of the Democracy Wall activists attacked the invasion, the war created an atmosphere in which any opposition could be painted as disloyal. But the invasion merely provided the occasion – Deng Xiaoping had used the movement to secure power, and now had no further use for it.

The limited tolerance was for international consumption. As the cynics of the *Far Eastern Economic Review* saw it:

Businessmen may not be the most concerned lovers of democracy and human rights but they see them as the best guarantee of smooth functioning of industrial and commercial structures... the major problem of China remains to modernise, but for that

---

15   Quoted in above, page 47.

there must be the wholehearted support of the population, support
which might be lost through a lack of democracy and legality.[16]

But the movement refused to go away, or do as it was told,
becoming smaller but tougher. There were further demonstrations of youth sent to the countryside in Beijing, Shanghai
and Hangzhou, and when Wei Jingsheng went on trial in
November 1979, his defence was printed as a pamphlet and sold
at Democracy Wall.

By early 1980 all unofficial newspapers were banned and the
Democracy Walls had been closed in most cities. Yet the ruling
class could not simply return to the old style of repression. At the
same time as the movement was being further restricted, new
political avenues opened up.

In August 1980 elections were held for local People's
Congresses across the country. Though the congresses had as
much real power as a British parish council, the activists used
the elections to produce leaflets and posters, and to hold numerous meetings and debates.

In two colleges, official attempts to tamper with the election
produced large protests. At Changsha University, it was reported
that local factories had held collections for the students, raising
between 2,000 and 3,000 yuan[17] (about three years' average
industrial wage). This raised an ironic historical echo: Mao had
begun his political career as a student activist in Changsha...

One chronicler recorded twelve such election contests (five in
factories) and argued that:

...the fact that the known cases include so many examples from
Beijing [four out of the twelve] suggests that other tumultuous

---

16 *Far East Economic Review*, 11 May 1979.
17 *FEER*, 31 October 1980.

contests may have occurred in places where there were no foreign observers and simply went unreported.[18]

The same month, a movement of youth from Shanghai demanding to be allowed home exploded in the town of Aksu in Xinjiang. At its height the movement drew in more than 70,000 people and effectively took over the town. Though the majority of the youth had to stay in the countryside, the protests effectively ended the policy of sending them there.[19]

The movement managed to survive illegally for several more years. In September 1980 representatives of more than 50 unofficial journals met in Guangzhou to set up a nationwide organisation. At least some of the activists turned towards organising workers. Following the rise of Solidarity in Poland, there were reports of attempts to organise unofficial unions in Shanghai, Wuhan and Xian, and strikes in Taiyuan.[20] After surviving hundreds of arrests in 1981, the movement was finally destroyed in the repression that began in the summer of 1983.

Repression and its limits

Following the elections, the balance began to tip decisively against further reforms, and back towards repression. This shift culminated in the law and order crackdown of 1981-3 and the campaign against 'spiritual pollution' of late 1983. The first targeted three main groups: the remnants of the Democracy Wall activists; corrupt officials; and unemployed or lumpen youth. The latter made up the vast majority of the victims.

The return of students who had been sent to the countryside, and the growing numbers of students leaving school without jobs, led to a marked rise in unemployment in the late 1970s

18   Nathan, *Chinese democracy*, page 220.
19   Benton, *Wild lilies, poisonous weeds*, pages 113-119.
20   As above, pages 85 and 120-121.

and early 1980s. Many more youth were formally self-employed in 'service collectives' (road-sweeping, clearing industrial waste, loading lorries and so on). The early application of the market reforms in retailing allowed large numbers of people to set themselves up as street traders selling everything from fast food to foreign currency. These overlapping groups came by the early 1980s to form, at least in the larger cities, a street culture largely outside the control of the state.

Dubbed *liumang* (hooligans), these individuals living on the margins of society were marked by an extreme cynicism about the ruling class, an exaggerated respect for all things Western, and an open defiance of traditional rules about sexual morality, respect for their elders and the law in general. For many of them, petty theft and prostitution became necessary simply in order to survive. The law and order crackdown was launched to reassert the state's control over the streets.[21]

At the start of the crackdown, some of the most spectacular cases (organised prostitution, large-scale swindles and even armed robberies) came not from the *liumang* but from one of the most privileged groups in Chinese society – the children of high officials. In 1981 there were a number of public executions of such people, helping to win a measure of popular support for the crackdown. But as it gathered pace, the bureaucracy became increasingly effective at protecting their own, and the vast majority of the victims came from the ranks of the unemployed.

By late 1983, at the height of the repression, one observer noted that 'The sight of convoys of lorries full of youths, heads shaved and pushed forward by armed police or army guards, have once again become a common sight in new China, as have

---

21   For an account of the growth of the 'street culture' see Fox Butterfield, *China: alive in the bitter sea* (Coronet, London, 1983).

the parades of convicted criminals on their way to be shot.'[22]

In August of that year, 30 people were shot in public executions in Beijing alone. Across the country, the death toll ran into thousands. Crowds of up to 50,000 were assembled to watch the executions.

At the same time, the conservatives pushed forward their attempt to reassert their control over social life by launching the campaign against 'spiritual pollution' – unwelcome Western influences. This gave every local official, prude and bigot the chance to interfere once again in the most trivial aspects of everyday life. The echoes of the Cultural Revolution this aroused and the sheer absurdity of some of the prohibitions, meant that it was quickly wound up as counterproductive.

As one Western journalist described it:

> Women had been told not to let their hair descend below the shoulders; soldiers had been ordered to hand over pictures of their girl-friends; the Beijing Party Committee posted a notice banning long hair and high-heeled shoes; young people had their sunglasses confiscated in the streets. More seriously, some newly rich peasants committed suicide because their bank accounts were frozen; cadres and soldiers from the countryside were forbidden to seek spouses in the towns; and foreign investors were postponing signature of contracts.[23]

The campaign exposed a central contradiction facing the ruling class. Any return to the old methods of dealing with opposition or unwanted social changes risked undermining their whole economic strategy. Central to this strategy was an attempt to persuade Chinese workers and peasants that they had a stake

---

22   Andy Williams, 'Repression in China', in *Socialist Review* 62 (February 1984).

23   John Gittings, *China changes face*, page 197.

in the reforms. The threat that the state might again dictate every aspect of everyday life would ruin that attempt. The ruling class thus had to rein in the conservatives, and accept that they had lost a degree of control.

But they could not relax that control completely. Expectations of higher living standards and personal freedom produced constant demands for greater change. There was thus a constant zig-zagging between repression and relaxation. While the challenge to everyday control posed by the growing 'street culture' could be dealt with by higher levels of policing, consciously political opposition posed a far tougher set of dilemmas.

National minorities: racism and resistance

The national question in China never assumed the central importance it had in Russia. On official figures, more than 93 percent of the Chinese population are Han (ethnically Chinese). Many minority nationalists argue that these census figures are too low; while that may have been true for some groups, the figures in other ways overstated the reality. Of the ten major 'nationalities', four (including the largest single group) are thoroughly assimilated, with everyday speech and customs indistinguishable from their Han neighbours.[24] The 1982 census listed 4.3 million people as Manchus, for example, but the language has been almost extinct in northeastern China since the early 20th century. The largest single group of Manchu speakers live in a valley in the far west of Xinjiang, descendants of border guards posted there in the eighteenth century.[25]

Other nationalities have faced forced assimilation as emigration of Han Chinese into their sparsely-populated areas has turned them into minorities even in their own provinces.

---

24 S Robert Ramsey, *The languages of China* (Princeton University Press, Princeton, NJ, 1989), pages 167-168 and 243.

25 As above, page 215.

In Inner Mongolia, for example, Mongolians are now less than 20 percent of the population. Officially, the regime has always encouraged minorities to keep and develop their own languages and customs – in practice, their treatment has ranged from paternalism to outright racism.

Resistance came from two main groups: Muslims and Tibetans. The 15 million Muslims in China belong to a number of different nationalities. Roughly half of them are ethnically and linguistically Chinese, officially classified as a minority (Hui) only because of their religion. Most of the rest are Uyghurs, but there are substantial numbers of Kazaks and Kyrgyz, who maintain close links with the much larger groups over the Russian border.

Xinjiang, where the majority of Muslims live, was only annexed by China in the eighteenth century, and it is still ruled effectively as a colony (the name itself means 'new dominion'). The Red Army arrived in 1950 as a conquering army, and there was armed resistance in the north of the province for several years. The impact of forced collectivisation (which involved forcing nomadic herders to live in settled villages) and the disasters of the Great Leap Forward sparked off several abortive rebellions, while more than 60,000 Kazakhs fled over the Russian border.[26]

During the Cultural Revolution, mosques were forcibly closed and prayers forbidden, while the Arabic and Cyrillic scripts in which both the Uyghur and Kazakh languages are written were abolished, and replaced with a romanised script. In the early 1980s Muslim anger broke out into open warfare. In April 1980, two days of rioting broke out in the town of Aksu after a Uyghur child was killed. (Muslims also joined in the protests of Shanghai youth in the same town later that year.) The following year, the shooting of a Uyghur in the city of Kashgar

---

26   Kamow, *Mao and China*, page 135.

drew thousands of Muslims into street fighting which led to the calling-in of the army.[27]

Since then a considerable liberalisation took place. Old mosques were reopened and new ones built; the ban on the use of Arabic fell into disuse; limited numbers were allowed to make the *hajj* (the pilgrimage to Mecca); and new editions of the Koran were printed. (Muslims in Russia were then importing copies of the Koran in their languages from China.)[28]

Despite these concessions, resentment continued to simmer, both over Chinese racism and economic backwardness. In December 1985 more than 1,000 students demonstrated in Urumchi both against nuclear testing (most Chinese nuclear testing facilities and waste-dumps are in Xinjiang), and against family planning policies. The following month students from Xinjiang held a sympathy march in Beijing.[29] Minority nationality students (especially in Beijing) are an elite being trained to take up token posts in government. The fact that even they were moved to protest against Chinese domination gave an indication of the depths of feelings in Xinjiang.

But the most important demonstrations took place during the Tiananmen protests of 1989. They began over the publication of a book on the sexual habits of national minorities, which was from the few accounts available grossly offensive to Muslims. On 12 May 1989 two thousand people marched in Beijing demanding the banning of the book. The following day more than 10,000 marched in Lanzhou, where rioting followed. The state's response was swift and instructive; by 15 May 90,000 copies of the book had been burned by officials in Shaanxi province.[30] But that same day saw

---

27 Tizano Terzani, *Behind the forbidden door* (Unwin-Hyman, London, 1987) page 224.

28 *FEER*, 5 July 1990.

29 Gittings, *China changes face*, page 172.

30 British Broadcasting Corporation, *Survey of World Broadcasts*, (London) FE/0458, 16 May 1989. Hereafter *SWB*.

the largest Muslim protests yet, as 'nearly 100,000' marched in five cities and towns in Qinghai province (Qinghai's official population is slightly over four million).[31] In Urumqi several thousand people 'attacked party headquarters and the defending armed police squads with rocks and steel bars.'[32] Two days later the government banned the book nationally.

This was the first pan-Muslim movement seen in China since the 1930s. Previous revolts had at best united Uyghurs and Kazakhs: given the spread of the movement, substantial numbers of Huis must have been involved in it. The rise of Islamic fundamentalism in the 1970s and early 1980s almost entirely passed China by, partly because 90 percent of China's Muslims are Sunni, but more important because the state became skilled at buying off the religious leaders. The government's swift reaction showed the extent of their fears about the potential of such a movement.

It is impossible to say to what extent the Muslim movement became fused with the general revolt against the government, but clearly the protests were inspired by the general atmosphere of rebellion. Clearly, too, the state's hasty climbdown will have given heart to all those involved in the protests. What is certain is that the anger among Muslims did not disappear after the Tiananmen massacre. In April 1990 there was serious fighting in a small town near Kashgar between armed Islamic separatists and police, in which at least 22 people were killed. The fighting came after several months of reports of increased agitation by both Islamic fundamentalists and nationalists.[33]

But the major nationalist revolt against Chinese domination was then in Tibet. Tibetans have suffered more than any other nationality from Chinese domination, and there has been

---

31   BBC, *SWB*, FE/0460, 18 May 1990.

32   *FEER*, 3 August 1989.

33   *FEER*, 19 April and 3 May 1990.

resistance since the mid-1950s. CCP officials first arrived in Tibet in 1951, but initially attempted to rule the country through the existing ruling class. From 1956 open guerrilla warfare raged throughout eastern Tibet (now part of Sichuan province), and in 1959 the Chinese army occupied the whole country, imposing a military administration and partition. Most Tibetans now live in areas which were added onto the neighbouring provinces of Yunnan, Sichuan and Qinghai. Some 55,000 people (out of a population of roughly three million) fled the country, led by the Dalai Lama, Tibet's political and spiritual ruler.

Since then Tibet has been ruled almost exclusively by Chinese. The first time an ethnic Tibetan was appointed to a senior government post was in 1979. In the 1980s, only 10 percent of the Chinese in Tibet spoke any Tibetan, and only 10 percent of Tibetans spoke Chinese (in itself a comment on what they felt about the occupation).[34] Practically all Chinese treat Tibetans and Tibetan culture with racist contempt, as constant official documents attacking 'Han chauvinism' admit,[35] and Tibetans face systematic discrimination in every area of work outside agriculture.

Tibet before the Chinese occupation was far from the earthly paradise defenders of the old order paint. It was a desperately poor and desolate country, with a declining population among whom famine and venereal disease were endemic. Its rulers were a particularly vicious feudal ruling class who held the power of life and death over their serfs. Some socialists have used this to defend the Chinese occupation, arguing that they have wiped out feudal superstition and backwardness. The reality is that, while health and educational standards have improved, the

34   A. Tom Grunfeld, *The making of modern Tibet*, (Zed Books, London, 1987), pages 207 and 213.

35   As almost every book of travellers' tales documents. Two of the best from the 1980s are Vikram Seth, *From heaven lake* (Sphere Books, London, 1984) and Charles and Jill Hadfield, *A winter in Tibet* (Impact Books, London, 1988).

majority of Tibetans in 1989 were as poor and as powerless as they were before 1959. One brutal ruling class was replaced by another equally brutal (and much better armed). There could be no greater condemnation of the Chinese occupation than the fact that, more than 30 years later, the vast majority of Tibetans wanted the old ruling class back.

That hatred of the Chinese occupation was rooted in two major factors: economic disasters and the near-extinction of Tibetan culture during the Cultural Revolution. The economic disasters began in the early 1960s when Chinese technicians insisted on the peasants planting winter wheat instead of the traditional barley. This, together with the large Chinese migration into Tibet and the consequent increased exploitation of the land, caused enormous damage. As one historian of Tibet explained:

> [The] wheat was unsuited to Tibet's soil as it depleted the soil's essential nutrients at a far greater rate than did the native barley-resulting in rapidly diminishing outputs after some initially huge harvests. Moreover, hunting and fishing, coupled with precipitous population growth... have altered the delicate balance of the Tibetan plateau, making large segments of it uninhabitable for perhaps generations.[36]

The result was widespread famine which persisted for several years. Coming soon after the Great Leap, little or no spare grain was available for relief, and untold numbers died. The horrors of the Cultural Revolution followed almost immediately.

The systematic attacks on every aspect of Tibetan culture did not stop with the formal end of the Cultural Revolution in 1979. Thousands of people continued to rot in jail, and the attempts to suppress Tibetan language and culture continued throughout

---

36   Grunfeld, *The making of modern Tibet*, page 212.

the 1970s. It was only after Hu Yaobang visited Tibet in 1981 that any relaxation of this policy was decreed. But while some monasteries were rebuilt, and people were no longer attacked in the streets for wearing Tibetan clothing, the systematic racism of the Chinese-dominated state machine ensured that nothing fundamentally changed.

Large-scale riots broke out in October 1987 and March 1988 in Lhasa, and there were several smaller demonstrations both before and after these. Two events in January 1989 decisively altered the climate. The first was the removal of the provincial CCP secretary (the only one ever to speak Tibetan) for being 'soft' on Tibetan nationalism. The second was the death of the Panchen Lama, the second figure in the Tibetan political-religious hierarchy after the Dalai Lama, and one of very few Tibetan leaders to have collaborated with the Chinese.

A number of funeral marches for the Panchen Lama in February 1989, held by Buddhist monks and nuns, turned into pro-independence rallies but were dispersed peacefully by the police. However, on 5 March – the anniversary of the 1988 riots and a major religious festival – another such demonstration attracted hundreds of urban youth, and became considerably more militant. The police opened fire, killing at least ten people and wounding many more. In the next two days huge crowds of urban youth, many of them seeming consciously to copy the dress and the tactics of the Palestinian intifada, took over most of the Tibetan quarter of Lhasa, burning Chinese shops and businesses and defending their territory with barricades. For the first time in 30 years, the Tibetan independence struggle had challenged the state and won, albeit briefly.

But the odds against them were enormous. Martial law was declared on 7 March, and thousands of extra troops drafted into Tibet. Mass arrests, beatings and shootings followed, and Lhasa remained under martial law for the rest of the year.

Both Tibet and the Muslim areas of China remain running

sores for the ruling class. In both cases, limited liberalisation in the 1980s merely allowed pent-up hatreds to be expressed openly, and provided greater opportunities for organisation. The revolts of the nationalities, though far less important than in Russia, added yet another dimension to the ever-worsening crisis of the 1980s. Moreover, Lhasa in March 1989 showed in miniature the power of the cities to shake the ruling class – which was to explode across China in May. It showed, too, the murderous lengths they would go to in defending their power.

The growth of student opposition

China's student population grew enormously in the 1980s. In 1989 there were more than 1,000 universities and colleges (compared with only 400 in 1978) with a student body of more than two million (two percent of the 18-24 age group), 400,000 of whom were in Beijing. The modernisation strategy placed great emphasis on education and training, with students being told that their scientific and technical expertise would be essential to China's future development.

Yet they lived six or eight to a dormitory four metres square, their lives ruled by a host of petty rules and regulations which enforced a near-total sexual segregation. Campus facilities were overcrowded and insufficient – at Beijing University, China's equivalent of Oxford, there were seven dining rooms for 12,000 students. The student grant, for those who got it, was barely enough to cover the cost of food. Classroom teaching was based on rote learning and the teacher's absolute authority. The yawning gap between the glittering future they were promised and the misery of everyday life produced a state of permanent discontent.

Students were by no means alone in feeling that discontent. It was their particular position in society that made it easier for them to express it. For while the atmosphere on the campuses was far more repressive than in Western universities, by comparison with Chinese factories or offices it was much less so. Free from the daily discipline of the factory or the office, and with far more leisure to read and discuss, they had a relatively greater freedom of action than most workers. The very fact that many of them come from privileged backgrounds, as sons and daughters of high officials, gave them a deeper insight into the corrupt nature of the system.

In many ways their position was similar to that of students in Western Europe and North America in the mid-1960s. Chris Harman's explanation of the roots of student revolt then applied equally to China:

> Elements of ideological confusion in society at large become magnified in the student milieu. Whole sections of the student population are expected to absorb the ruling ideology, so as to be able to transmit it to others when they graduate. If that ideology is in palpable contradiction with reality as they experience it, they are themselves thrown into intellectual turmoil and can react with moral indignation.[37]

In the mid-1980, that ruling ideology in China was not so much in contradiction as in crisis. The experience of the Cultural Revolution left a deep cynicism about politics in the minds of most urban Chinese. Deng Xiaoping's junking of Maoism merely deepened the cynicism. In 1979 he attempted to replace the canons of Maoist ideology with what he called the 'Four Cardinal Principles' to guide the CCP.

But as Orville Schell noted in 1987:

> In the past, when I had asked Chinese friends to locate a certain phrase in Mao's collected works... they had been able not only to recite the full quotation but also, like game show contestants,

---

37   Chris Harman, *The fire last time: 1968 and after* (Bookmarks, London, 1988) page 42.

to cite its chapter and verse as well. However, when I asked party members... simply to list Deng's Four Cardinal Principles, I often found them at a loss. They would come up with two or three... before foundering in an orgy of embarrassed demurrals. Even those few who could recall all four usually got bogged down in meaningless platitudes when asked what each principle meant...[38]

In practice, the ruling class was reduced to two operational ideas which still retained any purchase on the minds of most Chinese: 'To get rich is glorious' and simple nationalism. The first was increasingly discredited by the massive inflation of the late 1980s, and by the enormous growth in social inequality which the economic reforms generated. Nationalism remained an enormously powerful idea, but one that worked both for and against the ruling class. Although the opposition of the 1980s defined itself as nationalist and patriotic, this did not mean simply accepting the ideas of the ruling class. On the contrary, a key part of their arguments was that the government was acting 'unpatriotically' in ignoring the wishes of the people. Nationalism became a terrain of struggle, as the movement opposed its own understanding of it to that of the ruling class.

Student protest began to reappear in mid-1984 with a rash of protests against living and working conditions. Though these were restricted to individual campuses, with few attempts even to link up with other students, a number of political demands were also raised. The following year students took to the streets again, with large marches against Japanese 'domination' of the Chinese economy in Beijing, Wuhan and Chengdu. While this was a relatively safe issue to protest about, it allowed expressions

---

38   Schell, *Discos and democracy*, page 257. The four were: We must keep to the socialist road; we must uphold the dictatorship of the proletariat; we must uphold the leadership of the Communist Party; we must uphold Marxism-Leninism and Mao Zedong Thought.

of more general anger. One placard on the march in Beijing read 'What has all our sacrifice of blood given us? Police and refrigerators.'[39] In Chengdu the march ended in fighting with the police.

Beijing students announced that they would march again on 9 December, the anniversary of mass student protests against Japanese imperialism.[40] The authorities' response was deliberately restrained – mass meetings were convened on campuses to talk the students out of it, with eventual success. The message was clear – a certain measure of dissent was to be tolerated, but within strict limits. Indeed, the following year saw a deliberate attempt to promote greater argument and discussion.

An article in the People's Daily in May 1986 clearly spelt out official fears:

> If a person is constantly anxious when putting pen to paper or giving a lecture, and constantly worrying which of his formulations will go beyond the bounds of what is considered to be an academic problem to become a political problem, then he has no choice but to keep his mouth shut... If citizens do not have the right to air their views on politics, then politics remains a forbidden zone, and people will still unavoidably warn each other that 'disaster comes from careless talk', and will try to avoid 'incriminating themselves by what they say',[41]

The semi-official opposition that grew up in 1985-6 had few formal structures, being rather diffuse groupings of students, journalists, lower party officials and academics around various figureheads. Prominent among these were Fang Lizhi, then

---

39 Gittings, *China changes face*, page 172.
40 9 December 1935 was the beginning of the student movement which demanded a united front against Japan between the CCP and the Guomindang.
41 Quoted in Schell, *Discos and democracy*, page 32.

vice-president of the University of Science and Technology of China (USTC) in Hefei; Liu Binyan, a journalist on the People's Daily; and Wang Ruowang, an investigative journalist in Shanghai. All three were Communist Party members; but all three had been persecuted in the Hundred Flowers movement of 1956 and in the Cultural Revolution, which gave them credibility among the disaffected. In late 1985 and throughout 1986 all three, as well as a number of lesser-known figures, used the easing of restrictions to make speeches at campus after campus, attracting hundreds and sometimes thousands of students.

The opposition was not defined by any particular programme, but rather by their advocacy of rather vague concepts – human rights, democracy, justice, freedom of the press, reform, nationalism – capable of a variety of interpretations. The Western media usually painted them as simply being concerned to see the introduction of 'Western democracy' into China, but the reality was far more complex.

Illusions in the West were widespread among most oppositionists in China. But the image they aspired towards was far removed from the realities of the West. What it represented above all was a searching for ways of reforming the political set-up. That produced a continual ferment, extending far beyond the limited circles of those who had access to the media or to semi-official platforms.

Their searching had a number of key limitations. The opposition accepted the leading role of the Communist Party – indeed most of its leaders were until their expulsion CCP members, and all refused the label of 'dissident'. It accepted the modernisation strategy and the consequent need for sacrifices from workers. It shared, too, the nationalism of the ruling class, posing its arguments in terms of what was best for China as a whole. Most important of all, it saw any real change as coming from above. In short, what the opposition offered in terms of ideas was an alternative strategy for the ruling class for more effectively running Chinese society.

Indeed, their key argument was that without democracy there could be no modernisation – that it was China's 'backward' or 'feudal' political structure that held back real economic development. In this they drew on a number of seminal works by leaders of the Democracy Wall movement. Their attitude was best summed up by something written by Xu Wenli, editor of one of the most influential Democracy Wall journals:

> Reform from below is impossible. For Chinese society and the Chinese people do not want disorder, nor have they created disorders. The historical experience of Chinese reform also makes it clear that reform from above cannot be carried through to the end. For the reform power of an upper stratum alone is not enough to overcome the bureaucratic resistance of the old system. Evidently the only practical road is a combination of reform from above and reform from below.[42]

But to judge the opposition's impact on the student movement simply in terms of these alternatives was to see only one side of the contradiction. The role of loyal opposition they aspired to was one that brought them into constant conflict with the ruling class. The self-imposed limits within which they worked were far wider than those that the state would allow.

In the absence of any real change from above, they necessarily stressed the need for pressure from below. Liu Binyan argued that:

> In European revolutionary history, the first step in the fight for the establishment of a constitution was freedom of speech. Of course, freedom of speech... wasn't just a matter of some king being particularly enlightened or some chief minister being especially generous and just announcing that from this day on

---

42   Quoted in Nathan, *Chinese democracy*, page 44.

people will be permitted to publish newspapers… Freedom of speech was created by the people themselves.[43]

Most important of all, whatever the weaknesses and contradictions in the alternatives that the opposition offered, their audience were attracted above all by their ringing denunciations of what was wrong with China – lack of democracy, bureaucracy, corruption – and by the simple fact that it was possible openly to organise meetings at which all these issues could be argued out.

The anger erupts

The contradiction between the limited changes from above and the much greater demands for change from below finally exploded in December 1986. Students in Hefei marched through the city protesting against the rigging of elections to the local People's Congress. They won a re-opening of the nominations, and there was initially suspicion that some elements of the ruling class had backed them in order to upset their opponents. But news of the protest and the victory spread quickly and were to set off far more important protests elsewhere.

The movement eventually spread to more than 20 cities and some 150 campuses, but the most important were Shanghai and Beijing. Hundreds of Shanghai students had heard Fang Lizhi deliver a blistering attack on the government the previous month; thousands more had been angered when police attacked dancers at a rock concert just days after the Hefei protest. On 18 December thousands of students marched to the city centre demanding a meeting with the local authorities. While the students in Hefei had seen themselves as marching in favour of Deng Xiaoping and against his 'conservative' opponents, the Shanghai protests were far more radical.

'If you want to know what freedom is, ask Wei Jingsheng,'

---

43   Quoted in Schell, *Discos and democracy*, page 159.

read one poster. Another changed the traditional salute to leaders 'Long live' (*wan sui* – literally, ten thousand years) into 'Deng Xiaoping *wan shui*' (ten thousand taxes). For five days crowds of up to 70,000 blocked the city centre, among them large numbers of workers. One told a Western reporter he was there because his bosses got all the benefits of reform while he got nothing. The Shanghai protests were stifled by armed police surrounding the campuses – but the next day Beijing students moved.

For four days running students from a number of Beijing universities demonstrated, calling for solidarity with Shanghai and freedom of the press. On 26 December city officials announced restrictions on marches, placing Tiananmen Square completely off bounds. Two days later hundreds of students from Beijing Teachers' University defied the ban, breaking open the locked gates of two other universities. And on 1 January several thousand students set out for Tiananmen, which was not only ringed with police but also flooded to turn it into a sheet of ice! After scuffles with the police a number of students broke into the square and 25 were arrested.

The next day more than 4,000 marched on the square to demand their release. Told halfway that they had won, the majority dispersed, but about a thousand carried on to make their original protest. As the arrested students returned to Beijing University, another thousand marchers set off to prove that the ban could not be enforced. The police just stood and watched, clearly under orders to do nothing to stop them. The final act of the movement was a mass burning of a Beijing paper which had carried the most vicious attacks on them.[44]

Initially the ruling class were split on how to respond. But as the protests died down it seemed that while those pressing for

---

44   For a fuller account of the protests see Schell, *Discos and democracy*, pages 223- 241.

greater controls had won, the repression would be measured. Hu Yaobang, then CCP general secretary, was sacked for 'liberalism', and a number of leading oppositionists were expelled from the CCP. But they were neither publicly disgraced nor jailed. Among the students, a number of the organisers were disciplined by the campus authorities, and many of those graduating in 1987 found themselves allocated to jobs in Inner Mongolia or the far west. But others were allowed to carry on their studies, and some of the leaders in 1986 were to be central to the May events of 1989.

Out of the 1986 protests came a realisation among a small minority of students of the need for organisation. Their work was necessarily clandestine, leaving nothing behind in the way of writing, but the fruits of their organisation were to be seen in the revival of the student movement in mid-1988. For much of 1987, however, the campuses remained quiet as a conservative campaign against 'bourgeois liberalisation' took off.

Launched by 'conservatives' building on their success in removing Hu Yaobang, the campaign targeted 'Western influences' and the oppositionists for daring to challenge the CCP's monopoly of power. It looked like a rerun of the campaign against 'spiritual pollution' – and like that campaign, it quickly turned into an embarrassment for the government. At the 13th CCP Congress in October it was unceremoniously dumped. In what seemed to have been an unplanned revolt by the lower ranks, the campaign's main instigator, Deng Liqun, who had been expecting election to the Politburo, was dropped from the central committee. The congress once again reaffirmed that – within strict limits – a certain amount of opposition would be tolerated.

The spring of 1988 saw students testing out those limits time and time again. In Beijing alone, there were demonstrations in April outside the National People's Congress (China's rubberstamp parliament) against inflation and poor living conditions. Li Peng suggested that intellectuals take second jobs to make ends meet, so one group of students set up shoe-shine stalls outside the congress![45] In May there were abortive attempts to organise pro-democracy marches on the anniversary of the May 4th nationalist demonstration of 1919. In June protests against the murder of a student by *liumang*, which started out demanding greater law and order, turned quickly into more general protests against CCP leaders. 'Do we have to wait until someone from Zhao Ziyang's home county is killed before we get protection?' read one poster. Beijing was not alone - in the first six months of 1988 there were protests at some 77 colleges in 25 cities.[46]

But the anger, in the absence of any clear focus, could easily be deflected in any direction, even the most reactionary. At the end of 1988 there were mass racist attacks across a number of Chinese campuses, with crowds of up to 3,000 students attacking African students' quarters. Where the police intervened, they came in on the side of the attackers. Though these racist outbursts seemed to come out of the blue, they were the continuation of a terror campaign on the campuses that had been going on for several years. One black Canadian student who was at a Shanghai university in 1988 spoke of living with the daily threat of attack, both from individuals and gangs of up to 30 people, and of black students having to move around the campus and the city in large groups for their safety.

But he also noted that there was a clear minority prepared to defend black students (even though some of them argued that blacks shouldn't 'provoke' trouble by going out with Chinese women) and to stand up to the racists. One of the anti-racists told him prophetically: 'One day we're just going to explode.'[47]

---

45   *FEER*, 16 June 1988.

46   *FEER*, 3 November 1988.

47   My thanks to Cameron Haynes of Montreal International Socialists for this information.

The ruling class were happy to see students venting their anger on innocent scapegoats. But as I argued in *Socialist Worker Review* at the time:

> As recent events in Yugoslavia have proved, state tolerance of racist outbursts as a safety valve can easily backfire. The current spate of racist attacks on Chinese campuses is a sign of the deep anger and alienation felt by most Chinese students. The ruling class has no guarantee that the anger will not turn on the students' real enemies.[48]

---

48 *Socialist Worker Review*, January 1989.

CHAPTER 7

'We are still ruled by wolves' – the revolt of 1989

In 1985 the ruling class faced a clear crisis of economic strategy; by 1988, this had turned into a full-blown economic crisis. In the countryside their efforts to stem the decline in grain output had led to intolerable strains in both the state purchasing system and in supplies to farmers. By the end of the year grain rationing had returned to parts of the countryside. Provincial governments were banning the export of grain to other provinces, and by December less than 90 percent of the state purchasing quota had been met. This was not primarily due to a massive drop in output (grain production fell back only slightly in 1988), but rather to the way in which the ethos of the market had seeped into the state organs in the countryside.

Seeing township grain management centres buying up grain at state prices and then reselling it on the free market (at a 150 percent mark-up), many peasants decided to cut out the middleman and sell directly to rural workers. In many areas the incentive to do this was greatly increased when the state purchasing authorities announced that they had insufficient funds to meet their contracts, and would have to give IOUs in part payment.[1]

---

1   One county in Anhui could only pay for half of its contracts in cash; the rest were paid for with a bank-deposit receipt. (*FEER*, 2 March 1989).

1989 was even worse than 1988. In the Kaifeng region of Henan province (north China's main wheat-growing area), 40 percent of the state-supplied fertiliser had by March been resold on the open market-by the company's officials, to other state officials![2] In May the Ministry of Commerce and the Agricultural Bank of China announced that they needed 20 billion yuan to meet purchases of summer wheat and oil but 'at most only half the funds can be supplied'.[3]

Throughout industry, as growth continued to outstrip the supply of most raw materials, competition for supplies became more intense. In the silk industry, for instance, silkworm cocoons were traditionally reared in southern inland provinces (principally Sichuan) and sold for processing to the silk mills of Shanghai and Guangdong. But in 1988, because the silk-producing provinces were building their own mills, deliveries slowed to a trickle. Provincial governments sent armed guards to border crossings to enforce export controls and, by October, 1,400 of Shanghai's 1,600 silk looms were standing idle.

Guangdong managed to keep a higher level of supplies – but its solution showed the extent of the anarchy pervading the Chinese economy. Provincial officials sent agents into Sichuan to buy silkworm cocoons on the black market, and then used local army trucks to get their booty through the border guards![4] There was similar fierce competition for scarce cotton and wool.

Inflation continued to soar to heights never seen in the lifetimes of most Chinese. In December 1987 pork and sugar

2   *Beijing Review*, 10 April 1989. According to the article: 'a district discipline inspection committee [the Fraud Squad!]...requested three tons of fertiliser for the relatives of one official... [who] had only two-thirds of a hectare of land.' The article finished not with a bang but with a whimper: 'With corruption chewing into China's agricultural policies, the nation waits for its leaders to take measures that will clean up this mess.'

3   BBC, *SWB*, FE/0458, 16 May 1989.

4   *FEER*, 27 October 1988.

had been rationed at fixed prices in all major cities. Yet the strains this put on a state budget already in deficit could not be borne for long. Early in 1988 Sichuan ended pork rationing because the provincial government could no longer afford the subsidies, and a number of cities quietly decontrolled prices, promising 'income subsidies' to compensate for the increased prices.

When this became known, panic buying began on a massive scale, and fears about restrictions on imports, as well as skyrocketing food prices, led to major runs on the banks. In the northeastern city of Harbin, more than 12 million yuan (US$3.3 million) was withdrawn from personal accounts in just three days. In Guangzhou, where it was announced that, as an experiment, rice prices would be 'decontrolled' (that is, doubled) from 1 July, queues began to appear from the end of May.[5]

By August similar bank runs had spread across the country and a number of strikes had broken out. But at the same time wages jumped enormously. In July the official state payroll for workers and urban staff was 25 percent higher than the previous year, and bonuses and subsidies rose by 36 percent.[6] Workers' ability to push up wages – particularly through bonus payments – had risen greatly since the early 1980s. Because factory managers now controlled their finances, they could be pressured to concede higher wages to cover inflation, irrespective of profitability.

Yet only a minority of urban workers could cover themselves in this way. Even among those workers who could push up their bonuses, it is unlikely that this did more than slow down the rise in the cost of living. Workers on fixed salaries (which was most white-collar and professional workers), students and the unemployed had no way of protecting themselves. Meanwhile,

5   *FEER*, 3 November 1988.
6   *FEER*, 29 September 1988.

they could see local officials and the minority of successful small businessmen living better than ever before.

The ruling class ended up with the worst of both worlds: mass anger against inflation and corruption on the one hand, and a spiralling wage bill on the other. In autumn 1988 they decided on an even harsher credit squeeze. Banks were ordered to scrutinise all requests for credit or withdrawals, and given sweeping powers to refuse either as they saw fit. The effect was to send large parts of the economy into wholesale recession.

In the construction industry, several million temporary workers from the countryside were sacked. As they returned home, they found that many of the rural industries were closing for lack of raw materials and credit. By March 1989, it was officially admitted that more than a million unemployed rural workers from four provinces had flooded into Guangzhou alone.[7]

In many areas the banks responded by stopping all payments or refusing to transfer money out of their city or province. Many enterprises got round the restrictions by returning to a cash-only economy. By November 1988 one-quarter of Sichuan's money supply was held in cash in factory safes – one firm had to hire an armoured car to pay over US$150,000 to a supplier who (quite rationally) refused to take a cheque![8]

In short, the squeeze worsened the chaos inside the economy, without increasing the state's control over the crisis. The most powerful local officials and managers used their autonomy to avoid or mitigate the effects of the slowdown, and because the government's weapons were such blunt ones, their effect was random, varying greatly from area to area. By early 1989 it was clear that China was in the grip of the worst economic crisis the majority of the population could remember; it was equally clear that the government had no solution.

---

7   *Beijing Review*, 13 March 1989.
8   *FEER*, 5 January 1989.

One common feature of the squeeze was the most concerted effort yet to make workers pay the costs of the crisis. In May 1989 it was reported that in twelve provinces, from the northeast to the southeast:

> Local banks issued mandatory savings targets to enterprises, demanding that they withhold wages according to proportion – (generally 10-50 percent of a worker's wage) and replace them with various deposit slips and reward tickets, otherwise the bank would not honour cash withdrawals for wages.[9]

The report concluded by saying that 'Discontent has been aroused among some workers.' Events were already proving this something of an understatement.

A single spark...

> The saying 'A single spark can start a prairie fire' is an apt description of how the current situation will develop. We need only look at the strikes by the workers, the uprisings by the peasants, the mutinies of soldiers and the strikes of students which are developing in many places to see that it cannot be long before a 'spark' kindles 'a prairie fire.'[10]

Mao wrote those words in January 1930. But if any of the Chinese ruling class still read his works in 1989, they must have seemed only too relevant. The 'spring revolt' became one of those great moments in working-class history, like Spain 1936, Hungary 1956, May 1968 in France, Portugal 1974 or Poland 1980, when all the old certainties were thrown into confusion and suddenly everything seemed possible.

---

9   BBC, *SWB*, FE/045816 May 1989.

10   Mao Zedong, *Selected Works*, volume 1, page 121.

The explosion had its roots in a combination of political and economic crisis that was simply waiting for a spark. But the organisations that came to the fore in the movement had been active for several months previously. Small-scale, regular meetings had been held on a number of Beijing campuses, with speakers arguing the case for democracy and the need for students to act. On 3 April, Wang Dan, a student who was to become a leading figure in the events in Tiananmen Square, publicly protested against attempts to interfere with these 'democracy salons'. Fifty-six students signed the protest, demanding a regular meeting place and a promise of no victimisations.[11] So the explosion did not come out of nowhere; but the sheer scale of it went far beyond anything that anyone had hoped for.

The spark was provided by the death of Hu Yaobang on 15 April. Hu had been responsible for many of the political reforms of the early 1980s, and his sacking in 1986 after the student protests had added to his image as a liberal. The rumour quickly spread across the campuses that he had died of a heart attack while arguing with conservatives (specifically, Premier Li Peng), during a meeting of the Politburo. The following day students began to gather in Tiananmen Square, draping the Monument to the People's Heroes in the centre of the square with wreaths and listening to an endless succession of speakers.

In the next couple of days, hundreds became thousands, thousands became tens of thousands (including increasing numbers of workers), and the speakers went from simply eulogising Hu to placing political demands on the government: for democratic elections, freedom of the press, freedom of assembly and an end to corruption and nepotism among the bureaucracy.

---

11 Han Minzhu, *Cries for democracy* (Princeton University Press, Princeton, NJ, 1990) pages 15-19. Quotes not otherwise referenced are taken from this source.

Even in that first week, the mood was angrier and more militant than any Beijing protest since 1976. One poster read 'Those who should have died live; those who should have lived have died.' One group of Tianjin students sent a letter of support which said 'Seventy years after the May 4th movement, our country is still poverty-stricken and ruled by wolves.'[12] By Thursday 20 April there were reports of sympathy marches and protests in at least eleven cities across the country; 3,000 students marched in Shanghai, and a similar number in Tianjin.

Twice that week crowds of students attacked the gates of Zhongnanhai, the old imperial Forbidden City where China's top rulers live. The students' confidence came not only from the sheer numbers involved, but also from a sense of their own history. As one student prophetically told *The Guardian*: 'The police don't dare to do anything. If there's trouble, the workers will join in and it will be like 1976, and the party doesn't dare risk that.'[13]

In April 1976, the same monument had been the focus for the Tiananmen riots, and for Deng Xiaoping and those around him it was an ominous reminder of the past. Deng's supporters had backed the 1976 protests, which had been crucial to his return to power. Now, thirteen years later, a similar movement was drawing larger and larger crowds in opposition to him. That movement was now organised, not by the lower levels of the bureaucracy, but by independent student bodies openly defying the CCP.

The extent of their organisation was shown on Saturday 22 April, the day of Hu's funeral. The ruling class banned all demonstrations, and brought thousands of police and soldiers into Tiananmen. But throughout Friday night well-disciplined columns of students (some marching to funeral music played

---

12   *The Guardian*, 22 April 1989.
13   *The Guardian*, 20 April 1989.

on ghetto-blasters!) marched into the square, brushing past the police lines. By dawn the square was a sea of red flags, banners and placards, with some 150,000 protesters sitting in ranks listening to speaker after speaker, and singing over and over again the song that would become the movement's anthem – the *Internationale*.

It was not the first time the *Internationale* had been sung on student protests; it had been a regular feature of both the Democracy Wall protests and the marches of 1986. But then it had been used to affirm the legitimacy of the movement and to stress its loyalty to Deng's reforms. Now, as 150,000 people assembled in open defiance of a state ban and in open contempt of the ruling class – 'these men aren't Communist, they're just feudal old guys who are afraid of the people and despise us'[14] as one lorry driver told *The Observer* – it began to mean something very different. When they sang:

Arise you prisoners of starvation
Arise you wretched of the earth
For justice thunders liberation
And a better world's in birth

there was a sense that they were reclaiming it as an anthem of rebellion.

Faced with the reality that it would be impossible to clear the square without mass bloodshed, the government climbed down. For the duration of the funeral a truce was agreed – the soldiers guarding the square and the protesters would all sit in silence to hear the service. But as it finished, the students marched out again in disciplined columns chanting 'Long live the people', 'Up with democracy, down with autocracy' and 'We will return'.

That weekend there was serious rioting in Xian and

14   *The Observer*, 23 April 1989.

Changsha, where thousands of workers and unemployed joined student marches. At Chongqing, in Sichuan province, crowds filled the city centre, while in Wuhan 30,000 marched in the largest demonstration since the Cultural Revolution.

An emergency meeting of the Politburo on Monday 24 April endorsed Deng Xiaoping's call for the movement to be suppressed 'by bloodshed if necessary', and the press began to call it an 'organised conspiracy to overthrow the Communist Party'. But hundreds of journalists began to demonstrate for their right to tell the truth about the movement. On the campuses, an indefinite class boycott started which by the following day had extended to practically every college in Beijing.

Though divisions were already appearing inside the movement – one mass meeting at Beijing University ended in fighting over the microphone – they agreed to call another mass march for 27 April, and to send students out into the streets to agitate among workers and citizens for support.

That march took over the city for the day. Some 150,000 people – half students, half workers, on one estimate – took fifteen hours to cross the city:

Work came to a complete halt in every factory, office block and building site along the more than 25-mile route. Traffic ground to a standstill and onlookers climbed up trees, onto rooftops and billboards to urge the protest on. Clinging to scaffolding, construction labourers banged tin lunch boxes with chopsticks and roared their support. Factory workers in overalls leaned from workshop windows, flashing victory signs and applauding.[15]

On at least three occasions, crowds of thousands of workers intervened to surround hundreds of army troops and prevent them from approaching student marchers. Workers surrounding the

---

15   *The Independent*, 28 April 1989

students sometimes pushed aside police blockades even before the students drew near... The perception of government impotence was most vivid when the crowds burst through the last police barricade to get to Tiananmen... Nearly 1000 army troops in twenty trucks did not flee quickly enough, and mobs swarmed around the trucks... when it became obvious that the soldiers were terrified and thinking only of retreat, the crowd magnanimously cleared a way for them to escape. 'Brothers, go home and till your fields', the crowds shouted as the trucks moved off.[16]

A BBC radio journalist reporting on the march was interrupted by the presenter in London saying: 'This sounds more like a revolution than a protest.' He was wrong, but he caught an important point about the movement. The joyful, carnival nature of the demonstration illustrated the beginning of something essential to every revolution: the realisation by masses of people of their power to defy the old order releases angers, frustrations and hatreds that have smouldered for years. This 'festival of the oppressed', as Lenin described it, marked an enormous step forward for Beijing workers, as they moved from sympathising with the students to becoming part of the protests – and in so doing taking the movement a crucial step forward.

The march ended with calls for nationwide demonstrations on 4 May, the 70th anniversary of the first nationalist movement. The response was patchy. In Beijing, Shanghai, Wuhan and other cities, where the movement had been going on for some time, the marches were smaller than previous ones – though 100,000 marched in Beijing, and some 20,000 in Shanghai, where the police continually blocked the march.

But in other cities where nothing had so far happened, 4 May marked the beginning of the protests. In the northeastern city of Dalian:

---

16   *International Herald Tribune*, 28 April 1989.

Some 4000 people marched from Dalian University of Technology to the government offices downtown. it was quite lively, very good-humoured, very friendly. In the square the students milled around, sat down and chanted 'Dialogue, dialogue' – as the students in Beijing were still doing at the time. Some nurses came out of one of the hospitals, and they were applauded.[17]

There were the first reports of marches in Changchun, in the northeast, and the western cities of Taiyuan, Lanzhou and Xining.

The sheer size of China, and the enormous distance between the major cities, made for vast discrepancies in the rise and fall of the movement. While telephone and telex links between student leaders in different cities made it far easier to spread news than ever before, the fact that those links seem to have all gone through Beijing only accentuated the importance of Beijing as a leader.

After 4 May the movement in Beijing went into a lull. The college class boycott was called off, and in the absence of a clear focus the crowds moved off the streets. The city mayor's offer of talks with student leaders, which began on 7 May, served further to demobilise the movement. For there was an enormous gap between the anger and potential power of the movement on the one hand, and its aspirations on the other.

Among the core of the movement, there was no question that the problem was seen as the ruling class as a whole. One poster at Qinghua University spelt this out with particular clarity. It simply consisted of two lists of names. On the left were listed the old guard of the party and state leadership, and on the right their children and relatives holding senior positions. Every single senior leader was involved – Zhao Ziyang no less than the rest.

---

17   Eye-witness account. In June 1989 I interviewed a number of
     eye-witnesses returned from China, whose accounts I have drawn on
     heavily in this chapter and the next. My thanks are due to all of them.

To quote just a few examples: the governor of Guangdong was the son of the former head of the army; the then CCP secretary in Shanghai – later to become CCP general secretary – was the son-in-law of the former president; the sons-in-law of Deng Xiaoping, president Yang Shangkun and Zhao Ziyang ran China's overseas arms sales agency; Zhou's son ran a state trading company on the southern island of Hainan, where Li Peng's son was director of the local development corporation – Li Peng himself being the adopted son of former prime minister Zhou Enlai.[18]

Mass anger against such corruption, and the growing – and highly visible – inequalities between workers and officials, made it easy for the students to draw large numbers into their protests. But the movement's leaders had no real perspective for what might happen after 4 May, other than wanting to gain recognition for the Autonomous Students' Federation. The state's attempt to co-opt them therefore met with a certain degree of success. It seemed for a while as though the force of the movement had been dissipated.

From hunger strikes to martial law

The hunger-strikes that began in Tiananmen on 13 May aroused the movement to new heights, yet they were called by only a minority of its leaders, against the opposition of the majority. Russian president Gorbachev was due to arrive in Beijing on 15 May, to end the 30-year-old Sino-Soviet split. The most important foreign policy initiative since Nixon's visit in 1972, this was bound to attract media attention around the world. Many student leaders wanted to call the protests off, so as not to embarrass the government. But the minority understood that it was essential to use that opportunity. As one of them later explained:

---

18 *The Independent*, 9 May 1989.

After Gorbachev's visit… they would be ready to crush these troublesome students… we would have to increase the pressure, and do so before Gorbachev arrived. We had to do something that would threaten to embarrass the leadership during the state visit – and acutely enough to force them into the dialogue they had been avoiding.[19]

Only 200 students began the strike, but by Monday they had swelled to more than a thousand, with thousands more sympathisers camped out in Tiananmen. The hunger strikers for the first time laid down specific demands: for Li Peng's sacking and Deng Xiaoping's resignation.

Gorbachev's visit was relegated to second place. By the time he arrived for the first official meeting, at the Great Hall of the People to the east of Tiananmen, there were some 500,000 people in the square, and he was unceremoniously hurried inside by a side door. The next day there were more than a million people in the square, as workers came from all over Beijing to join the students. Workers from the Capital Iron and Steel Works marched into the demonstration in a body, as did journalists from the *People's Daily*. The day after, as Gorbachev flew to Shanghai, the crowds had doubled to two million, and the area of Beijing directly under the students' control spread far beyond Tiananmen.

The organisation of the hunger strikes showed how quickly the movement had learned to run its own affairs. As one eyewitness put it, Tiananmen:

…was organised in concentric circles, with the central organisation at its centre and the hunger strikers grouped around them. There were pathways kept open for ambulances and food which people were bringing in on lorries and cooks from restaurants

---

19   Li Lu, *Moving the mountain* (Macmillan, London, 1990) page 130.

with big cauldrons and stuff... and then there were pathways
kept open for demonstrators. And so to get right in you were
meant to show an ID card as a student.

By the Tuesday the vast majority of those joining the sit-in
were not hunger-strikers but supporters, many of them workers
and even some peasants. Student marshals kept order and
directed traffic, while workers across the city ensured that the
out-of-town supporters were fed and sheltered.

Elsewhere the hunger strikes brought the movement to
its highest pitch yet. Hunger strikes broke out in Shanghai
– where 30,000 students were camped out in the city centre –
Hangzhou, Guangdong, Hefei and no doubt many other cities.
A hundred thousand people marched in Nanjing, and the
movement spread to many cities and towns where previously
little or nothing had happened.

On 18 May alone, 100,000 people marched in the southwestern
city of Guiyang, where there was serious rioting; 15,000 marched
in Hohhot, the capital of Inner Mongolia, and there were demonstrations in two other Inner Mongolian towns; 'tens of thousands'
took to the streets in Kunming, another south-western provincial capital; while no less than eleven cities and towns in Sichuan
province saw protests. At Ningbo, in Zhejiang province, about a
thousand people 'broke into the city government compound', while
in Urumqi there was a 'grave riotous incident'.[20]

Even in Tibet, where martial law had been stepped up since
the start of the movement (meaning that there were armed
soldiers on every street corner) students went on strike; 400 were
still holding out at Lhasa University on 21 May.[21] Throughout

---

20 BBC, *SWB*, FE/0462 and 0467, 20 and 26 May 1989. The quotes and
    figures are taken from various provincial radio stations. Obviously the
    figures (like all those quoted) are estimates rather than exact counts – but
    the official media would have no interest in exaggerating them.

21 BBC, *SWB*, FE/0472, 2 June 1989.

that week and the next tens of thousands of students set off for Beijing from cities around the country, on trains provided free by railway workers.

Little is known in detail about the growth of the movement in provincial cities and towns. But it is obvious that it was not a linear process, with demonstrations growing steadily day after day. In the vast majority of places it started with very small groups giving a lead (the Autonomous Student's Federation in Dalian began with just two people), and keeping the agitation going until suddenly the confidence of much larger numbers grew sufficiently for them to join in. It is worth quoting at some length one eyewitness report to give a sense of that dynamic. Hefei was one of those cities where nothing had happened until the hunger strikes. But on the Monday the strikes started:

About 2000 students from Anhui Provincial University arrived at USTC [the University of Science and Technology, where the 1986 protests had begun]. They rattled the gates, chanted a lot of slogans and at a command pushed very hard at the gates, smashed the lock, and instead of pouring through the gates, there was a guy came to the front with a whistle, got everyone back, cleared away the people who had been pushing down the gates and they marched in a body with their banners, all the way round the campus... they all marched down to the town and the atmosphere that night was a little bit scared really, not very noisy except in the core people...

The next day they came again to the gates and this time a delegation came out of USTC numbering about 200-strong and again they marched around the town and this was a much more confident demonstration, much more noisy, more people. Because it was in the afternoon it got much more response from the people in the town; a lot of clapping, a lot of support, no hostility.

What happened the day after [Wednesday 17th] was that USTC managed to get their own act together. A person or small group of people put up half a dozen posters that there would be a rally at two o'clock and come the rally something in the region of 2000 students marched out of this campus. This again brought the whole centre of the city to a standstill; there were just bands of students and other supporters marching, criss-crossing around the streets. And this is when we started to get a glimpse of the way that the organisation was running.

They started collecting money so you saw them going past buses, and I went to one box which was a static collection point. I went across to this box and put some money in, and looked in-it was full up to the brim with money... it was on the Wednesday that it was absolutely clear that the vast majority of people who weren't in hiding behind closed doors in Communist Party headquarters were totally in support of the demands of the students... any leaflet that was posted up or any poster, you immediately had a crowd. And people not just reading it but copying it down, word for word. A student would produce half a dozen leaflets and they'd be immediately snatched up.

Very few workers joined the marches; most of the time it was individuals. But on the Friday [19th] there was a delegation of railway workers, and delegations of teachers... On that Friday workplace after workplace in the town would be festooned with slogans supporting the workers and there would be a crowd outside clapping away. And these firecrackers, absolutely spectacular, were long strings of things which they let off and they make a hell of a racket and everybody applauding...[22]

Thursday 18 May was a decisive day in Beijing. From Hu's funeral to the beginning of the hunger strikes the government had barely moved in response to the revolt, either because they

---

22   My thanks to Ersy Contogouris for transcribing the tape of this interview.

realised that doing nothing was their best move or (more probably) because they were split on how to react. But from the start of the hunger strikes they alternated blustery threats with hollow expressions of sympathy, both of which simply strengthened the determination of the hunger strikers, by now swelled to some 3,000 people, with hundreds more in hospitals suffering from exhaustion.

At noon Li Peng, three other Politburo members and the mayor of Beijing met leaders of the hunger strikers. The official transcript, published in *Beijing Review* of 29 May (an astonishing thing in itself) gave a sense of the hunger strikers' almost unbelievable courage and determination. Li Peng began with his customary tact and diplomacy:

> Today we will talk about only one thing: how to get the fasting students out of their present plight… You are all young, no more than 22 or 23 years of age. My youngest son is older than you. I have three children. None of them is engaged in official profiteering. To us, you are like our own children.

He was answered by Örkesh Dölet,[23] one of the leaders of the movement from the outset: 'It was not you who invited us to be here; rather it was so many people on Tiananmen who asked you to come out and talk with us. So as to how many questions we should discuss, it is for us to decide.'

He went on to spell out their demands:

> First, we think Zhao Ziyang or Li Peng had better go to Tiananmen and talk directly to the students there. Secondly,

---

23 A member of the Uyghur minority, he was known in most press reports as Wuerkaixi (the Chinese transliteration of his name) but attached importance to being known by his Uyghur name, according to an interview in *Der Spiegel*, 10 July 1989. My thanks to Einde O'Callaghan for the translation.

the *People's Daily* should… acknowledge the significance of the
current student movement… As for the dialogue, it should be an
open, equal, direct and sincere one with representatives of the
mass of students… here, open means a live television broadcast.

If all these were conceded, he concluded, it might be possible
to convert the hunger strike into a sit-in – there was no mention
of clearing the square. Another student openly threatened even
worse trouble: 'The student movement may have become a
people's movement. The students are relatively reasonable. We
cannot ensure that a people's movement can be reasonable.'

Later that same day Li Peng, Zhao Ziyang and two other
members of the Politburo Standing Committee visited some of
the hunger-strikers in hospital. They were jeered, heckled and
argued with; one student rose from his sick-bed to cry out: 'It is
your duty to fight corruption. You should start with your own
sons!' Faced by a student demanding to know why they had not
come before, one of them was forced to apologise: 'We were busy
that day. You must understand – we had Mr Gorbachev.'[24]

One last attempt was made to defuse the protests, with a dawn
visit to the hunger strikers by Li Peng and Zhao Ziyang. On one
report, Zhao Ziyang went on his own and was followed by Li Peng.
In the square Zhao simply wept as students put their demands to
him, while Li Peng stayed barely five minutes. This was later inter-
preted to prove that Zhao was sympathetic to the students. What
it rather showed was that, while he may have opposed the use of
force, he had no means of meeting their demands.

That night martial law was declared and troops began
advancing on Beijing. As workers turned out in their millions to
defend their struggle from the army, the protest that had turned
into open revolt now flared up to its highest point yet.

---

24   *South China Morning Post* (Hong Kong) 19 May 1989.

CHAPTER 8

Revolt and repression

The military operation that began late in the evening of 19 May had been in preparation for several weeks. Some 300,000 troops – 10 percent of the army – were drawn up around Beijing. As news of their coming spread across the city, students and workers sped off in trucks, cars, convoys of motor-cycles and commandeered buses to halt them on the outskirts:

> From Wanxi intersection, west of the city centre, it looked as if the revolution had made a return visit to the capital. Under street lights it was possible to see army trucks stretching the entire length of the road, their cab doors open and their engines cold. Green-uniformed troops, many not much older than the students who had forced them to a halt stood by helpless as hundreds of people danced across the roadway singing songs and chanting patriotic slogans…One or two soldiers talked to the students but most just listened or scanned the pamphlets handed around…[1]

The human barricades were quickly reinforced with buses, trucks and construction vehicles. The army trucks' tyres were let

---

1   *Financial Times*, 20-21 May 1989.

down, and their petrol drained. Underground workers, hearing that troops were being brought into the heart of the city by tube train, cut off the power to the system. There were widespread calls for a general strike on the Saturday (then a normal working day for most Chinese workers). Large numbers of workers did stay away from work that day, though more from lack of transport than because of any conscious decision to strike. As two eyewitnesses explained:

> Capital Iron and Steel Works was out on the Saturday afternoon... that was the widest strike action. That was the only time the students called for strike action... We heard 70,000 out of 200,000 had come out... We heard elsewhere that nobody went to work on Saturday, but there was no transport so the question we kept asking was whether people would have stayed away from work if there had been transport... We got a number of different answers. Most said only a minority.

Whatever the extent of direct strike action, there is no question that the barricades were run overwhelmingly by workers. One eyewitness described the scene on Saturday night, when the barricades were spread across all the entrances to the city:

> The direct experience we had was the crossroads looking out to where the tanks were coming from. There literally was not one student there. If you put together all the places that the army was stopped – these particular tanks were stopped at Dongshan which is ten miles up the road... When we went to one of the key places where the army had been stopped we suddenly realised how it's possible. This absolutely massive housing estate slap bang on the crossroads and working people concentrated there. And so you get the call and enough people flooding onto the streets...

Another eyewitness said:

Saturday night was the most amazing human spectacle I've ever seen. It was unreal, the amount of people who came out onto the streets. There was everybody there: the very old, sitting, waiting; families with young children, babies being carried in mothers' arms... They thought the crunch was coming that night and they were fully prepared to try and stop them.

An old man said that there were more people on the streets than he'd ever seen in his life – certainly more than in 1949. And there was a fantastic air of toughness, of determination, almost a matter-of-fact attitude... it was a situation of tumult, but of immense sense of purpose and importance. There were people getting up and instructing others what to do, but it seemed to be fairly spontaneous.

But there was a sense of direction; on the one hand chaos, but on the other hand great efficiency, because everybody's willing to do it, because they want to achieve a common purpose.

There was definite organisation within the housing estate. People by and large stayed out till two or three in the morning, but then went to bed. And there was a system within each residential block to get people out again at short notice, if the army were to move in at four or five o'clock. I even saw walkie-talkies and cordless telephones being used.

On the Sunday night two eyewitnesses wrote:

For 48 hours now the city of Beijing has been entirely in the hands of the people. Though the atmosphere is tense, there is no drunkenness, no looting and no violence... We are on the main road in the east of the city. The avenue is wide. Three articulated buses span it. Behind this for over 1000 metres there must be over 100 buses arranged in intricate patterns blocking the road. There is just enough room for a small vehicle. More buses sit waiting to be pushed into position to close the gaps if needed. People sit chatting in the buses. At the last barricade people stand looking into the distance through the dark.

The barricade won't, and isn't meant to, stop tanks. The idea is to halt and slow up moving troops to allow people to argue with the soldiers and turn them back, as has happened so often in the last couple of days. The barricades are for people to stand in front of, not behind... A teenage boy reads a leaflet out loud. It's from the students in Tiananmen, dated 21 May, 5.30pm... it says that Li Peng wants to fill the jails, that the future is worth fighting for... The students call on the people of Beijing to unite with them. The crowd, workers from the local district, roar with approval. The workers say they are prepared to die if need be. A woman, about 50 years old, emphasises the point with a gesture of slitting her throat. The courage is unbelievable...

All of the city centre, maybe six miles wide and six miles deep or perhaps more, is now under the control of workers and students. People talk of five million people, over half the entire population, out on the streets yesterday. Most of them are workers. Everywhere open-topped trucks packed with workers and students are passing. They all have red flags and banners flying as they speed from barricade to barricade, checking on the situation, seeing where help is needed. And everyone sings the Internationale over, over and over.[2]

Trotsky wrote of the revolutionary importance of barricades, in words that could have come from Beijing that weekend:

In every revolution, the significance of barricades is not at all the same as that of fortresses in a battle. A barricade is not just a physical obstacle. The barricade serves the cause of insurrection because, by creating a temporary barrier to the movement of

---

2   *Socialist Worker*, 27 May 1989.

troops, it brings them into close contact with the people. Here at the barricades, the soldier hears – perhaps for the first time in his life – the talk of ordinary honest people, their fraternal appeals, the voice of the people's conscience; and as a consequence of such contact between citizens and soldiers, military discipline disintegrates and disappears... And this is why, in our opinion, a popular rising has been 'prepared', not when the people have been armed with rifles and guns – for in that case it would never be prepared – but when it is armed with readiness to die in open street battle.[3]

That was exactly what happened on the Beijing barricades. It has to be said that the soldiers had not been fully prepared for what they were sent to do. Although they had been confined to barracks for two weeks, deprived of radios and any newspaper except the army daily, at most they had been told they were going to Beijing to put down a 'small counter-revolutionary disturbance' – some had even been told they were going to act as extras in a film![4] One eyewitness recalls:

A soldier running into the square at four in the morning, going to the students' public address system and saying that he and his battalion had been stopped a few streets away by barricades, and that they had joined the students, joined with the movement. He said that 80 percent of the army supported the students...

That weekend the revolt reached its highest point. Workers and students were in control of the whole of Beijing, and the government seemed helpless. It had assumed that the declaration of martial law and the sight of the troops would be enough to frighten the movement into submission; instead, it had risen to even greater heights. Troops fraternised with the workers and

---

3   Leon Trotsky, *1905* (Penguin, Harmondsworth, 1973) pages 411-12.

4   *The Guardian*, 24 May 1989.

students, and by Monday 22nd some army leaders were openly defying the call to apply martial law. Rumours started to spread that Li Peng had resigned, and that Deng Xiaoping had fled to Wuhan or Jinan.

The experience of power transformed everyday life. Everywhere there were crowds of workers and students discussing, arguing over wallposters; agitators who got up on a box and began to speak were guaranteed a large audience. Women, who play little or no part in official Chinese politics, were to the fore as agitators, organisers and stewards. One eyewitness estimated the crowds as 40 percent female, adding that she'd never felt so safe as a woman in her life. One British student, who had found the sexism of Chinese male students almost intolerable, noted that 'it stopped completely once the movement began'.

The same transformation of ingrained prejudices applied to minority nationalities, who normally face open discrimination in Beijing. The central student organisation feared that minority nationality troops who spoke no Chinese would be sent to break the barricades, as happened at least twice. Their response was to organise minority students to go out to the barricades to address the troops in their own languages.[5]

That one detail shows the extent of the organisation at the centre of the revolt, and the extent to which they could spread their ideas to masses of people. Yet they saw the insurrection almost entirely in defensive terms, designed purely to keep the troops out and defend the students in Tiananmen. The near-universal sense of dissatisfaction with the ruling class was not matched by any coherent sense of how to take the struggle forward, of how to press home their advantage. One eyewitness was told: 'Look, everybody is united in supporting the students, everybody here, but if you ask what they want, there's no unity on that, no idea.'

---

5   Eyewitness report.

The workers organise

One such opportunity to take the struggle decisively forward was the call for a general strike for the Monday which was put out by the Beijing Autonomous Workers' Federation. The strike never happened – on one account, the army contacted the student leadership in Tiananmen to ask for it to be called off.[6] It was to be a decisive turning point.

The students' approach to the workers was contradictory. On the one hand, they had consciously reached out for workers' support through street agitation and factory meetings. But the movement's leaders saw the workers' role as adding to the numbers on the streets, rather than using their collective power inside the factories and offices. Workers were just one of the groups of *shimin* (citizens) who were called on to support the students. In Shanghai, the movement even argued against strike action because this would damage the economy. As two eyewitnesses saw it:

> We just got the impression that the students very much saw themselves as the leaders and there certainly wasn't the idea that to go out and bring the workers out was the key thing, or to talk to workers was the key thing. And there wasn't really a belief in workers' power… But some people were absolutely clear that in order to get real change, then you had to get the workers out.

However, from the beginning of the movement, some workers at least had a different idea of their role and of how best to bring the mass of workers into the struggle. One poster which appeared on 28 April, signed simply 'A worker', argued for specific tactics to draw workers into the protests, and showed the depths of anger waiting to be tapped:

---

6   Eyewitness report.

Dear students,

As you continue your struggle over the following days, you must try to gain the broad support of workers, peasants, soldiers and businessmen. How can you do this? First, do not emphasise the treatment of intellectuals and the budget for higher education, and do not demand impractical democratic change; for this will alienate the workers and farmers.

The propaganda aimed at the workers, farmers and soldiers must emphasise the fact that the words 'owned by the people'[7] actually means 'owned by a small group of bourgeoisie'. That group calls us 'the masters of the country', yet we live in overcrowded conditions from generation to generation. On the other hand, those 'civil servants' build villas, and have police escorts for their luxury cars – while we 'masters' travel on overcrowded buses... Can we turn a blind eye to their draining of the national treasury? For where does that money come from? From our sweat and blood...[8]

The experience of mass involvement in the movement, through the demonstrations and the barricades, led a minority to see the necessity for an independent workers' organisation. The largest of these was the Beijing Workers' Autonomous Federation, but similar groups seem to have existed in Shanghai, Hangzhou, Xian, Tianjin and Guangdong, as well as several others in Beijing itself.[9]

Very little was known about the size or influence of these

7   'Ownership by the people' is the term used in China for state-owned industries.
8   Mok Yu Chiu and J Frank Harrison (editors) *Voices from Tiananmen Square,* (Black Rose Books, Montreal, Canada, 1990), pages 110-11.
9   For the first four cities, see *Amnesty International* press releases ASA 17/33/89, 17/35/89, 17/37/89 and 17/41/89, dated respectively 15, 16, 16 and 21 June 1989; for Guangdong and Beijing see *October Review* (Hong Kong Fourth Internationalist magazine) 25 June 1989.

other groups, and some may well have been just a handful of people. What is important is that the idea of autonomous workers' organisation could spread so quickly. The Beijing Workers' Autonomous Federation was founded on 21 April, and first appeared publicly in Tiananmen on 20 May:

> Between 50 and 100 workers erected a tented headquarters on the outskirts of the students' tents... Among the core members, there were steelworkers, railway workers, aviation workers, restaurant cooks, students and lawyers... hundreds and sometimes thousands of workers and residents crowded round the Federation's loudspeakers listening to· the speeches... The wide wage discrepancy between the workers and plant managers, the lack of workplace democracy, the lack of genuine workers' representation in the policy-making process, poor labour protection and working conditions, and the deterioration of workers' living standards in recent years were among their main grievances.[10]

In one early document they argued that:

> there is not yet an organisation which can truly express the wishes expressed by the working masses. Therefore, we recognise that there is a need to set up an autonomous organisation which will speak for the workers and which will organise the realisation of workers' participation and consultation in political affairs.[11]

Yet at the same time they stressed that they did not oppose the rule of the CCP, and that they wanted to work with sympathetic sections of the official unions – they wanted to work for

---

10   *Echoes from Tiananmen*, number 1, (Friends of Chinese *Minzhu* [democracy], Hong Kong, 1989), pages 12/13.

11   As above, page 14.

reforms within the law. One Hong Kong independent union activist summed the group up in this way:

> From what I gathered, they were very much in line with the students' demands... They had no clear economic demands, though they talked about safety issues. But they were not talking about their wages... 'We are against the bureaucrats', they said, 'they should not rip so much profit out of the people. The wealth should be shared out among the people. They should not be so rich while we are so poor.'... what impressed me most was they had a very strong conviction for their own organisation; they were very committed to the workers having their own organisation.[12]

Whatever the weaknesses and confusions in their positions (which must have been evolving from day to day), that last point was the most important one. Never before had workers consciously organised as workers to challenge the rule of the bureaucracy. Workers in state industries in China depended on their workplaces for housing, food subsidies and their children's schooling. The very real threat of losing all that, though it had never prevented economic strikes, had traditionally kept them on the sidelines of protest movements. Now a significant minority had broken free of those fears. Tragically, the potential of that giant step forward was not to be realised.

The retreat from strike action on the Monday after the weekend of the barricades both demonstrated the weaknesses of the movement's leadership, and allowed the government to regain the offensive. The nationalism of the student leaders,

---

12 From an interview with Lee Cheuk Yan, general secretary of the Clothing Workers General Union, 14 June 1989. My thanks to Nigel Paramour for a tape of this interview. (An independent union in Hong Kong is one that is neither pro-Beijing nor pro-Taiwan.)

which led them to accept the existence of a 'national interest' that they had in common with the government, was played upon to argue down a general strike as 'damaging to the economy'.

More important, a general strike would have led the movement to go on the offensive. There was no better time to do this than immediately after the 'weekend of the barricades'; the government had lost control over Beijing and the army was openly split. Workers taking the offensive could at the very least have split the government wide open; at best it could have opened up the possibility of workers' councils springing up, which could begin to challenge for real power.

From stalemate to repression

Across the rest of the country, the declaration of martial law raised the struggle to even greater heights. Hundreds of thousands took to the streets in Nanjing and Shenzhen, and the centres of Shanghai, Wuhan and Changsha were taken over for several days by the largest crowds yet seen in those cities. Martial law was extended (apparently successfully) to Wuhan on 22 May. In Xian the local radio station reported that '...the main roads have been seriously blocked... the main roads and side-streets are a sea of large and small-character posters and banners...'[13]

Lanzhou Radio made it clear that the unrest was not confined to the big cities: 'In recent days, an unstable situation in the social order has occurred in the Lanzhou area, and in a fairly large number of prefectures, autonomous prefectures and cities... a very tense situation exists in industrial production.'[14]

But the biggest demonstration was that in Hongkong on

---

13   BBC, *SWB*, FE/0471, 1 June 1989.
14   BBC, *SWB*, FE/0467 29 May 1989. A prefecture was a sub-provincial
      administrative area; an autonomous prefecture was one mainly inhabited
      by minority nationalities. [Updated]

21 May. Left-wing students had previously organised a couple of small solidarity marches, the largest of which had drawn some 6,000 people (large by Hong Kong standards). With the declaration of martial law, everyone knew that 21 May would be bigger - one leader of the independent unions hoped for 100,000 people, while the police expected 8,000 and originally deployed just 50 officers to control it![15]

In the teeth of a raging typhoon, more than one million people, one-sixth of the entire population, took over the streets of Hong Kong island in the largest protest ever seen in the colony. Significantly, the pro-Beijing unions mobilised heavily for the march, joining in the calls for the sacking of Li Peng and Deng Xiaoping. While the march was a slap in the face for the Chinese ruling class, it was equally one for the British rulers of the colony, as demands for democracy in China were echoed by demands for democracy in Hong Kong itself in the run-up to its reversion to China in 1997.

While the movement advanced elsewhere in China, in Beijing itself there was an effective stalemate. Inside Tiananmen Square there were constant arguments about the future direction of the movement. Increasing numbers of Beijing students gave up the hunger strike, to be replaced by students from outside Beijing, who were continuing to pour into the city, though in smaller numbers. The numbers in the square and on the streets dropped steadily.

The movement now had little clear focus beyond the nightly assemblies to barricade the roads against the army, which gradually became smaller as the likelihood of the army's arrival got less and less. As workers went back to work during the days, the pressures from managements to halt all action became stronger and stronger. Revolts can never stand still – if they do not go forwards, they allow the enemy time to regroup. As the

---

15   Interview with Lee Cheuk Yan and eyewitness account.

momentum of the movement faltered, so the initiative began to pass back to the ruling class.

To turn that initiative into regaining control, however, would take another two weeks. For while the movement had ceased to go forward, there were still enormous crowds on the streets of Beijing, with hundreds of thousands joining the afternoon marches. Throughout the evenings people continued to throng the street corners where the barricades had been erected. One eyewitness said of this period:

> The barricades were going and by Tuesday night [23rd] they'd more or less gone... they just put up a token one on Tuesday night where we were but the meeting got bigger. This flyover had a permanent propaganda bus parked underneath it. And this bus would have-on Tuesday night it had two or three thousand people around it. And this was a crowd which kept coming and going. They would listen twenty minutes or half an hour, and then they'd go, so you can imagine how many people there were there.

Attention began to focus on the manoeuvres inside the ruling class. For a couple of days hopes were pinned on the president, Wan Li, who cut short a visit to Canada to return home. He alone possessed the constitutional power to dismiss Li Peng, and it was rumoured that he was returning home to do that. There may have been some truth in this; when he arrived in Shanghai he was arrested, on the pretext of entering hospital for medical tests, and flown secretly to Beijing.

But more importantly, a military solution was being prepared. On 24 May Deng Xiaoping held a secret meeting with the commanders of six of China's seven military regions[16]

---

16 The commanders of the seven military regions (the others are Shenyang, Jinan, Nanjing, Guangzhou, Chengdu and Lanzhou) are the operational commanders of the armed forces, and the most important political figures

(excluding Beijing, where the regional commander had refused to move against the students) to put together a task force to finally crush the movement. Yet by the end of May it began to look as though this would be unnecessary – a movement began in the provinces to empty the colleges, and by 1 June many students had left for home. In Tiananmen morale was dwindling even faster than numbers. It seemed the ruling class had only to wait. If the trend had continued, Tiananmen would soon have emptied to the point where a small-scale police operation would have been sufficient.

But on Monday 29 June students erected the now famous 'Goddess of Liberty' statue in Tiananmen, and by midnight more than 150,000 people had gathered in the square. A fresh hunger strike began, intended to last until the convening of the National People's Congress set for 20 June. News of the first arrests, of leaders of the Autonomous Workers' Federation and of the motorcyclists who had kept the barricades connected, only added to the anger evident in the crowds. It was as though everything was set to start all over again.

Blood on the streets

Exactly why the army went into Beijing with such ferocity on 3 June is still unclear. It may be that it was a last-minute decision, prompted by panic at the sight of the crowds returning to the streets; it is equally possible that the necessary troops were only in place on that date, or that the arguments inside the ruling class and the military leadership were only resolved the previous day.

Whatever the reason, the horror of 3 June was highlighted by the farce played out the previous night. In the early hours of Saturday morning, unarmed soldiers, many of them out of uniform, appeared on the main road to the east of Tiananmen.

---

inside the military. Their political as well as military support was essential for any frontal attack on the students.

They had jogged some ten miles from their bases outside Beijing. As the news spread, crowds of workers came out onto the streets to stop them. Traffic signs, fences, buses and ambulances were used to erect makeshift barricades.

East of the square a jeep ran down a group of cyclists, killing two of them outright. Derision turned to anger as workers and students jeered and spat at the troops. Isolated soldiers were caught and stripped, and they retreated in disorder, many of them crying. Some simply deserted, wandering off into the crowds. The government had once again been humiliated. Whether this farce was a cynical manoeuvre, designed to fail, or a last attempt to clear the square peacefully, or simple incompetence, may never be known. Whatever the reason, it pulled greater numbers onto the streets, convinced that the troops would be back. But no one expected what followed.

They came in their thousands in the early hours of Sunday morning. Armoured cars and tanks and guns smashed through the barricades along the Avenue of Eternal Peace, driving across the Gate of Heavenly Peace to the steps of the Monument to the People's Heroes, firing as they came. One Chinese eyewitness described their approach:

…by 11.30pm there were around 10,000 citizens with us. Teams made up of people wearing black and yellow spotted armbands to symbolise that they were not afraid of death were organised to go and guard the main routes into the city centre in order to stop the soldiers. At 1am my team of 100 students went to the western Xidan area where we immediately confronted troops.

The front rank was composed of special riot police, while behind them were the army. Immediately the riot police used tear-gas… As we withdrew we heard shots for the first time in the campaign. At first we couldn't believe the troops were firing at us but as more people fell we realised they were, and that they were using real bullets. At this we retreated south down Xisinan

Avenue, carrying the wounded with us. We lay down to avoid the bullets and watched as tanks and armoured trucks full of soldiers passed down Changan Road towards Tiananmen. The procession lasted an hour.[17]

As tens of thousands of workers poured onto the streets in disbelief, rage and terror, the armoured personnel carriers fired at random into their midst. In Tiananmen itself, students pleaded with the army to negotiate and refused to run. Sometime after 5am, the last 2,000 students remaining in the square held a meeting and arranged to withdraw. As they left, the army opened fire on them. One wounded student wrote in his own blood on the pavement 'Li Peng, you will never live in peace.'

Every minute gunshot casualties were brought into the hospitals, their numbers growing as the troops began to fire on ambulances. One small hospital:

...looked like an abattoir. There were bodies on benches and beds or on blood-soaked mattresses on the floor. Many had gaping bullet wounds on the chest, legs, or head. A doctor, voice hoarse with emotion, told us that 300 wounded had come in. 'Most were so bad we sent them on elsewhere... Four have died, including a nine-year-old girl shot through the throat'... Another doctor said twelve people had died under his hands; out of 300 injured, 30 had died. He thought 50 had died in every one of the 20 major hospitals in the capital.[18]

All that night across the city the same terror was unleashed. The student leaders in Tiananmen had opposed to the last any resistance, insisting that theirs was a peaceful movement. There were major arguments as workers and some students insisted on

17   Eyewitness account from a provincial student.
18   *The Guardian*, 5 June 1989.

the need to take up arms, but the leadership refused to budge, even handing back to the army some arms they had captured. Li Lu, one of the student leaders, later argued that none of the arms were functional, and that they were given to the students to trap them.[19] Even if that was true, the fact remains that the leaders in Tiananmen not only refused to organise any resistance, but tried to stop any form of self-defence.

Beijing's workers fought back, however, with a heroism that almost defied belief. Buses were dragged into place as barricades and set alight, while crowds rained stones, bricks, and petrol bombs onto the troops. Isolated soldiers were caught, disarmed and hanged. The few guns that the workers managed to acquire were turned on the army. Tanks and troop carriers were surrounded and set alight or broken into, and here and there troops either surrendered to the crowds or turned their guns on one another. But there was never any hope that individual acts of rebellion could turn into a general mutiny – the movement was simply not strong enough to convince the soldiers it could win.

Yet it could have been possible to win over sections of the army even at that stage. When Franco launched his military rising in Spain in 1936, Spanish workers stormed the barracks in the major cities and pulled over to their side large numbers of troops. In the Hungarian revolution of 1956:

> The troops in Budapest, as later in the provinces, were of two minds: there were those who were neutral and there were those who were prepared to join the people and fight alongside them. The neutral ones (probably the minority) were prepared to hand over their arms to the workers and students so that they could do battle against the AVH [secret police] with them. The others brought their arms with them when they joined the revolution.[20]

---

19   Li Lu, *Moving the mountain*, page 193.
20   Peter Fryer, *Hungarian tragedy* (New Park, London, 1986) page 39.

But in both these cases there was one essential precondition: that the movement was prepared to take up arms and fight to the death. This gave the soldiers the confidence that they would not simply be shot for mutiny, and that there was a chance of winning. Without that determination, in Beijing there was never a chance of turning isolated acts of heroism into a general refusal to repress the movement.

The following morning Beijing looked like Budapest in 1956 or Beirut in 1982: huge palls of smoke hung over the city, tanks and troops were everywhere, and gunfire rang out continually. The Chinese Red Cross put the death toll at 2,600 (a claim they later denied) and one anonymous Red Cross official told journalists: 'It's in the thousands. Obviously it's going to be impossible to ever know'.[21] Yet the resistance continued. Crowds of workers and students assembled on the outskirts of Tiananmen, yelling 'fascists' and 'murderers'. As the soldiers opened fire, they retreated, only to regroup and continue taunting the troops. That night there was again scattered fighting; troop carriers careered up and down the main avenues, firing at random into crowds and workers' housing blocks.

It took all the next day for the troops finally to crush the struggle. Yet the defiance and hatred continued to smoulder, symbolised by the single most unforgettable image to come from Beijing in those days. On the morning of 6 June Wang Weilin, the 19-year-old son of a factory worker, confronted the army with the bravery that had made the revolt possible. Standing in front of a column of tanks, he forced them to swerve, then come to a halt, and climbed up onto the lead tank before he was led off by his friends. He was later executed in secret, but his example will not soon be forgotten.

21   Amnesty International, *Death in Beijing*, (London, 1989) page 51.

After the massacre

The June massacres were no acts of random savagery, nor the work of individual soldiers running amok; they were a calculated and deliberate declaration of civil war by a ruling class who had no other means of restoring their authority. Across the country, mass protests erupted. Two nights of street fighting in Chengdu left more than 300 dead. More than 100,000 people marched in Shanghai and Nanjing, while thousands more took to the streets in city after city. Most important of all, in many cities the students moved to organise strike action. In Guangzhou, one student argued:

> There must be a total strike – no more hunger strikes, they are useless. Only if the workers stop the steel production and the power stations and the railways can we bring these people down. There are not enough soldiers in all of China to keep the vital industries running. The workers have the power, let the workers have their say. It is the only way.[22]

In Hefei:

> There was a six-hour funeral march through the city, calling on factories and workers' estates, broadcasting news and urging strike action... On the Tuesday, USTC students picketed all the gates of Anhui Iron and Steel factory claiming 30 percent strike action. They controlled the six main intersections in the city centre in an attempt to stop workers going to work. There were large crowds at the barricades, and buses were used to block the roads.[23]

The centres of Wuhan, Lanzhou and Changsha were

---

22 *The Guardian*, 5 June 1989.

23 Eyewitness account.

blockaded for several days, while millions of workers stayed away from work or organised go-slows in the factories. Yet the resistance could only show the depth of hatred for the regime, and the extent to which the regime's power now rested on brute force alone - it could not win back consent.

On the afternoon of 7 June a nationwide call went out from the student leadership left in Beijing to stop the blockades in order to avoid further bloodshed, and for the activists to go underground to carry on the struggle. 'The aim was to preserve the living leadership and in all cities the call was followed. The exception was Shanghai where the movement was strongest. There the students staged a very skilful withdrawal over the next three days.'[24]

While the students were able to organise some sort of retreat in the days following the massacre, the regime seemed in utter disarray. The rumours became wilder and wilder: other troops were marching on Beijing to attack those who had carried out the massacre; Deng Xiaoping was dying of cancer in a Shanghai hospital; Zhao Ziyang had been shot on Li Peng's orders; an army general had attempted to assassinate Li Peng. The ruling class were thrown into turmoil by their victory, as they desperately tried to work out what to do next.

By the end of that week, all the rumours appeared to be false. Li Peng and Deng Xiaoping reappeared on Chinese television claiming to be in control. But both appeared surrounded by army officers, and when Deng made a major speech on Friday 9 June he read from a prepared script, and was twice corrected or prompted from off-screen. On 24 June the formal question of the CCP leadership was decided when Zhao Ziyang was sacked (along with a number of his supporters) and replaced as CCP general secretary by Jiang Zemin, previously CCP secretary in Shanghai.

---

24   Eyewitness account.

By the end of 1989 more than 30,000 people had been arrested, many of whom were shot in secret. According to the Hong Kong paper *Ming Pao*, between 7 and 12 June more than 1,700 people were arrested in Bejing alone, some 400 of whom (almost all workers) were shot.[25] In the city of Jinan, capital of Shandong province, seventeen people were publicly executed on 21 June, and nine others were given suspended death sentences.[26] For weeks after the massacre Chinese television showed an unending succession of arrested workers and students, handcuffed and with bowed heads, who had clearly been badly beaten. The arrests and killings continued throughout the year and well into 1990. Meanwhile the press and television lied about the massacres on a scale not seen since the Cultural Revolution.

Though the repression was vicious beyond belief, it failed to exterminate the opposition. Even if the worst figures for arrests and murders are true, the toll was less than in the law-and-order crackdown of 1982-3, when far fewer people had been active in the Democracy Wall movement. Moreover, numbers of the leading activists escaped the crackdown. Of 21 student leaders on the 'most wanted persons' list, the government had announced the arrest of only seven by the end of 1989 (three of whom were turned in by their families); at least five had escaped to the West. The leaders of the Beijing Autonomous Workers' Union arrested after the massacre were all caught far outside Beijing; one had managed to hide out for two weeks in Chengdu. These were people whose pictures had been circulated across the whole country; the chances of lesser activists must have been far better.

The activists' ability to go on the run marked a major break from past episodes of repression. In 1976, the police simply went to the houses of those they wanted to arrest after the Tiananmen riots. Given the tight controls over everyday life, escape was

---

25 *Amnesty International* press release, ASN17/36/89, 16 June 1989.
26 *Amnesty International* press release ASN17/49/89, 28 June 1989.

simply unthinkable. In 1989 it was incredibly risky (anyone caught harbouring a wanted person shared their fate), but it was possible. The fact that Örkesh Dölet, Chai Ling, Li Lu and a number of other leaders could escape to Hong Kong testified to the existence of a sophisticated underground network.

In Beijing at least, the resistance took a long time to die out. In the last week of June, the bodies of two soldiers who had been garrotted were dragged from a canal, and reporters spoke of hearing gunfire practically every night. One writer vividly illustrated the extent of the ruling class' fears:

> You would hardly know during the daytime in Beijing that martial law is still in effect. But at night, when Beijing is as still and almost as empty as a northern Chinese village, things are different. All along the streets after dark and until the early hours of the next day, the soldiers, like shadows in the dim light, are on duty.
>
> AK-47 semi-automatic rifles cradled in their arms, they emerge from under the black trees, stopping passers-by to check identity papers, examining the cargoes of night delivery trucks, scrutinising the passengers and also the trunks and even the glove compartments of every car that passes.[27]

On the campuses, there was at least one public display of mourning for those who died in Tiananmen. Students were required to take part in self-criticism sessions denouncing the movement and confessing their errors. They were openly cynical about these sessions. In one college, one group avoided saying anything at all by asking the official leading the session to read Deng Xiaoping's speech over and over again – 'to make sure we don't miss anything!'[28]

---

27 *International Herald Tribune*, 27 June 1989.
28 Eyewitness account.

The international revulsion against the massacres forced a number of Western governments to impose partial sanctions against China. Japan, West Germany, France, Denmark, Holland, Canada and Australia all froze loans packages, as did the World Bank and the Asian Development Bank. Yet businessmen who fled Beijing in the days following the massacres were all too quick to return – the Japanese government even had to warn its nationals against looking like 'ghouls around a corpse'! By early July most Japanese companies based in Beijing had reopened their offices, as had half of the British companies.

But their eagerness to resume business as usual was tempered by fears about the economic climate – China's worst-ever trade deficit was announced in July – and the effects of public opinion on their operations elsewhere. One anonymous American explained their quandary with callous cynicism, even managing to put a price on it:

> The way things are here, people are torn between trying to protect what business they have and weighing up the negative effects on their corporate image of being seen to be eager to trade with butchers. What's the point of getting $20 million worth of bad publicity for $5 million worth of business?[29]

By August the loans were once again flowing, and most of the sanctions had been quietly dropped. There was no shortage of hypocritical denunciations of the killings from world rulers. Possibly the most sickening was George Bush's assertion that 'you cannot crush an idea with tanks' – just six months before US troops murdered over 7,000 people in the invasion of Panama. Yet behind the rhetoric it was business as usual. Britain, Australia, France, and the United States all refused political asylum to Chinese students who had been active in

---

29   Quoted in *The Independent*, 11 July 1989.

solidarity movements. In 1990 Britain even tried to deport 30 activists who had escaped via Panama. The 'Western democracies' in which the students had placed such hopes showed all too quickly whose side they were really on.

The Monday after the massacres, Beijing Radio announced that 'order has been restored in Beijing'. Seventy years ago, after the defeat of a workers' rising in Germany, Rosa Luxemburg wrote an answer to that which is worth repeating today:

> 'Order reigns in Warsaw!' – 'Order reigns in Paris!' – 'Order reigns in Berlin!' And so run the reports of the guardians of 'order' every half-century, from one centre of the world-historical struggle to another. And the rejoicing 'victors' do not notice that an 'order' which must be periodically maintained by bloody butchery is steadily approaching its historical destiny, its doom.[30]

She went on to say that:

> The whole path of socialism, as far as revolutionary struggles are concerned, is paved with sheer defeats. And yet, this same history leads step by step, irresistibly, to the ultimate victory. Where would we be today without those 'defeats' from which we have drawn historical experience, knowledge, power, idealism?!… we are standing on precisely those defeats, *not a one of which* we could do without, and each of which is a part of our strength and clarity of purpose.[31]

The revolutionary fervour that gripped China in 1989 left an enduring legacy that no amount of repression can erase. Millions of workers and students discovered the power to challenge and

---

30   Rosa Luxemburg, 'Order reigns in Berlin', in *Selected political writings* (Monthly Review, New York, NY, 1971) page 410.

31   As above, pages 413-14.

humiliate their rulers, and to run their own lives without the police and the bureaucracy. Thousands paid with their lives for that knowledge, but their heroism will endure as an example for future generations of fighters. Rosa Luxemburg's conclusion is a fitting tribute to the hopes for which they died:

> The masses were up to the task. They fashioned this defeat into a part of those historical defeats which constitute the pride and power of international socialism. And that is why this defeat is the seed of the future triumph.
>
> 'Order reigns in Berlin!' You stupid lackeys! Your order is built on sand. The revolution will raise itself up again clashing and to your horror it will proclaim to the sound of trumpets: *'I was, I am, I shall be!'*[32]

---

32   As above, page 415.

.

CHAPTER 9

What next?

Within six months of the Tiananmen Square massacre, the governments in East Germany, Czechoslovakia and Romania had fallen, and members of the once-banned Solidarity were being drawn into the Polish government. The 'peaceful revolutions' of late 1989 seemed to prove that non-violent mass protest could indeed topple unpopular regimes and begin the process of democratisation. Many exiled Chinese opposition leaders took this as proof that their strategy had been right – what had worked in Eastern Europe could work next time in China.

But the comparison was misleading. In the first place, the revolutions of 1989 were far less peaceful than they are now painted. In Romania it took two weeks of the fiercest street fighting seen in Europe since Hungary in 1956 to get rid of Ceausescu. In both East Germany and Czechoslovakia, the ruling classes originally considered trying to shoot the opposition movements off the streets. Two things stopped them: fears that the army would refuse to obey orders, and Gorbachev's express opposition to any repeat of Tiananmen Square in Eastern Europe.

But there was a deeper difference. Eastern Europe's rulers

were caught in a closing vice of economic stagnation at home and increased competition from the West. In all three countries, a large section of the ruling classes could see that the old methods of central direction of the economy could not solve the crisis. A fundamental change of economic direction was essential, and they were prepared to use the protests from below to put pressure on the old guard to change. The oppositions in Eastern Europe were pushing at half-open doors (even if, as in Romania, they had to shoot their way through).

The Chinese ruling class could not take the same course for the simple reason that they had already done so. Between 1976 and 1978, the same combination of mass pressure from below and the recognition of the need for change among many CCP leaders brought Deng Xiaoping to power and set the economic reforms in motion. (Although events unfolded at a quite different speed in China, as in Romania, Czechoslovakia and East Germany, it was the pressure from below that was decisive in forcing the rulers' hands.)

The revolt of 1989 sprang out of the economic and political crisis that the market reforms had created in China. Because of that crisis, the Chinese ruling class could not offer any real economic or social change; they feared the much wider explosion that any concessions to the protest movement would have engendered. Cornered, they resorted to massacre as the only short-term solution. Yet while it saved their skins in the short term, it only worsened their crisis.

On the first anniversary of the massacre, Beijing was flooded with troops and police to prevent any public demonstrations. Yet hundreds of students marched on several college campuses to mourn their colleagues, and even in Tiananmen Square itself, a number of brave individuals defied the police to stage personal protests.

The size of the security operation was a sign of the regime's weakness, not its strength. As China entered the 1990s, the tensions that produced the spring revolt of 1989 were worse than ever. The economic crisis deepened, while the arrests and killings of activists only intensified the isolation of the ruling class. In December 1989, news of the Romanian revolution led the rulers of China to order troops to be stationed around the television stations in Beijing, for fear that the example of Bucharest would be followed. The repression was still too recent, and the opposition too fragmented, for this to be a real possibility, but the events in Romania were certainly an inspiration for many. One Westerner teaching in northeast China reported hearing constant conversations about 'Ceausescu-Bucharest-Timisoara' among his students and fellow teachers.[1]

In the countryside, the austerity measures begun in 1988 continued to cause real hardship. The government admitted that more than 370,000 rural enterprises closed in 1989 for lack of raw materials or credit, throwing almost 1.8 million people out of work[2] – the real figure was certainly much higher. In addition, millions more workers who had lost their temporary jobs in the cities returned to the villages. Meanwhile those still working the land became poorer, because of both the austerity measures and the workings of the market.

According to official figures, peasant incomes dropped by more than three percent in 1989.[3] Given the enormous inequalities in the countryside, that figure masked much worse cuts in living standards in the more backward areas. Though the 1989 grain harvest was a good one, that only made matters worse. Free-market grain prices dropped substantially, and the state purchasing agencies didn't have enough money to pay for the increased output. Production of essential industrial crops such as cotton also fell, forcing the state to increase imports.

---

1   Personal communication.
2   *Beijing Review*, 25 June 1990.
3   *FEER*, 14 June 1990.

But workers in the cities paid the highest price for the crisis. Open wage-cutting began in September 1989, with around 10 percent of wages being forcibly invested in government bonds, while bonuses were cut or abolished in many factories. Between fifteen and twenty million workers – about one in seven of the urban workforce – had been laid off by the end of 1989.

Yet working-class resistance had not been crushed. One sign of this was the sharp drop in labour productivity reported for 1989, the biggest fall being registered in Beijing. Workers in Chengdu, Wuhan and other cities held protest marches against the cuts, and there were numerous short-lived strikes. The government was forced to announce that bonuses would not be abolished altogether, and to increase lay-off pay from 70 to 100 percent of salaries.[4] The scale of these scarcely-reported protests was massive. According to one report:

> ...workers in more than 30 Chinese cities had applied to carry out legal demonstrations involving a total of more than half a million workers. [CCP] sources could not confirm that figure, but said that worker discontent was widespread and encompassed most provinces.[5]

By the end of 1989 the austerity measures had hit Chinese industry so hard that the state was forced to lend factories money so that they could pay their taxes! Yet as the credit squeeze was gradually eased in early 1990, the old problems of the economy – overheating, shortages of raw materials and energy, and excessive investment-began to re-emerge.

China's new rulers had ditched Mao's economic strategy because it had led to stagnation and technological backwardness. As they saw it, abolishing centralised control from Beijing was

---

4   *FEER*, 25 January 1990.
5   *International Herald Tribune*, 8 January 1990

the only way to make the Chinese economy more efficient and competitive. The realities of international competition dictated that China had to enter the world economy in order to develop. 'Socialism in one country' was dead.

This did not mean that they were abandoning state capitalism in favour of private capitalism. Private capitalism had returned to China, most notably in the countryside, but it remained a tiny proportion of the economy as a whole. The reforms were rather about shifting the balance of power and responsibility within the ruling class. Direct control over the economy was devolved from a few hundred top officials in Beijing to the mass of lower-level officials and factory managers. The state remained in command – but it was those members of the ruling class at the sharp end who now had the real authority in their factory, city or province.

That strategy led to the fastest economic growth ever in Chinese history. In the 1980s, China had the highest rate of economic growth anywhere in the world. Yet the faster the economy grew, the more the ruling class lost control over the pace and direction of that growth. In devolving economic power to local officials, they created tens of thousands of localised and sectional decision-making centres, whose adherence to the wishes of the ruling class as a whole could not be relied upon. That development took on a dynamic of its own, leading to ever greater unevenness and dislocation of national planning.

In the same way, as China was pulled deeper into the world economy, the rhythms of the world economy came increasingly to dictate the terms on which its integration took place. Time and again, long-term export strategies and priorities have been rewritten or abandoned as world markets have changed unpredictably.

Yet the CCP's power was based precisely on their ability to control and direct the economy: the modernisation strategy demanded that ability even more than Mao's did. The contradiction between planning and 'market forces' meant that the state had to constantly intervene to reassert its control. But that reassertion could only go so far. Whatever some members of the ruling class might have wished, they could not revert to a siege economy. For all practical purposes, the reforms were irreversible. In the countryside, there was simply no force large enough to impose collectivisation of the fields again. In the cities, while they could discipline local officials and managers, they could not completely subordinate them to central control. Meanwhile China's integration into the world economy had now gone too fat to be reversed without incalculable economic damage.

The ruling class were thus forced to try to stabilise an inherently unstable economy. Each time they intervened, they risked making the situation even more irregular and unpredictable. It was a vicious circle, from which there was no escape inside the nation-state, even one as big as China.

None of the problems facing the ruling class were unique to China – the same problems face every capitalist class attempting to guide their national economy in an uncontrollable world system. In China the problems were worse because of the economy's backwardness and Mao's disastrous attempts to overcome it. Yet the 1980s strategy proved no more capable of solving the fundamental problems than the old one. The roots of that failure did not lie in the mistakes or inadequacies of the Chinese ruling class, but in the nature of capitalism as a world system of production, in which the nation-state had become a brake on any real economic development.

Indeed, as the world economy slid once again into recession, the modernisation strategy could possibly have presaged worse for the mass of the population. The World Bank concluded a major survey of the Chinese economy in the early 1980s with a warning which now sounds like a prophecy:

An enlarged role for markets and competition, though it will undoubtedly improve efficiency and accelerate technological progress, could potentially also have undesirable social and economic consequences, including unemployment, unacceptably low (and high) wages, bankruptcy of enterprises and dismissal of workers, and the poor and backward being left further behind... Very few countries have combined state and market regulation in such a way as to produce rapid and efficient growth, and fewer still have also managed to avoid intolerable poverty among substantial segments of their population...[6]

Forty years after the brave promises of Liberation, it was a sobering conclusion. Yet there was an alternative, first shown in the revolution of 1925-27. The risen working class then defied the power of the warlords and imperialists, and drew the mass of the peasantry into a struggle which could have wiped out their oppression and exploitation. It was the crushing of that alternative which ultimately made Mao's victory possible.

That power was shown again in the revolt of 1989. When the workers joined the students in the streets of Beijing and other cities, what had begun as a protest movement blossomed into the biggest threat to the Chinese ruling class ever. Tragically, there was no revolutionary party that could make the mass of workers aware of their real power and take the struggle through to the end. But the experience of their own power could make it easier to create such a force the next time that China explodes. As the Beijing Autonomous Workers' Union wrote, the day that millions thronged to the barricades that briefly liberated Beijing:

The working class is the most advanced class and we, in the Democratic Movement, should be prepared to demonstrate its

---

6   World Bank, *China: long-term development issues and options*, pages 181-182.

great power. The People's Republic of China is supposedly led by the working class, and we have every right to drive out the dictators... To bring down dictatorship and totalitarianism and promote democracy in China is our undeniable responsibility... we have nothing to lose but our chains, we have a world to win![7]

---

7   Quoted in Mok Yu Chiu and Harrison, *Voices from Tiananmen Square*, page 115.

Further reading

In the introduction to the original edition, I wrote that 'there is a vast literature on modern Chinese history', which seems today like a gross understatement – since 1991, the sheer volume of writing about China has grown almost as fast as the society and economy it is attempting to understand. However, much of what is written becomes outdated within a couple of years. This lists some of what I think are the most important or most accessible works, with a bias towards left-wing and socialist writers.

Au Loong-Yu, *China's rise: strength and fragility*, (Merlin Press, London, 2013) and *Hong Kong in revolt: the protest movement and the future of China* (Pluto, London, 2020)

Hongwei Bao, *Queer comrades – gay identity and* tongzhi *activism in post-socialist China* (NIAS Press, Copenhagen, Denmark, 2018)

Jasper Becker, *Hungry ghosts*, (John Murray, London, 1996) – the best general account of the Great Leap Forward.

Gregor Benton, *Prophets unarmed: Chinese Trotskyists in revolution, war, jail, and the return from limbo* (Haymarket, Chicago, IL, 2014)

David Brophy, *China panic – Australia's alternative to paranoia and pandering*, (La Trobe University Press/Black Inc., Carlton, Vic, 2021)

Jeremy Brown, *June Fourth: the Tiananmen protests and Beijing massacre of 1989,* (Cambridge University Press, Cambridge, 2021)

Adrian Budd, *China: rise, repression and resistance*, (Bookmarks, London, 2024)

Darren Byler, *In the camps: China's high-tech penal colony,* (Atlantic Books, London, 2022)

Leslie T Chang, *Factory girls: from village to city in a changing China* (Random House, New York, 2009)

Anita Chan, Richard Madsen and Jonathan Unger, *Chen village: revolution to globalization* (3rd edition), (University of California Press, Berkeley, CA, 2009) – multi-generational account of changes in one village from 1949 to 2007.

Elizabeth Croll, *China's new consumers*, (Routledge, London, 2006)

Fan Shigang, *Striking to survive*, (Haymarket, Chicago, IL, 2018)

Jonathan Fenby, *The Penguin history of modern China* (third edition), (Penguin, London, 2019)

Leta Hong Fincher, *Betraying Big Brother: the feminist awakening in China* (Verso, London, 2019)

Eli Friedman, *The urbanization of people* (Columbia University Press, New York, NY, 2022)

Eli Friedman, Kevin Lin, Rosa Liu, and Ashley Smith, *China in global capitalism*, (Haymarket, Chicago, IL, 2024)

John Gittings, *China changes face* and *Real China*, (Simon & Schuster, London, 1996)

Nigel Harris, *The mandate of heaven: Marx and Mao in modern China* (Haymarket, Chicago, IL, 2015)

Peter Hessler, *River town*, (John Murray, London, 2001) – insightful account of change in an isolated provincial city.

Richard Javid Heydarian, *Asia's new battlefield: the USA, China and the struggle for the Western Pacific* (Zed Books, London, 2015)

Ben Hillier, *The art of rebellion* (Spark Publishing, Melbourne, 2020)

Ho-fung Hung, *The China boom* (Columbia University Press, New York, NY, 2015)

Harold Isaacs, *The tragedy of the Chinese revolution* - also available online at: https://www.marxists.org/history/etol/writers/isaacs/1938/tcr/index.htm

Ed Jocelyn and Andrew McEwen, *The Long March*, (Constable, London, 2006) – not a history, but a 2002 retracing of the route by two British bikers, which gives a vivid picture of changes in the countryside.

Jung Chang, *Wild swans*, (HarperCollins, London, 1991)

Ching Kwan Lee, *Against the law: labor protests in China's rustbelt and sunbelt* (University of California Press, Berkeley, CA, 2007)

Simon Leys, *The Chairman's new clothes: Mao and the Cultural Revolution* (Allison & Busby, London,1981), *Chinese shadows* (Penguin, London, 1978), and *Broken images: essays on Chinese culture and politics* (Allison & Busby, London,1979)

Zhongjin Li, Eli Friedman and Hao Ren, *China on strike: narratives of workers' resistance* (Haymarket, Chicago, IL, 2016)

Louisa Lim, *The People's Republic of amnesia : Tiananmen revisited* (Oxford University Press, New York, NY, 2014)

Roderick MacFarquhar and Michael Schoenhals, *Mao's last revolution*, (Harvard University Press, Cambridge, MA, 2006)

Maurice Meisner, *Mao's China and after* (third edition), (The Free Press, New York, NY, 1999)

James A Millward, *Eurasian crossroads : A History of Xinjiang* (Columbia University Press, New York, NY, 2009)

Hsiao-Hung Pai, *Scattered sand: the story of China's rural migrants* (Verso, London, 2013)

Pun Ngai, *Migrant labor in China* and *Made in China* (Duke University Press, Durham, NC, 2005)

Denny Roy, *Taiwan: a political history* (Cornell University Press, Ithaca, NY, 2003)

Ralf Ruckus, *The left in China: a political cartography* (Verso, London, 2023) and *The communist road to capitalism* (PM Press, Oakland, CA, 2021)

Robert K Schaeffer, *Red Inc.*, (Paradigm Publishers, Boulder, CO, 2012)

John Sexton, *Red friends*, (Verso, London, 2023) – the international left and China from the 1930s to the 1960s

Wade Shephard, *Ghost cities of China* (Zed Books, London, 2015),

Richard Smith, *China's engine of environmental collapse* (Pluto Press, London, 2020)

Jonathan D Spence, *The gate of heavenly peace* (Penguin, London, 1982)

Sun Shuyun, *The Long March*, (HarperPress, London, 2006)

Leon Trotsky, *On China. Problems of the Chinese revolution (1927-1931)*, a shorter collection of Trotsky's writings, is available online: https://www.marxists.org/archive/trotsky/1932/pcr/index.htm

Tsering Woeser, *Tibet on fire* (Verso, London, 2016)

Margery Wolf, *Revolution postponed: women in contemporary China* (Stanford University Press, Stanford, CA, 1985)

Emily Yeh, *Taming Tibet: landscape transformation and the gift of Chinese development* (Cornell University Press, Ithaca, NY, 2013)

Yu Hua, *China in ten words*, (Duckworth, London, 2005)

WEBSITES – China and Taiwan

Asian Labour Review https://labourreview.org/

China Labour Bulletin – the best source for news of strikes and other workers' actions in China https://clb.org.hk/en

China Worker – longstanding orthodox Trotskyist group in Hong Kong, affiliated with International Socialist Alternative https://chinaworker.info/en/

Chuang – blog and occasional journal which publishes left-communist analyses from both inside China and the diaspora https://chuangcn.org/blog/

Gongchao – German-based multilingual blog focused on workers' and social struggles https://www.gongchao.org/

Lausan – radical left perspectives from Hong Kong, east Asia and its diasporas https://chuangcn.org/blog/

Made in China – open access online academic journal, with a focus on workers' rights and social movements https://madeinchinajournal.com/journal/

New Bloom – Taiwanese radical left journal https://newbloommag.net/

Sixth Tone – offbeat and eclectic site covering multiple aspects of contemporary China, particularly strong on climate change and environmentalism https://www.sixthtone.com/

WEBSITES – Socialist websites with regular China/east Asia coverage

Europe Solidaire Sans Frontières – French-based site that reprints articles from across the far left, affiliated with the Fourth International https://www.europe-solidaire.org/spip.php?rubrique2

ISO Aotearoa – revolutionary socialist website in Aotearoa/New Zealand https://iso.org.nz

Red Flag – website and paper of Socialist Alternative (Australia) https://redflag.org.au/

rs21 – revolutionary socialist website in Britain https://www.rs21.org.uk/

Spectre – North American Marxist journal and website https://spectrejournal.com/

Tempest – revolutionary socialist website in the USA https://tempestmag.org/

Acknowledgements

(1991)

Parts of this book have previously appeared in a pamphlet, *China: Whose revolution?* (Socialist Workers Party, London 1987), and in articles in the quarterly journal *International Socialism*. All the material has been revised and updated for this edition. Many comrades have given me useful advice and encouragement which improved those writings: my thanks to Chris Bambery, Pete Binns, Duncan Blackie, Norah Carlin, Sue Clegg, Ersy Contogouris, Pete Green, Chris Harman, Derek Howl, John Molyneux, Nigel Paramour, Sam Pryke, John Rees, and Lawrence Wong. I would particularly like to thank Fran Belbin, Alex Callinicos, Paul McGarr, Peter Marsden, Julia Richmond and Dave Sellars for their criticism and comments on the present text, Peter Court and Peter Marsden for editorial production and design, and Bookmarks for publication and distribution.

(2024)

I have drawn on articles in *International Socialism*, *International Socialist Review*, *Jacobin* and *rs21.org.uk* for the introduction, though again all material has been revised and updated. My thanks to Robert Narai for suggesting this new edition, to Matthias Radja and Oscar Sterner for overseeing the production, to Susan Miller for cover design and layout, and to Gareth Dale, Rob Hoveman, Mousa Sha, Sue Sparks and WA Standley for providing or suggesting material for the new introduction. Adrian Budd, April Holcombe, Matthias Radja, Shail Shah and Colin Wilson gave me valuable comments on the first draft of the introduction. I have benefitted greatly from being part of an online group of Trotskyist writers on China, including again Adrian Budd and April Holcombe as well as Au Loong Yu, Tom Bramble, Promise Li, Kevin Lin, Pierre Rousset and Ashley Smith – my thanks to them all for several years of stimulating discussion. I have corrected a number of errors, infelicities and typos from the first edition, and updated some references, with major changes indicated in [square brackets].

A note on transliterating Chinese names

In transliterating Chinese place and personal names I have used the official Chinese *pinyin* system, both because it bears the closest relation to their pronunciation, and because it is the style used in almost all contemporary writings on China. To avoid confusion, I have also amended some transliterations in quotes. The only exceptions are those where the *pinyin* forms are completely different from the names by which they are known in the West – Chiang Kaishek and Hong Kong, for instance – and for names in Hong Kong and Taiwan, where *pinyin* is not used. I have also updated the transliterations of Uyghur names.

Charlie Hore, October 2024